Quantification

Quantification forms a significant aspect of cross-linguistic research into both sentence structure and meaning. This book surveys research in quantification starting with the foundational work in the 1970s. It paints a vivid picture of generalized quantifiers and Boolean semantics. It explains how the discovery of diverse scope behavior in the 1990s transformed the view of quantification, and how the study of the internal composition of quantifiers has become central in recent years. It presents different approaches to the same problems, and links modern logic and formal semantics to advances in generative syntax. A unique feature of the book is that it systematically brings cross-linguistic data to bear on the theoretical issues, discussing French, German, Dutch, Hungarian, Russian, Japanese, Telugu (Dravidian), and Shupamem (Grassfield Bantu), and pointing to formal semantic literature involving quantification in around thirty languages.

Anna Szabolcsi is Professor of Linguistics at New York University. Her books include *The Possessive Construction and Existential Sentences* (in Hungarian, Akadémiai Kiadó, 1992), *Lexical Matters* (contributor and co-editor with Ivan A. Sag, CSLI Publications, 1992), *Ways of Scope Taking* (contributor and editor, Kluwer, 1997), and *Verbal Complexes* (with Hilda Koopman, The MIT Press, 2000).

T0382599

Research Surveys in Linguistics

In large domains of theoretical and empirical linguistics, scholarly communication needs are directly comparable to those in analytical and natural sciences. Conspicuously lacking in the inventory publications for linguists, compared to those in the sciences, are concise, single-authored, non-textbook reviews of rapidly evolving areas of inquiry. Research Surveys in Linguistics is intended to fill this gap. It consists of well indexed volumes that survey topics of significant theoretical interest on which there has been a proliferation of research in the last two decades. The goal is to provide an efficient overview and entry into the primary literature for linguists – both advanced students and researchers – who wish to move into, or stay literate in, the areas covered. Series authors are recognized authorities on the subject matter as well as clear, highly organized writers. Each book offers the reader relatively tight structuring in sections and subsections and a detailed index for ease of orientation.

Quantification

ANNA SZABOLCSI

New York University

CAMBRIDGE
UNIVERSITY PRESS

CAMBRIDGE
UNIVERSITY PRESS

University Printing House, Cambridge CB2 8BS, United Kingdom

One Liberty Plaza, 20th Floor, New York, NY 10006, USA

477 Williamstown Road, Port Melbourne, VIC 3207, Australia

314-321, 3rd Floor, Plot 3, Splendor Forum, Jasola District Centre, New Delhi - 110025, India

79 Anson Road, #06-04/06, Singapore 079906

Cambridge University Press is part of the University of Cambridge.

It furthers the University's mission by disseminating knowledge in the pursuit of education, learning and research at the highest international levels of excellence.

www.cambridge.org
Information on this title: www.cambridge.org/9780521715935

© Anna Szabolcsi 2010

First published 2010

A catalogue record for this publication is available from the British Library

ISBN   978-0-521-88796-0   Hardback
ISBN   978-0-521-71593-5   Paperback

Contents

Figures

Tables

Acknowledgements

Many sections of this survey have benefited from the help of colleagues; I am grateful for their generosity and thank them by name at the pertinent places in the book. I am indebted to Zoltán Gendler Szabó, Eytan Zweig, Chris Collins, Oana Savescu Ciucivara, and an anonymous reviewer for reading earlier versions of the manuscript and giving me innumerable insightful comments, and to Anikó Csirmaz for recent discussions of Hungarian quantifiers.

Some of the chapters are reincarnations of my lecture notes for introductory graduate courses and seminars at UCLA and at NYU. I thank especially the participants in the past two or three years, Rahul Balusu, Eric Besson, Jon Brennan, Andrea Cattaneo, Simon Charlow, Amanda Dye, Stacy Dickerman, Tricia Irwin, Dan Lassiter, Inna Livitz, Txuss Martín, Salvador Mascarenhas, Violeta Vázquez Rojas, and Jim Wood for their endurance and inspiring feedback.

The shaded Hasse-diagrams, multi-level towers, and other nice pieces of LaTeX were done by Salvador Mascarenhas; he also kept me out of trouble when my own type-setting skills were not up to the task. Autumn Gerami and Kayley Squire helped compile the index.

1

What this book is about
and how to use it

1.1 The proper treatment of quantification in ordinary Human

In *The proper treatment of quantification in ordinary English* Montague sets forth his goal as follows:[1]

> "The aim of this paper is to present in a rigorous way the syntax and semantics of a certain fragment of a certain dialect of English. For expository purposes the fragment has been made as simple and restricted as it can be while accommodating all the more puzzling cases of quantification and reference with which I am acquainted." (Montague 1974a: 247)

The goal of this book is to survey a good chunk of the research that has been directed at Montague's puzzles and their natural extensions in the past 35 years. The survey has a dual focus. One is on how the understanding of "quantification" and "quantifier" has been changing over time. The way I see it, we have witnessed three main stages of research:

Grand uniformity (the 1970s and 1980s)
Foundational work that affords a uniform treatment of initially disparate-looking phenomena: generalized quantifiers for all noun phrases, a kind-based treatment of existential and generic readings of bare plurals, etc.

Diversity (the 1980s and 1990s)
Dynamic semantics for definites and indefinites, choice-functional indefinites vs. others, the differential behavior of quantifiers

Internal composition (from 2000 on)
Quantifier-phrase-internal and, most recently, quantifier-word-internal compositionality

The other focus is on the core notion of scope and its implementation in several varieties of generative syntax and categorial grammar. We may disagree about what the best syntax is, but any serious attempt at compositionality must be built on a credible syntax. It is important to see that at least the core ideas can be implemented in various different ways.

Montague's puzzles include the interaction of quantifier phrases among themselves and with intensional predicates, and the binding of pronouns by quantifiers. We will not attempt to cover the research on intensionality, save for a brief discussion in **§5.7**, although Chapter 3 takes up quantification over individuals vs. worlds and times. Another major self-imposed limitation has been to set aside quantificational binding (see **§2.3.3**).

The structure of the discussion is as follows.

Chapters 2 through 4 offer an introduction to generalized quantifiers, with an eye on the implications for scope and the syntax/semantics interface, non-nominal domains of quantification, and on semantic properties that turn out to be significant for empirical work. These chapters do not attempt to rehash what existing excellent introductions do (see some recommended readings in **§2.1**); they attempt to give a picture that cannot be found elsewhere.

Chapters 5 and 6 pull together some of the questions and data that led to the major transformation in how we approach "quantifiers" and "scope". (The transformation explains why this introduction does not start with a substantial definition of "quantification" – there is no need to set up a strawman and fight with it throughout the book.)

Chapters 7 through 10 discuss some of the issues that have been in the focus of much research: existential scope, distributivity, numeral indefinites, and modified numeral expressions. Here a major limitation is that the discussion of plural noun phrases (especially of collective readings) is kept to the minimum.

Chapter 11 surveys recent approaches to the syntax of clause-internal scope, with special attention to how they account for the diversity of scopal behavior. Chapter 12 pulls together the even more recent work on the internal structure of universal quantifiers – quantifier phrases as well as quantifier words.

The last four chapters survey more controversial and more preliminary ideas than the ones preceding them. Seeing that this is a research survey, not a textbook, it hopes to stimulate further work by giving a sense of where we actually are.

Throughout the book I attempt to link up the results of serious semantics and serious syntax. Occasionally I am mainly talking to the semanticist or to the syntactician, but my hope is that many readers will put themselves in the shoes of both.

Although a great many formal semanticists are native speakers of languages other than English, the bulk of our efforts has been directed at analyzing English or, sometimes, at disguising research on another language as work on English. This survey makes an attempt to bring multiple languages to bear on the questions under discussion, or at least to point out the existence of some high-quality literature on various languages. I am definitely not doing as good a job as I would like to, simply because I have not processed all this literature in sufficient depth.

1.2 How to use this book

This is not a textbook. Many things follow from this. It does not single out one theory and endow the reader with a working knowledge of it. It selects a story-line and shows what a relatively wide range of literature has to say about it. Although some formalization is offered, the discussion is kept as informal as possible, to maintain readability and to remain neutral as to technicalities. Sometimes it does not make sense to avoid the formalism; if the reader feels that a part is too difficult, they should breeze through it and rest assured that they will be able to pick up the thread afterwards.

The endnotes typically supply further important empirical or formal detail. Their contents are an integral part of the text, at least for some readers. They are relegated to note status to avoid disrupting the train of thought in the main text. The best thing is to keep a bookmark at the notes and consult them systematically.

The chapters and sections address theoretical issues, rather than descriptive topics, whenever possible. For this reason the discussion is somewhat fragmented and repetitive: a particular descriptive topic and a particular piece of work may be relevant for various different questions. So one descriptive topic may be discussed in many places in the book, and different claims made in one and the same piece of work may be brought to bear on various different issues. Usually there are pointers to the other relevant sections and occasionally brief summaries are given of what has already been said; the reader is encouraged to also make good use of the index. A certain amount of repetition is necessary in any case, because not every reader will want to go through the whole book. No issue or piece of work is discussed completely. It is assumed that the reader will go on to consult some of the literature surveyed herein.

The publisher and the author were unanimous in wanting a slender volume, so a certain amount of background is presupposed. For the basics I recommend the syntax and semantics chapters of the twelve-author textbook Fromkin (2000). A good thorough introduction to syntax is Koopman, Sportiche and Stabler (to appear). For formal foundations, the ideal background is a combination of Gamut (1991) and Chapters 2, 6, and 7 of Landman (1991). For lighter fare, use Allwood et al. (1977) and Szabolcsi (1997d). It will be extremely helpful if the reader is comfortable with

λ's. For a boost I recommend Chris Barker's famed Lambda Tutorial, http://homepages.nyu.edu/~cb125/Lambda/.

Where appropriate the text will point to handbook articles or textbooks, or to original works that have acquired comparable status, for background on the topic under discussion. To draw the reader's attention to these items the authors' names appear in small capitals.

1.3   Notation and terminology

As Montague (1974a,b) points out, the syntax of the object language may be directly interpreted in models, or translation into a suitably rich logical language may induce a model-theoretic interpretation for the object-language syntax. Montague uses the translation strategy; HEIM AND KRATZER (1998) use direct interpretation. The present book follows the translation strategy, because it makes it much easier to calculate with somewhat complex expressions. The reader should be aware of the following: (i) Expressions are translated into a logical language; the λ-operator for example is not used as part of the English meta-language; (ii) Square brackets indicating scope are not abandoned in favor of right-unbounded dots; (iii) The domain of quantification is either not indicated or its type appears as an index on the prefix. For example:

$$\text{Heim and Kratzer: } \lambda x \in D \; . \; P(x) = 1$$
$$\text{this book: } \lambda x_e [P(x)]$$

Following current syntactic practice we refer to syntactic units like *every dragon* as "quantifier phrases", "noun phrases", "DPs", or "QPs". The label "NP" is reserved for the complement of the determiner, as in the schematic form *every NP*. Notice that "NP" is not short for "noun phrase": *every dragon* is a noun phrase but *dragon* is a NP.

Plain italics, as in *every dragon*, indicate a mention of a natural-language expression. Adding a prime (in the text or in numbered examples), as in *every dragon′*, signifies both the counterpart of a natural-language expression in the syntax of some logical language, and the interpretation (denotation, meaning) of the expression. This convention allows us to avoid clumsy things like $[\![every\ dragon]\!]^{M,g}$. Although the convention is obviously sloppy and can be seen as complicit in promoting the confusion of logical syntax with model theoretic semantics, if the reader bears the distinction in mind it will always be clear which of the two things we are talking about in a given context.

Sometimes the interpretation of a linguistic example is prefixed with OK or #. Such annotation indicates that the example is acceptable or unacceptable on the given interpretation, and that no claim is being made as to whether the example has other interpretations.

2

Generalized quantifiers and their elements: operators and their scopes

2.1 Generalized quantifiers – heroes or old fogeys?

Starting with Montague (1974a) but at least with the almost simultaneous appearance of BARWISE AND COOPER (1981), Higginbotham and May (1981), and Keenan and Stavi (1986) generalized quantifiers became the staple of formal semantics. For decades it has been taken for granted that they serve as the interpretations of the most widely researched grammatical category in the field, i.e. noun phrases. Nevertheless, there is mounting evidence that generalized quantifiers are not the panacea magna they were once thought to be, and these days one reads more about what they cannot do than about what they can. So are generalized quantifiers a thing of the past? If not, what are they good for? What are the main reasons for them to be superseded, and by what?

Like many other books, this one starts out with generalized quantifiers, but it does so bearing the controversy around them in mind. This will also make it easier to highlight some of the underlying assumptions and some of the firm advantages of generalized quantifiers. Building on these foundations the book will survey two areas of research. One has to do with alternative approaches to scope assignment. The other has to do with the diversity in the behavior of quantifier phrases and with recent attempts to explain it in a compositional fashion. In this way the book will place an emphasis on ongoing work. Apart from the hope of stimulating research in these newer areas, making the unquestioningly generalized-quantifier-theoretic part relatively brief is justified by the fact that there are so many superb texts available on the topic. From the 1990s one would recommend KEENAN (1996), KEENAN AND WESTERSTÅHL (1997), and LANDMAN (1991). In recent years the most comprehensive and authoritative text is PETERS AND WESTERSTÅHL (2006); GLANZBERG (2006) and RUYS AND WINTER (2008) are excellent handbook chapters.

2.2   Generalized quantifiers and their elements: operators and their scopes

In many logics, operators are introduced syncategorematically. They are not expressions of the logical language; the syntax only specifies how they combine with expressions to yield new expressions, and the semantics specifies what their effect is:

(1)   If ϕ is a formula, $\forall x[\phi]$ is a formula.
        $\forall x[\phi]$ is true if and only if every assignment of values to the variable x makes ϕ true.

The quantifier prefix $\forall x$ functions like a diacritic in the phonetic alphabet: $'$ is not a character of the IPA but attaching it to a consonant symbol indicates that the sound is palatal (e.g. [t$'$]). In line with most of the linguistic literature we are going to assume that operators embodied by morphemes or phrases are never syncategorematic.[2] But if *every* and *every dragon* are ordinary expressions that belong to some syntactic category, then, by the principle of compositionality, they must have their own self-contained interpretations. This contrasts with the situation in predicate logic. In (2) the contributions of *every* and *every dragon* are scattered all over the formula without being subexpressions of it. Everything in (2) other than *guard treasure$'$* comes from *every dragon*, and everything other than *guard treasure$'$* and *dragon$'$* comes from *every*.

(2)   Every dragon guards treasure.
        $\forall x[dragon'(x) \rightarrow guard\ treasure'(x)]$

Not only would we like to assign a self-contained interpretation to *every dragon*, we would also like to assign it one that resembles, in significant respects, the kind of interpretations we assign to *Smaug* and *more than three dragons*. The reason why these are all categorized as DPs in syntax is that they exhibit very similar syntactic behavior. It is then natural to expect them to have in some respects similar semantics. If they did not, then the syntactic operations involving DPs (e.g. merging DP with a head, in current terminology) could not be given uniform interpretations. To a certain point it is easy to see how that interpretation would go. Assume that the DP *Smaug* refers to the individual s and the predicate (TP, a projection of Tense) *guards treasure* to the set of individuals that guard treasure. Interpreting the DP–TP relation as the set theoretical element-of relation, *Smaug guards treasure* will be interpreted as $s \in guard\ treasure'$. Now consider *Every dragon guards treasure*. The DP *every dragon* does not denote an individual, but we can associate with it a unique set of individuals, the set of dragons. Reinterpreting DP–TP using the subset relation, *Every dragon guards treasure* is compositionally interpreted as *dragon'* $\subseteq$ *guard treasure'*. To achieve uniformity, we can go back and recast $s \in$ *guard treasure'* as $\{s\} \subseteq$ *guard treasure'*, with $\{s\}$ the singleton set that contains just Smaug. But indefinite DPs like *more than three dragons* still cannot be accommodated, because there is no unique set of individuals they could be associated with. In a universe of just 5 dragons, sets of more than three dragons can be picked in various different ways.

One of Montague's (1974a) most important innovations was to provide a self-contained and uniform kind of denotation for all DPs in the form of generalized quantifiers, introduced mathematically in Mostowski (1957) based on Frege's fundamental idea. The name is due to the fact we generalize from the first order logical $\forall$ and $\exists$ and their direct descendants *every dragon* and *some dragon* to the whole gamut, *less than five dragons, at least one dragon, more dragons than serpents, the dragon,* etc., even including proper names like *Smaug*.

A generalized quantifier is a set of properties. In the examples below the generalized quantifiers are defined using English and, equivalently, in the language of set theory and in a simplified Montagovian notation, to highlight the fact that they do not have an inherent connection to any particular logical notation. The main simplification is that we present denotations extensionally. Thus each property is traded for the set of individuals that have the property (rather than the intensional analogue, a function from worlds to such sets of individuals), but the term "property" is retained, as customary, to evoke the relevant intuition. This approach fits all three of our examples equally well:

(3) a. *Smaug* denotes the set of properties that Smaug has. If Smaug is hungry, then the property of being hungry is an element of this set.

 b. *Smaug* denotes $\{P : s \in P\}$. If Smaug is hungry, then $\{a : a \in hungry'\} \in \{P : s \in P\}$.

 c. *Smaug* denotes $\lambda P[P(s)]$. If Smaug is hungry, then $\lambda P[P(s)]$ (*hungry'*) yields the value True.

(4) a. *Every dragon* denotes the set of properties that every dragon has. If every dragon is hungry, then the property of being hungry is an element of this set.

 b. *Every dragon* denotes $\{P : dragon' \subseteq P\}$. If every dragon is hungry, then $\{a : a \in hungry'\} \in \{P : dragon' \subseteq P\}$.

 c. *Every dragon* denotes $\lambda P \forall x[dragon'(x) \rightarrow P(x)]$. If every dragon is hungry, then $\lambda P \forall x[dragon'(x) \rightarrow P(x)](hungry')$ yields the value True.

(5)   a.   *More than one dragon* denotes the set of properties that more
            than one dragon has. If more than one dragon is hungry, then
            the property of being hungry is an element of this set.

      b.   *More than one dragon* denotes $\{P : |dragon' \cap P| > 1\}$. If
            more than one dragon is hungry, then $\{a : a \in hungry'\} \in$
            $\{P : |dragon' \cap P| > 1\}$.

      c.   *More than one dragon* denotes $\lambda P \exists x \exists y[x \neq y \wedge dragon'(x) \wedge$
            $dragon'(y) \wedge P(x) \wedge P(y)]$. If more than one dragon is hun-
            gry, then $\lambda P \exists x \exists y[x \neq y \wedge dragon'(x) \wedge dragon'(y) \wedge P(x) \wedge$
            $P(y)](hungry')$ yields the value True.

To make this set of sets of individuals more vivid, it is useful to invoke
some simple notions of set theory. The powerset of a set A is the set of
all A's subsets. The powerset is so called because a set of n elements has
2^n subsets (2 to the nth power). Imagine a universe of discourse with 4
elements. Its powerset, i.e. the set of all its 16 subsets, is as follows:

(6)   Let the universe of discourse be the set $\{a, b, c, d\}$. Then the set
      of all its subsets, i.e. its powerset is $\{\emptyset, \{a\}, \{b\}, \{c\}, \{d\}, \{a,b\},$
      $\{a,c\}, \{a,d\}, \{b,c\}, \{b,d\}, \{c,d\}, \{a,b,c\}, \{a,b,d\}, \{a,c,d\},$
      $\{b, c, d\}, \{a, b, c, d\}\}$.

Extensional semantics can distinguish just these 16 sets of individuals
(properties) in a 4-element universe. For example, if the set of dragons is
$\{a, b, c\}$ and the set of things that fly is $\{a, b, d\}$, then the properties of being a dragon and being a thing that flies can be distinguished. But if both
sets happen to have the same elements, then an extensional semantics
cannot distinguish them.

Some sets in the universe have names such as *dragon, flies*, etc. whereas
others do not. But for our purposes all these are on a par. The most useful
label for $\{a, b\}$ is not 'dragon that flies' but, rather, 'entity that is identical
to a or b'. When we ask whether a particular sentence, e.g. *Smaug flies* is
true, we are interested in sets with particular linguistic labels, but when
we study the quantifiers themselves, we are interested in all the sets that
are elements of the quantifier and in their relation to all the other subsets
of the universe.

To visualize a generalized quantifier we draw the Hasse-diagram of the
powerset of the universe. The lines represent the subset relation, thus $\{a\}$
is below $\{a, b\}$ and $\{a, b\}$ below $\{a, b, c\}$, because $\{a\} \subseteq \{a, b\} \subseteq \{a, b, c\}$.
Each generalized quantifier is represented as an area (a subset) in this
diagram. If Smaug is the individual a, and the set of dragons is $\{a, b, c\}$,
the generalized quantifiers denoted by the DPs *Smaug, every dragon*, and
more than one dragon are the shaded areas in Figures 2.1, 2.2, and 2.3,
respectively. Such diagrams will be used over and over in Chapter 4.

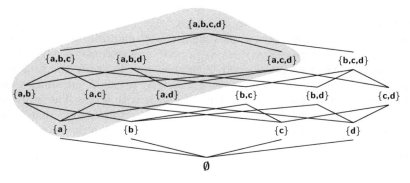

Fig. 2.1 The set of properties Smaug has: all the sets that have
a as an element

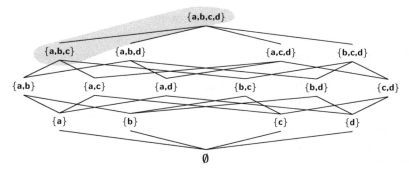

Fig. 2.2 The set of properties every dragon has: all the sets that have $\{a, b, c\}$
as a subset

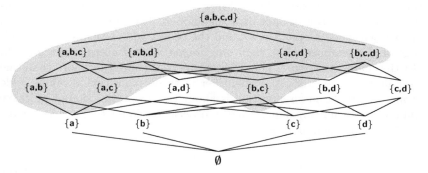

Fig. 2.3 The set of properties more than one dragon has: all the sets whose
intersection with $\{a, b, c\}$ has more than one element

Recall that our desire for a uniform interpretation stems from the fact that all DPs play similar roles in syntax.[3] We now have such an interpretation. The specific notion of a generalized quantifier is furthermore useful in two main respects. First, it provides a foundation for the treatment of quantifier scope. Second, it enables one to study the semantic properties of DPs, and to do so in a way that possibly subsumes them under cross-categorial generalizations. We start with scope. The property (*is*) *hungry'* mentioned above has a simple description, but that is an accident. Properties might have arbitrarily complex descriptions:

(7)   If every dragon flies or lumbers, then the property of being an individual such that he/she/it flies or he/she/it lumbers is in the set of properties every dragon has.

(8)   If there is more than one dragon that spotted every adventurer, then the property of being an individual such that he/she/it spotted every adventurer is an element of the set of properties more than one dragon has.

(9)   If every adventurer was spotted by more than one dragon, then the property of being an individual such that there is more than one dragon that spotted him/her/it is an element of the set of properties every adventurer has.

Properties with simple descriptions and ones with complex descriptions are entirely on a par. We are not adding anything to the idea of generalized quantifiers by allowing properties of the latter kind. But once the possibility is recognized, quantifier scope is taken care of. In each case above, some operation is buried in the description of the property that is asserted to be an element of the generalized quantifier. In (7) the buried operation is disjunction; thus (7) describes a configuration in which universal quantification scopes over disjunction. (8) and (9) correspond to the subject wide scope, S > O, and the object wide scope, O > S, readings of the sentence *More than one dragon spotted every adventurer*. In (8) the main assertion is about the properties shared by more than one dragon, thus the existential quantifier in subject position is taking wide scope. In (9) the main assertion is about the properties shared by every man, thus the universal quantifier in object position is taking wide scope.

This is all there is to it:

(10)   Scope
The scope of a quantificational DP, on a given analysis of the sentence, is that part of the sentence which denotes a property that is asserted to be an element of the generalized quantifier denoted by DP on that analysis.

2.3 Scope and constituent structure

2.3.1 The basic idea

The scope of an operator in logic is simply the constituent that it is attached to. All properties of absolute and relative scope follow from this.

In talking about natural language one has to distinguish between semantic scope, as in (10), and syntactic domain. In her pioneering and immensely influential work on syntactic domains for semantic rules, Reinhart (1979, 1983) hypothesized the following:

(11)   Hypothesis about Scope and Domain
        The semantic scope of a linguistic operator coincides with its domain in some syntactic representation that the operator is part of.

Reinhart defines the syntactic domain of an expression as its sister relative to the first branching node above it (the expression c-commands the nodes in its sister). Her specific assumption in these works is that the only relevant syntactic representation is surface structure, but the key idea is the more general one, namely, that syntactic structure determines semantic scope and does so in a very particular way. This is not the only possible view: for example, Cooper (1983) and Farkas (1997a) put forth non-structural theories of scope. So one important task for work on the syntax/semantics interface is to determine whether (11) is correct, and if yes, exactly what kind of syntactic representations and notion of domain bear it out.

On the structural view of scope the readings in (7), (8), and (9) correspond to the semantic constituent structures (12), (13), and (14), respectively:

(12)   (Every dragon)   ((flies) or (lumbers))

(13)   (More than one dragon)   ((spotted) (every adventurer))

(14)   ((More than one dragon)   (spotted))   (every adventurer)

How well do these semantic constituents match up with syntactic constituents? Initial encouragement comes from the fact that overt *wh*-fronting creates similar constituents. *Flies or lumbers, spotted every adventurer,* and *more than one dragon spotted* are semantic constituents in (12)–(13)–(14) and syntactic constituents in (15)–(16)–(17).

(15)   Who flies or lumbers?

(16)   Who spotted every adventurer?

(17)   Who did more than one dragon spot?

So such constituents are syntactically possible; but the question remains as to whether all scope-semantically motivated constituents are syntactically plausible.

In this section we consider two rather different ways to implement the above ideas concerning scope and to answer these questions. The approaches of Montague and May produce the above constituent structures in abstract syntax, whether or not there is independent purely syntactic evidence for them. In contrast, the approaches of Hendriks and of Barker and Shan dissociate scope from pure syntax. Their systems allow one to maintain whatever constituent structure seems motivated on independent syntactic grounds and still deliver all imaginable scope relations. Finally, the proof-theoretical perspective in Jäger (2005) and Barker (2007) offers a way to move between these as desired.

The goals of this discussion are twofold. One is to introduce some fundamental technologies. Another is to show that there is no deep semantic necessity to opt for one technology or the other; the choices can be tailored to what one finds insightful and what the empirical considerations dictate.

2.3.2   The (first) proper treatment of quantification: Montague

We consider two derivations of *More than one dragon spotted every man* in an extensionalized version of Montague's PTQ (1974a). Montague used a syntax inspired by but not identical to a categorial grammar and built sentences bottom-up. This was very unusual at the time when linguists used top-down phrase structure rules, but today, in the era of Merge in Minimalism, it should look entirely natural.

We assume verbs to denote functions of individuals (entities of type e).[4] Because quantifier phrases do not denote individuals, they cannot serve as arguments of such verbs. In line with the reasoning above, quantifier phrases combine with expressions that denote properties, and the semantic effect of the combination is to assert that the property is an element of the generalized quantifier. The subject being the highest, i.e. last, argument of the verb, inflected verb phrases denote a property anyway, so a subject quantifier phrase can enter the sentence without further ado. If the quantifier phrase is not the last argument, the derivation must ensure that a property-denoting expression is formed in one way or another. This is what HEIM AND KRATZER (1998: Chapter 7) refer to as Quantifier Raising forced by a type-mismatch.

Montague's PTQ offers several ways to build the subject wide scope, $S > O$, and the object wide scope, $O > S$, readings of a sentence. Those chosen below will make the relation between Montague's, May's, and Hendriks's methods the most transparent. We start by applying the verb to arguments interpreted as free individual variables and build a sentence without quantifiers. Montague notated such variables with indexed pronouns in the syntactic derivation; we employ indexed empty categories *ec*. Properties (of type $\langle e, t \rangle$) are then formed from this sentence by abstracting over the variables one by one. Abstraction is achieved by binding the variable by a λ-operator.

(18)   If α is an expression, $\lambda x[\alpha]$ is an expression. $\lambda x[\alpha]$ denotes a function of type $\langle b, a \rangle$, where b is the type of the variable x and a is the type of the function value α. When applied to some argument β of the same type as x, the value of the function is computed by replacing every occurrence of x bound by λx in α by β. E.g. $\lambda x[x^2](3) = 3^2$.

Each time a property is formed, a quantifier can be introduced. The later a quantifier is introduced, the wider its scope: other operators may already be buried in the definition of the property that it combines with, and therefore they fall within its scope. The derivation of the reading where the subject existential scopes over the direct-object universal is given first. Recall that it is to be read bottom-up, starting with "build a sentence with two free variables." The cardinality quantifier *more than one* will be abbreviated using $\exists_{>1}$. The last step is spelled out in (20).

(19)   Subject > Object reading

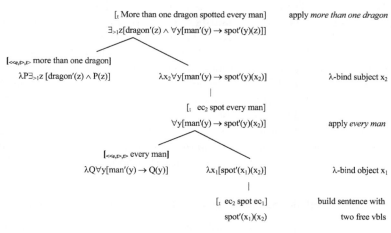

(20) $\lambda P \exists_{>1} z [dragon'(z) \wedge P(z)](\lambda x_2 \forall y [man'(y) \rightarrow spot'(y)(x_2)]) =$
        $\exists_{>1} z [dragon'(z) \wedge \lambda x_2 \forall y [man'(y) \rightarrow spot'(y)(x_2)](z)] =$
        $\exists_{>1} z [dragon'(z) \wedge \forall y [man'(y) \rightarrow spot'(y)(z)]]$

The derivation of the reading where the direct-object universal scopes over the subject existential differs from the above in just one respect: properties are formed by λ-binding the subject variable first and the direct-object variable second, which reverses the order of introducing the two quantifier phrases. The last step that introduces the universal is in (22):

(21)   Object > Subject reading

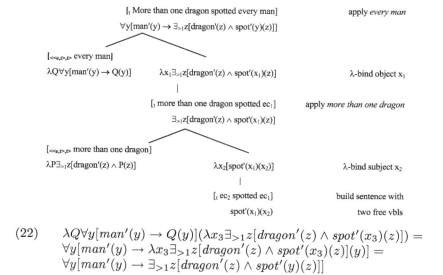

(22) $\lambda Q \forall y[man'(y) \rightarrow Q(y)](\lambda x_3 \exists_{>1} z[dragon'(z) \wedge spot'(x_3)(z)]) =$
$\forall y[man'(y) \rightarrow \lambda x_3 \exists_{>1} z[dragon'(z) \wedge spot'(x_3)(z)](y)] =$
$\forall y[man'(y) \rightarrow \exists_{>1} z[dragon'(z) \wedge spot'(y)(z)]]$

Montague's PTQ collapsed the two steps of λ-binding a free variable and applying a generalized quantifier to the property so formed into a single rule of quantifying-in. To make the derivation more transparent, we disentangled the two steps, as do HEIM AND KRATZER (1998), who construe λ-abstraction as the reflex of the movement of the index on the variable.[5] We followed PTQ in replacing the variable with the quantifier phrase in the surface string. This feature is syntactically unsophisticated and need not be taken too seriously; see May and Hendriks below.

Before turning to other ways to achieve the same interpretive results we take a brief look at quantifiers binding pronouns, among other reasons in order to explain why it makes sense for this book to set them aside.

2.3.3   Interlude: quantifier phrases do not directly bind pronouns

Predicate-logical quantifiers do not only bind variables that allow them to function as arguments of predicates. (23), which can be seen to translate one reading of (24), contains three bound occurrences of the variable x, of which the one in $room\text{-}of'(x)$ corresponds to the pronoun *his*.

(23) $\forall x[boy(x) \rightarrow in\text{-}room\text{-}of'(x)(x)]$

(24)   Every boy is in his room.

Is the relation between *every boy* and *his* a case of binding in the same sense as the relation between $\forall x$ and the x of *room-of'*(x) is, as has often been assumed? Nothing in our account of quantifier phrases as generalized quantifiers explains how they bind pronouns!

This is in fact as it should be. The bound reading of the pronoun in (24) does not come about in the same way as the binding of the x's in (23). In (23) the three variables are all directly bound by $\forall x$ because, in addition to being within its scope, they happen to have the same letter as the quantifier prefix. In contrast, pronouns are not directly bound by quantifier phrases in natural language. In the well-known parlance of syntactic Binding Theory, pronouns have to be co-indexed with a c-commanding item in argument position (subject, object, possessor, etc.), not with one in operator position (the landing site of *wh*-movement or the adjoined position created by Quantifier Raising). The claim that syntactic binding is a relation between argument positions is grounded primarily in data about reflexives but it is thought to extend to pronouns and offers a simple account of strong and weak crossover.[6]

If the pronoun is directly linked to the c-commanding argument position and not to the quantifier itself, what is the actual operator that binds it? It is the operator that identifies the pronoun with a c-commanding argument position. The technologies for achieving identification are varied, but the interpretive result is always the same. (25) presents three equivalent metalinguistic descriptions of the bound pronoun reading of the VP *saw his/her/its own father*:

(25)   a.   be an individual such that he/she/it saw his/her/its own father

   b. $\{a : a$ saw a's father$\}$

   c. $\lambda x[x$ *saw* x's *father*$]$

So the operator that binds the pronoun is the abstraction operator λ. (Montague's original grammar in PTQ makes the binding of pronouns part of the job of his rule of quantification. The reason is that, as was mentioned, he collapses predicate abstraction and applying the generalized quantifier to the predicate into a single rule. Decoupling the two, as in HEIM AND KRATZER (1998) and in the discussion above, is motivated not only by notational transparency but also by the reasoning in this section.)

The property in (25) combines with a noun phrase denotation as other properties do, and the pronoun's antecedent is specified:

(26)   If every girl saw her own father, then the property of being an individual such that he/she/it saw his/her/its own father is an element of the set of properties shared by every girl.

We should also mention that Sportiche (2005) as well as Barker and Shan (2008) differ from Reinhart regarding the role of c-command in the bound-variable readings of pronouns. See (30) below.

To summarize, although the interaction of quantifiers and pronouns raises many important questions and supplies an important set of data, by setting them aside in this book we do not deprive quantifiers of one of their fundamental roles. For general discussion see BÜRING (2005); SZABOLCSI (2008).

2.3.4   Quantifier Raising: May

May's (1977, 1985) generative syntactic treatment of quantifier scope is the most similar to Montague's. May first derives a syntactic structure leading to the surface string with quantifier phrases in argument positions. This structure is input to further syntactic rules whose output (Logical Form) feeds only semantic interpretation, not pronunciation. Such a rule is Quantifier Raising (QR), which adjoins quantifier phrases to VP or to S (Tense Phrase, TP in more recent terminology). The scope of the adjoined quantifier phrase is its c-command domain. We simply assume that a phrase c-commands its sister relative to the first branching node above it. Crucial is the consequence that the higher a quantifier is adjoined, the wider scope it takes.

Notice that (27) is parallel to Montague's (19) and (28) to Montague's (21). A syntactic difference is that Montague intersperses the steps that disambiguate scope with those that create the surface string, and May does not.

(27)

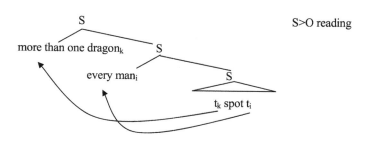

(28)

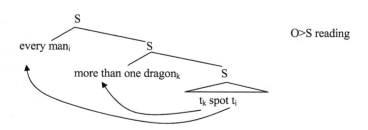

A difference more important to us is that while May treats the phrases *every man* and *more than one dragon* as normal categorematic expressions in deriving the surface syntax, in his Logical Form these phrases behave like the syncategorematic operators of the predicate calculus: they are co-indexed with the traces left by QR directly, without the mediation of λ-abstraction. This difference can be eliminated by imagining that there is an abstraction-step hidden between assembling an S and adjoining a quantifier phrase to it, such as $\lambda t_i[spot(t_i)(t_k)]$ preceding the adjunction of *every man* to S in (27). With that, the parallelism between the two pairs of derivations is essentially complete. Reversing historical order we might look at Montague's grammar as one that builds the output of May's compositionally, without invoking movement. HEIM AND KRATZER (1998) show that a compositional strategy may even include movement. Specifically within the copy theory of movement FOX (2002a,b) reinterprets the lowest copy of QR as a definite description with a bindable variable; see §4.2.2.

Looking back, both May's and Montague's scope assignment strategies conform to our basic assumption about scope in (10). May's is intended to conform to (11), the hypothesis about scope and syntactic domain as well because, May argues, the Logical Form (LF) representations produced by QR are part of syntax. That means that LF representations obey essentially the same principles that govern the well-formedness of syntactic representations that feed Phonetic Form. In May (1985) this claim is in fact only partially borne out. For example, QR indeed obeys certain principles that overt movement does, but it also operates more locally than its semantically plausible overt relative, *wh*-movement. A universal quantifier does not scope out of its tensed clause, but a *wh*-phrase may move out of it tensed clause. With the advent of feature-driven movement in Minimalist syntax (Chomsky 1995) the fact that QR is a non-feature-driven adjunction operation became another point of difference. Such reasons led HORNSTEIN (1995) to propose that QR does not exist, and scope is a by-product of movement motivated by Case-assignment, which is indeed clause-bounded (i.e. operates within the confines of one tensed clause). Kennedy (1997) demonstrates that antecedent-contained verb-phrase deletion can only avoid infinite regress if it involves an instance of QR that cannot be motivated by Case; this is a strong argument against Hornstein's proposal. Are we then back to square one with respect to the clause-boundedness of QR? Cecchetto (2004) points out that Chomsky's (2001) Phase Theory offers a natural way to accommodate it. A phase is a chunk of structure at the edge of which syntactic memory is emptied, similarly to Cooper's (1983) theory of quantification, where the so-called quantifier store is obligatorily emptied at the clause-boundary. As of date QR remains part of Minimalist syntax. (See SzABOLCSI 2000 and FOX 2002a for a more detailed overview of the syntax of scope, and Chapter 11 for some recent developments.)

It is not too difficult to argue that quantifier scope is syntactically constrained if in doing so one is allowed to postulate syntactic structures and syntactic constraints whose justification comes exclusively, or largely, from matters of interpretation. Among others, such is the constraint that the semantic scope of a linguistic operator coincides with its c-command domain, the most popular version of (11). It turns out that if one carefully discounts all cases where the non-c-commanding operator is also separated from the intended dependent element by a tensed-clause boundary, then evidence for the c-command restriction is slim. Consider for example (29), an example that would demonstrate that it is not sufficient for a quantifier to precede a pronoun to bind it.

(29)   That every boy was hungry surprised his mother.
          # 'for every boy, that he was hungry surprised his own mother'

In (29) *every boy* does not c-command *his mother* and, indeed, the latter has no bound-variable interpretation. But *every boy* is also separated from *his mother* by a tensed-clause boundary, so the latter does not even fall within the quantifier's scope. It is probably for such reasons that Sportiche (2005) does not make structural c-command a condition on scope and on pronoun binding, contra Reinhart (1979, 1983) and much literature following her; Barker and Shan (2008) advocate a similar revision.

(30)   Sportiche's Principles of Scope:
          (i) If X superficially c-commands Y, Y can be interpreted in the scope of X.
          (ii) X and Y can outscope each other only if X and Y are clause-mates.
          Principle of Pronominal Binding:
          A pronoun can behave as a variable bound by X only if it can be interpreted in the scope of X.

2.3.5 All the scopes, but a simple syntax: Hendriks

What emerges from the above is that any representation of the S > O and the O > S readings will have to boil down to the schemas in (31)–(32). $P(x)(y)$ is forced by the assumption that the natural language predicates at hand take individuals as arguments. The λ-binding (predicate-abstraction) steps are forced by the assumption that quantifier phrases denote generalized quantifiers. The two schemas differ as to which argument slot is λ-bound first and which second.

(31) $\quad QP_A(\lambda y[QP_B(\lambda x[P(x)(y)])])$ $\hspace{3cm}$ S > O

(32) $\quad QP_A(\lambda x[QP_B(\lambda y[P(x)(y)])])$ $\hspace{3cm}$ O > S

One of the key insights in Hendriks (1993) is that it is possible to abstract these interpretive schemas away from the specific quantifier phrases QP_A and QP_B. This in turn allows one to dissociate the interpretive schema from the syntactic constituent structure of the sentence.

Replace QP_A and QP_B with variables A and B of the same type as generalized quantifiers, $\langle\langle e,t\rangle, t\rangle$, and abstract over them with λ-operators. Because the variables A, B are not individual variables but are of the generalized quantifier type, the λ-expressions in (33)–(34) take quantifier phrases as arguments, rather than the other way around. The order in which the λA and λB prefixes appear determines the order in which the verb picks up its arguments, but it does not affect their scope, so it can be dictated by independent syntactic considerations; for example we may assume an invariant (S (V O)) structure. In both (33) and (34) the first quantifier phrase the λ-expression applies to will be the direct object. The relative scope of the quantifier phrases replacing A and B is determined by their relative order within the underlined portions of (33)–(34):

(33) $\quad \lambda B \lambda A[\underline{A(\lambda y[B(\lambda x[P(x)(y)])])}]$ $\hspace{2cm}$ schema of S > O

(34) $\quad \lambda B \lambda A[\underline{B(\lambda x[A(\lambda y[P(x)(y)])])}]$ $\hspace{2cm}$ schema of O > S

This is a nimbler logic than the first-order predicate calculus; it allows one to arrest the action of a quantifier at the point it enters the formula and to release it where desired. The quantifier's action is released where it actually applies to an expression that denotes a property. Notice that (33) and (34) fully conform to (10), although they abandon (11).[7]

Where are the schemas in (33)–(34) coming from, if they do not simply record the phrase-by-phrase assembly of the material of the sentence? Hendriks proposes to assign flexible types to verbs, so that two versions of *spot* for example anticipate two different scope relations between the subject and the object. (33) and (34) are two interpretations for the same transitive verb P. Below is a constituent-by-constituent derivation of the

O > S reading. The verb combines with both the direct object and the subject by functional application:

(35) $spot'$: $\lambda B \lambda A[B(\lambda z[A(\lambda v[spot'(z)(v)])])]$
$every\ man'$: $\lambda Q \forall y[man'(y) \rightarrow Q(y)]$
$spotted\ every\ man'$:
$\lambda B \lambda A[B(\lambda z[A(\lambda v[spot'(z)(v)])])](\lambda Q \forall y[man'(y) \rightarrow Q(y)]) =$
$=\ \ \lambda A[\forall y[man'(y) \rightarrow A(\lambda v[spot'(y)(v)])]]$
$more\ than\ one\ dragon'$: $\lambda P \exists_{>1} z[dragon'(z) \wedge P(z)]$
$more\ than\ one\ dragon\ spotted\ every\ man'$:
$\lambda A[\forall y[man'(y) \rightarrow A(\lambda v[spot'(y)(v)])]]$
$(\lambda P \exists_{>1} z[dragon'(z) \wedge P(z)]) =$
$=\ \ \forall y[man'(y) \rightarrow \exists_{>1} z[dragon'(z) \wedge spot'(y)(z)]]$

This is the gist of Hendriks's proposal. More generally, he shows two important things. First, the different interpretations for the verb can be obtained systematically by so-called type-change rules, in this case by two applications of Argument Raising, see (36). (33) and (34) are due to two different orders in which the subject and the object slots are raised, cf. the underlined segments. Second, all the logically possible scope relations in an arbitrarily multi-clausal sentence, including extensional–intensional ambiguities, can be anticipated by the use of three type-change rules: Argument Raising, Value Raising, and Argument Lowering. We ignore the last one, which turns an intensional relation into an extensional one between individuals, much like Montague's meaning postulate pertaining to $seek'$, because in this book we remain agnostic about the proper treatment of de re/de dicto ambiguities. Below are extensionalized Argument Raising and Value Raising. The simplified version of Value Raising is nothing else than the good old type-raising rule that turns proper names into generalized quantifiers.[8]

(36)   Argument Raising:
If α' is the translation of α, and α' is of type $\langle A, \langle b, \langle C, d \rangle \rangle \rangle$, then

$$\lambda x_A \lambda w_{\langle \langle b,d \rangle, d \rangle} \lambda y_C[w(\lambda z_b[\alpha'(x)(z)(y)])],$$

which is of type $\langle A, \langle \langle \langle b, d \rangle, d \rangle, \langle C, d \rangle \rangle \rangle$, is also a translation of α, where A and C stand for possibly empty sequences of types such that if g is a type, $\langle A, g \rangle$ and $\langle C, g \rangle$ represent the types $\langle a_1, \langle \ldots \langle a_n, g \rangle \ldots \rangle \rangle$ and $\langle c_1, \langle \ldots \langle c_n, g \rangle \ldots \rangle \rangle$.

Simplified by taking A and C to be empty:
If α' is the translation of α, and α' is of type $\langle b, d \rangle$, then

$$\lambda w_{\langle \langle b,d \rangle, d \rangle}[w(\lambda z_b[\alpha'(z)])],$$

which is of type $\langle \langle \langle b, d \rangle, d \rangle, d \rangle$, is also a translation of α.

(37)   Value Raising:
        If α' is the translation of α, and α' is of type $\langle A, b \rangle$, then
        $\lambda x_A \lambda u_{\langle b, d \rangle} [u(\alpha'(x))]$, which is of type $\langle A, \langle \langle b, d \rangle, d \rangle \rangle$, is also a
        translation of α, where A stands for a possibly empty sequence
        of types such that if g is a type, $\langle A, g \rangle$ represents the types
        $\langle a_1, \langle \ldots \langle a_n, g \rangle \ldots \rangle \rangle$.

        Simplified by taking A to be empty:
        If α' is the translation of α, and α' is of type b, then $\lambda u_{\langle b, d \rangle} [u(\alpha')]$,
        which is of type $\langle \langle b, d \rangle, d \rangle$, is also a translation of α.

Let us mention two other scope phenomena that involve the dissocia-
tion of the chronological order of introducing operators into the syntactic
structure from the scope they take, and have been handled in the linguistic
literature using pieces of logical machinery that are essentially identical
to Hendriks's Argument Raising and Value Raising.

Cresti (1995) analyzes "scope reconstruction" using a combination of
generalized-quantifier-type and individual-type variables, to an effect very
much like that of Argument Raising. Following Higginbotham (1993),
Cresti (1995) splits *how many people* into two quantifiers. "Reconstruction" is so called because in (i) *n-many people* is "put back" into a lower
position for interpretation.

(38)   How many people do you think I should talk to?
        (i) 'for what number n, you think it should be the case that there
        are n-many people that I talk to'
        (narrow scope, amount reading of *how many people*)
        (ii) 'for what number n, there are n-many people x such that you
        think I should talk to x'
        (wide scope, individual reading of *how many people*)

Cresti derives the two readings without actual reconstruction. In the
derivations below, x is a trace of type e (individuals), and X is a trace of
the same type as *n-many people* (intensionalized generalized quantifiers).
The latter, higher order variable plays the exact same role here as the
variables A and B do in (33) and (34). Working bottom-up, each trace is
bound by a λ-operator to allow the next trace or the moved phrase itself
to enter the chain. The lowest position of the chain is always occupied
by a trace x of the individual type, but intermediate traces (underlined)
may make one switch to the higher type X. The scope difference with
respect to the intensional operator *should* is due to the fact that in (39)
the switch from x to X takes place within the scope of *should*, whereas in
(40) *should* has no X in its scope. Note that the direction of functional

application is type-driven. In X $\lambda x[\ldots]$ the first expression applies to the second, whereas in X $\lambda X[\ldots]$ the second applies to the first.

(39)   narrow scope:
[$_{CP}$ how many people λX [$_{IP}$ ...think [$_{CP}$ $\underline{X}$ λX [$_{IP}$ ...should [$_{VP}$ $\underline{X}$ λx [$_{VP}$ ...x...]]]]]]

(40)   wide scope:
[$_{CP}$ how many people λX [$_{IP}$ $\underline{X}$ λx [$_{IP}$ think [$_{CP}$ $\underline{x}$ λx [$_{IP}$ ...should [$_{VP}$ ...x...]]]]]]

Moltmann and Szabolcsi (1994) use an idea very much like Value Raising (37) to account for the surprising 'librarians vary with students' reading of (41):

(41)   Some librarian or other found out which book every student needed.
    'for every student x, there is some librarian or other who found out which book x needed'

Every student in the complement can make the matrix subject referentially dependent; but under normal circumstances *every NP* is known not to scope out of its own clause. Moltmann and Szabolcsi argue that there is no need to assume that here, either. Instead, the clausal complement of *found out*, i.e. *which book every student needed*, receives a pair-list reading: 'for every student, which book did he need'. This "pair-list quantifier" as a whole scopes over the subject of *found out*, its clause-mate. The result is logically equivalent to scoping *every student* out on its own. (More on reconstruction in §**3.2**, and on pair-list readings in §**4.1.4**.)

Generally, let a "layered" quantifier be a QP_a that contains one or more other quantifier phrases. Besides pair-list readings, possessive constructions are a good example:

(42)   a.   every boy's mother
       b.   an inhabitant of every city

Let QP_b take wide scope within QP_a. Quantifying QP_a into a syntactic domain is logically equivalent to assigning QP_b wide scope over that domain. This is the basis for May's (1985) treatment of (42) without adjoining the universals to S: he adjoins the wide-scoping QP_b just to QP_a. We see that the equivalence is also an empirically welcome result when QP_a is a *wh*-complement. But reliance on it overgenerates when QP_a is a *that*-complement.

While neither Cresti nor Moltmann and Szabolcsi use flexible types for verbs, the proposals illustrate the naturalness of the logical tools, Argument Raising and Value Raising, that Hendriks employs. Bittner's

(1993) cross-linguistic semantics systematically exploits similar insights. Bittner's system differs from Hendriks's in that it is not designed to make everything possible. Its intention is to distinguish between universal, unmarked interpretations and language-specifically available marked ones.

Inspired by computer science, Barker and Shan (2006) associate linguistic expressions with their possible continuations. A continuation is the skeleton of a syntactico-semantic structure that the expression anticipates participating in. Continuized types are similar to Hendriks's raised types and to context change potentials in dynamic semantics.

2.3.6 Continuations and scope: Barker and Shan

Barker and Shan's system rests on this main idea:

(43)   The meaning of an expression is the set of its possible "continuations".

This builds on a rich tradition: Montague's generalized quantifiers as denotations for noun phrases; Cooper's (1983) quantifier storage; Hendriks's verb meanings that anticipate how their dependents will arrange themselves in a particular scopal configuration; dynamic semantics for pronominal anaphora; continuation-passing style in functional programming (Plotkin 1975), etc. Related notions are the sets of alternatives in Hamblin (1973) and Rooth (1992).

Beyond the basic insight, the implementation and its utility depend on what kinds of continuations are catered to. One way of looking at generalized quantifiers is that by virtue of being functions from properties to truth values they anticipate the kind of semantic objects they are going to combine with. Hendriks's scope grammar additionally makes a head, e.g. a verb anticipate (by Argument Raising), the whole derivation in which its dependents will be arranged in a particular scopal configuration; moreover, the head may anticipate (by Value Raising) its maximal projection being a complement of a higher head. In dynamic semantics, most intuitively sentences anticipate being continued with another sentence and to provide antecedents for pronouns in that sentence. So "anticipation" may pertain to argument structure, to scope, to anaphora, and other things.

Barker and Shan have developed a system whose formalism primarily specializes in scope taking and in the binding of pronouns by quantifiers (i.e. quantificational binding). Given the self-imposed thematic limitations of this volume we ignore binding, but we note that the way binding interacts with scope is essential in assessing the merits or demerits of this system. Regarding scope, one of the important ideas can be expressed in generative syntactic terms as follows:[9]

(44)   Pied piping everywhere
        When a phrase XP contains a wide-scoping operator of some sort,
        it becomes an operator-XP. I.e. it inherits the "operator feature"
        and behaves accordingly.

To take the simplest cases of pied piping, *about which* is a PP, but it is also a *wh*-expression, so it behaves like *wh*-phrases do in the given language. In English, it will be fronted under the appropriate circumstances, e.g. *(those secrets,) about which I cannot speak*. It is appropriate to call it a *wh*-PP. *About everyone* is a PP, but it is also a quantifier phrase, so it takes scope in the way quantifier phrases do; it is a quantificational PP. *About himself* is a PP, but it is also an anaphor, so it must find an appropriate binder; it is an anaphor-PP. Generalizing, *speak about which* is a *wh*-VP, cf. *(those secrets,) speaking about which would be dangerous*, *see everyone* is a quantificational VP, *see himself* is an anaphor-VP, and so on.[10]

What does this imply for the way sentences are built step by step? Focusing just on quantifiers, it implies that not only plain *everyone* must be introduced by some kind of a rule of quantification, but *about everyone* and *see everyone* must too. If we take a sentence where all the noun phrases happen to be quantifiers, then all the steps of building the sentence are quantifying-in steps.

Another implication is that the grammar must ensure that the expectation to be continued is passed from smaller expressions to the larger ones they build. A highly simplified picture of Groenendijk and Stokhof's (1990, 1991) dynamic semantics may be the best linguistic illustration of the "continuation-passing" idea (although as a matter of personal history Barker and Shan were inspired by computer science). One of the descriptive questions dynamic theories seek to answer is how singular indefinites support pronominal anaphora even in the absence of c-command – something that universals do not do:

(45)   a.   A dragon lumbered to the meadow. It hissed.
        b.   Every dragon lumbered to the meadow. # It hissed.

If *a dragon* is an existentially quantified expression, as we have been assuming with Montague, then it is mysterious how it is linked to the pronoun *it* despite the latter being outside the quantifier's scope. Heim (1982) proposes to equate the meaning of an expression with its context-change potential, especially its potential to serve as an antecedent for anaphoric expressions. She also proposes however that *a dragon'* is not a quantifier, but an open proposition (one with a free variable). Groenendijk and Stokhof adopt the first, fundamental innovation, but explore the possibility to maintain that indefinites denote quantifiers. For present purposes

the following simplification of the theory will suffice. First, Groenendijk
and Stokhof assume that all expressions are associated with the set of
their possible continuations. I.e. all sentences will be interpreted in the
following format: $\lambda p[\ldots p \ldots]$, where p is a variable over possible continuations. The contributions of indefinites and universals differ as to where
they force the continuation variable to be located. To model the fact that
indefinites are capable of extending their binding scope over the incoming
discourse, the continuation variable will find itself within the indefinite's
scope. To model the fact that universals cannot do the same, the continuation variable will find itself outside the universal's scope. If pronouns
are free variables, this machinery must be supplemented with abstraction
over assignments, so the pronoun can be brought within the scope of the
indefinite; binding itself is effected by an assignment-switcher. Because
this aspect is immaterial to present concerns, I will simply omit these
ingredients, although the omission makes the following logically plainly
incorrect.[11] (46)–(47) are the interpretations of the two sentences in (45a)
as sets of possible continuations:[12]

(46) $\lambda p \exists x[dragon'(x) \wedge lumber'(x) \wedge p]$

(47) $\lambda q[hiss'(x) \wedge q]$

Sets of continuations are combined by functional composition (whether
the two clauses are joined by *and* or simply form a sequence).[13] Functional
composition has two important consequences. First, the core of (47) fills
an argument slot in (46), that of the conjunct p. Second, (47) passes its
own expectation to be continued on to the result.

(48) $\lambda p \exists x[dragon'(x) \wedge lumber'(x) \wedge p] \circ \lambda q[hiss'(x) \wedge q] =$
         $\lambda r[\lambda p[\exists x[dragon'(x) \wedge lumber'(x) \wedge p]](\lambda q[hiss'(x) \wedge q](r))] =$
         $\lambda r \exists x[dragon'(x) \wedge lumber'(x) \wedge hiss'(x) \wedge r]$

What if we want to finish our story? To eliminate the possibility of further
continuations and to obtain a traditional sentence denotation (true or
false), the context-change potential is applied to (as opposed to getting
composed with) *Truth*, the tautologous continuation. This has the desired
effect, because for any p, $p \wedge Truth = p$.

(49) $\lambda r \exists x[dragon'(x) \wedge lumber'(x) \wedge hiss'(x) \wedge r](Truth) =$
         $\exists x[dragon'(x) \wedge lumber'(x) \wedge hiss'(x)]$

Returning to Barker and Shan, in addition to treating all expressions
that contain quantifiers as quantificational, they treat the quantificational
aspects of expressions in the continuation-passing style just illustrated.
To close off the continuation-scope of an expression they apply it to an
identity function. This plays the same role as *Truth* above: when an n-ary

function f is applied to the identity function, the first argument of f is eliminated.

The remarks above, together with the overview of Hendriks's technique in **§2.3.5**, provide sufficient background for a brief illustration of how the general ideas are implemented in Barker and Shan (2008) using what the authors call the "tower notation". This is essentially a simple and transparent proof-theoretic tool that enables one to calculate the results of combination quickly and efficiently. The "tower-operations" can be equivalently spelled out using λ-expressions.

All expressions are represented as towers with at least three levels: syntactic category, expression, logical form. The lexical items *ran* and *someone* will start out as below. (The system handles quantifier phrases like *some dragon*; we use *someone* just to simplify the exposition.)

(50)

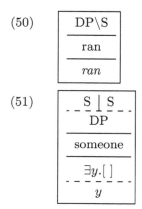

(51)

The two layers of the downstairs level of *someone* specify the argumental role and the scopal, or continuational, contribution of *someone*. "Below the dashed line" *someone* contributes a variable of type e (here: y). "Above the dashed line" it scopes over what will end up enclosed by the brackets [ ], and its contribution as a quantifier is to bind y by $\exists y$. The two layers of the upstairs level match these item-for-item. The category of *someone* is DP. *Someone* will scope over an S (the righthand-side one) and yield an S as a result (the lefthand-side one). That is, (51) conveys the following information about the behavior of *someone*:

(52)

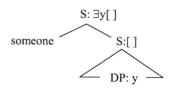

The factoring of the contribution of *someone* into an argumental and a scopal (continuational) part is inspired by Cooper (1983). Cooper was the first to introduce the idea that each quantifier fills an argument place in syntax, but its quantificational content is stored away. Both upstairs and downstairs the "above the dashed line" layers correspond to storage. Barker and Shan's system is more flexible than Cooper's in that the meanings of smaller units, e.g. quantificational determiners, can also be defined as storable.

The grammar has two type-shifters: Lift and Lower, and two ways of combination: Scope/ and Scope\. Lift, Scope, and Lower may apply to the whole item or just to its ground-floor level, with crucially different scope effects. The working of the rules is defined using the tower notation, but it is also spelled out using λ-terms.

The λ-expressions make it clear that Lift is nothing but the Montague-rule, or Hendriks's Value Raising. Lower applies its input function F to the identity function, as explained above. *Exp* abbreviates expression.

(53)   Lift: $\lambda x \lambda k[k(x)]$

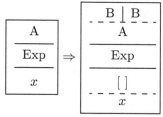

(54)   Lower: $\lambda F[F(\lambda x[x])]$

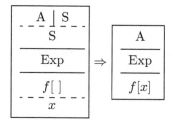

Lift maps one-layered levels to two-layered levels. At the upstairs level of the tower Lift takes an expression of category A and turns it into something that scopes over a B and yields a B, cf. the well-known lifted categories $(B/A)\backslash B$ and $B/(A\backslash B)$. At the downstairs level Lift takes the basic interpretation of *exp*, x, which matches its basic category A, and yields something that contributes the variable x but scopes over [ ]. In contrast, Lower collapses two-layered levels into one-layered levels (in Cooper's terms, retrieves quantifier meanings from storage).

The two Scope rules only differ from each other syntactically: Scope/ puts together a rightward-looking function of category B/A with its argument of category A, whereas Scope\ puts together a leftward-looking function of category $A\backslash B$ with its argument of category A. Recall now that Barker and Shan treat all expressions as sets of continuations, and that they combine any two expressions qua quantifiers. As the λ-expressions in (55) below show, the core of each Scope rule is $k(fx)$, where function f applies to argument x, and a higher function k applies to the result. f and x correspond to the two expressions combined. k corresponds to the anticipated continuation. Because Scope takes its input expressions to be quantifiers, it does not combine any f and x directly. Instead, in Scope/ a Left-expression L is quantified into $\lambda f[R(\lambda x[k(fx)])]$, and a right-expression R is quantified into $\lambda x[k(fx)]$. This implies that if the Left-expression and the Right-expression are not originally quantifiers (are not yet expecting to be continued), they must get lifted before they get combined.

The reader who has worked through §**2.3.5** will immediately notice the tell-tale signs of two instances of Argument Raising and one instance of Value Raising in the λ-expression that explicates Scope (see also the endnote with the derivations for *some student borrowed every book'*). Speaking in Hendriksese, the presence of k comes from Value Raising, and the quantifications involving L and R indicate that Argument Raising has been applied twice in the definition of Scope. It should be born in mind, though, that Barker and Shan do not use Argument Raising and Value Raising as rules in their grammar; the similarities with Hendriks consist in what general logical operations are needed to achieve a particular kind of result. Also, whereas in Hendriks's grammar AR and VR operate on linguistic expressions like *spot*, in (55) they operate on the basic combinator that applies f to x and derive a more complex combinator.

In the towers the "below-the-dashed-line" layers of both the downstairs and the upstairs levels continue to pertain to argument structure. In Scope/, f of category B/A applies to x of category A to yield $f(x)$ of category B. In the "above-the-dashed-line" layers the Right-expression (here the argument) is placed within the scope of the Left-expression (the function). Notice that g is whatever semantic content f affixes to its scope, and h is whatever semantic content x does. (In (55) the distinct category labels C, D, and E serve to make transparent that E is the label of the scope of x, D the label of the scope of f, and C the label of the result of putting the two together.)

(55)   a.   Scope/ $\lambda L \lambda R \lambda k[L(\lambda f[R(\lambda x[k(f(x))])])]$

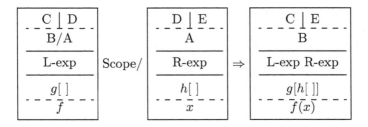

b.   Scope\ $\lambda L\lambda R\lambda k[L(\lambda x[R(\lambda f[k(f(x))])])]$

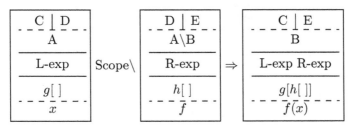

What we have already suffices to derive *Someone ran*, as well as a two-quantifier example on its direct, left-to-right scopal reading. We start by lifting *ran* and combine it with *someone* by Scope\.

(56) $\lambda x\lambda k[kx](ran) = \lambda k[k(ran)]$

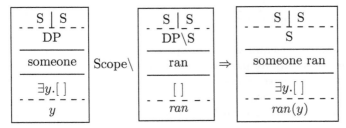

(57) $\lambda L\lambda R\lambda k[L(\lambda x[R(\lambda f[k(f(x))])])](\lambda P\exists y[Py])(\lambda k[k(ran)])$
$= \lambda k\exists y[k(ran(y))]$

$S \mid S$		$S \mid S$		$S \mid S$
DP		DP\S		S
someone	Scope\	ran	⇒	someone ran
$\exists y.[\,]$		$[\,]$		$\exists y.[\,]$
y		ran		$ran(y)$

The result is a set of continuations. To complete the derivation and obtain a traditional sentence, Lower applies. It collapses the "above the line" and the "below the line" material by inserting the latter into the former.

(58) $\lambda F[F(\lambda x.x)](\lambda k \exists y[k(ran(y))]) =$
$\lambda k \exists y[k(ran(y))](\lambda x.x) =$
$\exists y[ran(y)]$

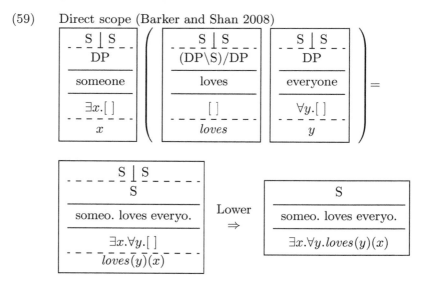

The derivation of *Someone loves everyone* on its direct scopal reading involves the same steps. First *loves* is Lifted. Then lifted *loves* combines with *everyone* by Scope/. The result combines with *someone* by Scope\. Finally, Lower eliminates the possibility of further continuations. Below is a compressed derivation:

(59)   Direct scope (Barker and Shan 2008)

In (59) *someone* acquires wide scope over *everyone* because Scope/ inserts $\forall y.[\ ]$ into the bracketed space representing the scope of $\exists x.[\ ]$. In this grammar inverse scope cannot be obtained by performing the same steps in the reverse order, which is what happens in the scope grammars reviewed above. Instead, both the inverse-scope-taker and the inversely-scoped-over expressions undergo extra lifts that create new layers. Lift applies to the "below-the-line" part to obtain the inverse-scope-taker, and to the whole expression scoped over. (Recall that Lift introduces [ ] without a quantifier prefixed to it.) The result will be lowered twice to complete the derivation.[14]

(60)   Inverse scope (Barker and Shan 2008)

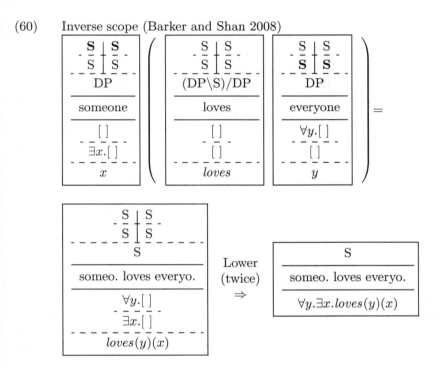

Barker and Shan have applied these basic ideas, in joint and/or separate publications, to the interaction of quantifiers and *wh*-phrases with pronominal binding (Superiority, Cross-over), donkey-anaphora and binding out of a quantifier phrase, the parasitic scope of the adjective *same*, and so on. Many of these topics are included in Barker and Shan (2009).

Moortgat's (1996) *q* type-constructor and the continuation semantics for symmetric categorial grammar in Bernardi and Moortgat (2007) represent convergent ideas; see Bernardi (2010) for discussion designed to be friendly to the linguist reader. In both these theories scope and binding are dependent on the order in which expressions are evaluated. This can be read off the way in which the sentences are constructed, but no structural condition like c-command is associated with precedence in evaluation. If the default evaluation order tracks left-to-right order, as Barker and Shan argue, that shows the empirical significance of the very thing that the introduction of c-command was meant to minimize, although it does not bring back left-to-right order as an inviolable condition.

2.4 Summary and Direct Compositionality

Section §2.2 presented DP-denotations as generalized quantifiers: sets of properties (extensionally, sets of sets-of-individuals). The scope of a quantifier A is the property that is asserted to be an element of A on a given derivation of the sentence. If that property incorporates another operator B (quantifier, negation, modal, etc.), then A automatically takes scope over B. The general lesson of Section §2.3 is that there are many different ways to implement this scenario. It may be acted out in the syntactic derivation of the sentence, but it may as well be squeezed into the flexible types of the participating expressions. Consequently, we may create abstract constituents by movement, but we may alternatively stick to some independently motivated constituent structure. We may bind syntactic variables (empty categories, traces), as Montague or May, but we may alternatively do without them and go "variable free", as Hendriks or Barker and Shan.[15] Notably, both Hendriks's and Barker and Shan's scope grammars are directly compositional, a property advocated in Jacobson (2002). Direct Compositionality means that each constituent built by the independently motivated syntax is immediately assigned its final and explicit interpretation.

The fact that one can take either approach is good news. But having to choose between them may not be so good, since both approaches offer their own insights. Barker (2007) makes the very important claim that it is in fact not necessary to choose. Building on Jäger's (2005) proof-theoretical proposal Barker points out that a grammar can deliver direct compositionality "on demand". Here the long-distance (Montague/May/Heim and Kratzer-style) and the local (Hendriks-style) analyses arise from one and the same set of rules, none of which are redundant. For every derivation in which an expression is bound at a distance or takes wide scope, there will be an equivalent derivation in which the semantic contribution of each constituent is purely local. As Barker explains, the interconvertibility follows from a natural symmetry in the grammar itself. The symmetry concerns rules of use and rules of proof in the Gentzen calculus (Gentzen 1935). Roughly, rules of use connect expressions directly over long distances, and embody the global view. Rules of proof help characterize the contribution of individual expressions within a complex constituent. Barker enriches Jäger's grammar and introduces rules of disclosure, which establish an explicit connection between the long-distance semantic effect of an element and its local denotation.

3

Generalized quantifiers in non-nominal domains

3.1 Domains of quantification

What kind of domains do generalized quantifiers quantify over? The traditional domain is that of individuals, and that is what the present book focuses on, but the same basic ideas and techniques extend to other domains, such as times and (indices of) possible worlds, and higher-order entities. Beyond its linguistic interest, this fact has some philosophical interest as well: Quine (1948) famously (and controversially) proposed that "To be is to be the value of a variable". The present section offers some pointers to the literature on various domains of quantification; §3.2 shows that the methods of scope assignment reviewed in Chapter 2 in connection with nominal quantifiers carry over to a new kind of expression: raising verbs.

Linguists and philosophers have argued that the domain of first-order entities is articulated into different sorts: alongside tangible individuals like people and books we have kinds (Carlson 1977), sums (Link 1983), individual correlates of properties (Chierchia 1984), events (Davidson 1967; Krifka 1989; Schein 1993; Lasersohn 1995; de Swart 1993; Borer 2005a,b), and more recently degrees or intervals of degrees (Kennedy 1999; Schwarzschild and Wilkinson 2002; Heim 2001, 2006a). Two other domains are moments or intervals of time, and possible worlds and parts thereof: situations (Hintikka 1962; Bennett and Partee 1972/2002; Cresswell 1990; Heim 1992; von Stechow 2003, 2004; Kratzer 1989, 2002; Kusumoto 2005).

Contemplating the cross-linguistic division of labor at the syntax/semantics interface Partee (1991) distinguishes D(eterminer)-quantification from A-quantification, where A stands for "the cluster of Adverbs, Auxiliaries, Affixes, and Argument-structure Adjusters". She hypothesizes that D-quantifiers range over individuals and A-quantifiers range over cases, events, or situations. Bittner and Trondhjem (2008) reject that division of labor based on cross-linguistic data. Specifically, they show that quantificational verbal roots and verbal affixes across languages quantify over objects of any type – events, individuals, places and, importantly, distributive dependencies. Balusu (2005) argues that distributive reduplicated numerals in Telugu quantify over event-aspects such as times and locations but never directly over event-participants like people and objects. (More on this in **§8.4**.) This case is interesting in that the semantics is much like that of pluractional verbs in Lasersohn (1995) but the reduplicated numeral resides in the noun phrase; see also Nakanishi (2007).

The best-known cases of abstraction and quantification over higher-order domains involve the interpretation of questions. Hamblin (1973) and Karttunen (1977) interpret questions as denoting sets of answer-propositions, i.e. sets of sets of possible worlds. Consider *Who walks?*:

(1) $\lambda p \exists x [{}^{\backsim}p \wedge p = {}^{\frown}walk(x)]$

Dayal (1994) extends the analysis to so-called "*wh*-scope marking" constructions (German, Hindi, Romani, Hungarian, etc.):

(2)   Was   glaubst du, mit wem   Maria gesprochen hat?
        what think   you with whom Mary spoken   has
        'Who do you think Mary spoke with?'

Dayal compositionally interprets such questions as, 'What, concerning who Mary spoke with, do you think?' This involves interpreting the question word *was* as an existential generalized quantifier over propositions, whose restriction is supplied by the complement question: $\lambda Q \exists p[who\text{-}Mary\text{-}spoke\text{-}with(p) \wedge Q(p)]$.

Let us return to the first-order domains of individuals, times, and possible worlds. Schlenker (2006b) observes that there are pervasive similarities both in the logical properties of quantification over the three domains and in the linguistic devices (quantifiers, definite descriptions, pronouns, demonstratives) that pertain to them. To remain with quantifiers, *some* and *all* pertain to individuals, *sometimes (when...)* and *always (when...)* to times, and the modal adverbs *possibly (if...)* and *necessarily (if...)* as well as mood markers to possible worlds. One of the logical similarities is the fact that the existential and the universal members of each pair are duals. Schlenker observes however that the treatment of the three domains has not been uniform in philosophical logic. Quantification over individuals is typically executed in a syntactically explicit manner, i.e. by binding variables in the object language, as in the language of first order logic. In contrast, quantification over times and especially worlds is typically executed in an implicit, or metalinguistic, manner. Here the object language uses non-variable-binding operators of a much more limited expressive power, such as the $\Box$ and $\Diamond$ of modal logic and Montague's ˆ. Notice that $\Box p$ expresses universal quantification over possible worlds just like $\forall x[f(x)]$ expresses universal quantification over individuals, but the latter makes this explicit in the syntax of the object language, whereas the former leaves it to the semantic metalanguage to spell out that $\Box p$ is true iff p is true in every world accessible from the world of evaluation. Ontological symmetry could be achieved if individuals, times, and worlds were treated alike. Schlenker (2006b) outlines various general ways to go about the ontological symmetry program.

Indeed, both in philosophical logic and in linguistics there have been significant precedents for deviation from the typical strategy. Quine (1960) recasts quantification over individuals along the lines of modal propositional logic, and Ben-Shalom (1996) makes the approach linguistically more relevant by presenting the nominal restriction of determiners as the accessibility relation associated with modal operators. From the other end, Groenendijk and Stokhof (1984) are among the first to demonstrate a need to quantify over worlds explicitly (see below). Cresswell (1990), Iatridou (1994), Percus (2000), Schlenker (1999, 2004), Pratt and Francez (2001), Kusumoto (2005), Lechner (2007), and von Stechow (2003, 2004) are among the growing number of authors who have proposed to treat certain cases of time and world quantification in a syntactically explicit manner. The primary linguistic diagnostic for explicit quantification is the existence of variable-like pronouns referring to the syntactically represented argument.[16] The primary logical diagnostics include the fact that the argument is not evaluated with respect to a single index, and the fact that the argument need not be linked to the closest suitable operator.

To illustrate the logical expressivity difference between implicit and explicit quantification, compare Karttunen (1977) with Groenendijk and Stokhof (1984) for *Who walks*. Karttunen uses the same translation for all interrogatives; see (1). Montague's ˘ allows Karttunen to evaluate the propositional variable p of type $\langle s, t \rangle$ with respect to the actual world, effectively saying that p is a true answer (although it may be partial). Montague's ˆ allows him to form the set of worlds in which *walk(x)*, with some name substituted for x, is true. Groenendijk and Stokhof differ from Karttunen in two respects. They require answers to be exhaustive, and they distinguish between complements of *know* and complements of *wonder*. They argue that as the complement of *know*, *who walks* is interpreted as a true and maximal answer-proposition, as in (3a), but as the complement of *wonder* it is interpreted as the intension thereof, as in (3b). The latter amounts to forming a set of pairs of worlds $\langle j, i \rangle$: those in which the walkers are the same.[17] This requires abstracting over worlds and, moreover, doing so crossing the abstractor of another world-variable. (The formulation of (3a) is geared towards this next step in (3b).)

(3)   a. $\lambda i \forall x [walk(i)(x) = walk(w*)(x)]$
        b. $\lambda j \lambda i \forall x [walk(i)(x) = walk(j)(x)]$

Montague's ⌣ and ⌢ would not make this expressible: ⌣ does not evaluate p with respect to an arbitrary world (index), and ⌢ does not abstract over an arbitrary world (index).

Quantification over (indices of) worlds requires an extension of Montague's type theory to the effect that, besides e and t, s is also a type; two-sorted type theory is introduced in Gallin (1975). Another kind of application of this extension is in Szabolcsi (1982), where explicit performatives are argued to denote changes, i.e. functions of type $\langle s, s \rangle$.

3.2   Raising verbs as quantifiers

The claim that syntactically explicit quantification over times and worlds is possible and sometimes necessary does not entail that all linguistic operators whose quantificational content pertains to times and worlds are to be treated in a syntactically explicit manner. One would want to have linguistic arguments for such a treatment in the individual cases. For example, it is clear that raising verbs, like propositional attitude verbs, have quantificational content. Very roughly,

(4)   *John knows in w that p*: In every world that is compatible with what John knows in w, p holds. (cf. Hintikka 1962)

(5)   *John wants in w [for it to be the case] that p*: Among the worlds sufficiently similar to w every one where p holds is preferred by John to those where p does not hold. (cf. Heim 1992; Villalta 2008)

(6)   *It seems in w that p*: In every world that conforms to the appearances in w, p holds.

The fact that the verb *begin* has a raising version in addition to its better known control version was first observed in Perlmutter (1970). The simplest evidence is that the subject of raising *begin* need not be sentient (*The paint began to dry*), nor an agent (*Mary began to get good roles*). Again, very roughly,[18]

(7)   *It begins [to be the case] at $\langle t, w \rangle$ that p*: There is an interval in w before t at which p does not hold, and there is an interval after t at which p holds.

This observation does not yet decide whether *seem* and *begin* are syntactically implicit quantifiers, along the lines of Hintikka's and Heim's classical analyses of propositional attitudes, or they are syntactically explicit quantifiers over worlds or times.

In this section I suggest that scope interaction with the subject indicates that at least certain raising verbs are syntactically explicit quantifiers. The gist of the argument will be this. In languages like Shupamem, Dutch, and possibly others raising verbs may acquire scope over the subject by overt fronting. This is only possible if the fronted verb binds a first-order time or world argument (whichever is appropriate) within the scope of the subject. In more general terms the argument offers a new diagnostic for explicit quantification.

As is well-known, English raising constructions can be ambiguous: one and the same string may receive what I will call a HI reading (subject scoping over the raising verb) or a LO reading (subject scoping under the raising verb). Starting with May (1985) this ambiguity is often attributed to reconstruction, i.e. to some kind of scopally significant lowering of the raised subject back into the infinitival clause. SPORTICHE (2006) offers a detailed discussion of the syntax and interpretation of reconstruction. (8) is the classical example. The HI reading entails the existence of a unicorn; the LO reading does not:[19]

(8)   A unicorn seems to be approaching.
       HI 'There is a particular unicorn and it seems it is approaching'
       LO 'It seems that a unicorn is approaching'

(9) exemplifies a HI/LO ambiguity reminiscent of (8). The two readings are logically independent. The HI reading is true in the little model described in the "HI scenario" in (10) and false in the "LO scenario"; conversely for the LO reading. The presence of a pertinent temporal adjunct facilitates the LO reading.

(9)   In April/from April on only Mary began to get good roles.
       HI reading of the subject: *only Mary > it began to be the case that*
       'Only Mary is such that previously she did not get good roles, but
       now she is getting good roles'
       LO reading of the subject: *it began to be the case that > only Mary*
       'It began to be the case that only Mary is getting good roles'

(10)

	HI scenario		LO scenario	
	Who is getting good roles		Who is getting good roles	
	before April?	after April?	before April?	after April?
	Mary: no	Mary: yes	Mary: yes	Mary: yes
	Susan: no	Susan: no	Susan: no	Susan: no
	Eva: yes	Eva: yes	Eva: yes	Eva: no

To determine how the HI and the LO readings come about it is useful to look beyond English. In some languages the two readings of *begin* are fully or partially disambiguated. The examples below are drawn from Hungarian, Italian, Dutch, and Shupamem (Grassfield Bantu), in this order.[20]

(11) a. Csak Mari kezdett   el jó   szerepeket kapni.
          only Mari began.3sg prt good roles.acc   get.inf
          HI 'Only Mary is such that she began to get good roles'
      b. Elkezdett   csak Mari kapni jó   szerepeket.
          prt.began.3sg   only Mari get.inf good roles.acc
          LO 'It began to be the case that only Mary is getting good roles'

(12) a. Solo Maria ha iniziato a   ricevere buoni incarichi.
          only Maria began.3sg prep get.inf   good roles
          HI 'Only Mary is such that she began to get good roles'
      b. Ha iniziato a   ricevere buoni incarichi solo Maria.
          began.3sg prep get.inf   good roles   only Maria
          LO 'It began to be the case that only Mary is getting good roles'

(13) a. Alleen Marie begon   goede rollen te krijgen.
          only   Mary began.3sg good roles to get.inf
          HI 'Only Mary is such that she began to get good roles'
      b. In mei begon   alleen Marie goede rollen te krijgen.
          in May began.3sg only   Marie good roles to get.inf
          HI 'Only Mary is such that she began to get good roles'
          LO 'It began to be the case that only Mary is getting good roles'

(14) a. Ndùù Maria ka   yeshe inget   ndàà li?.
          only Maria past begin have.inf good roles
          HI 'Only Mary is such that she began to get good roles'
      b. A   ka   yeshe ndùù Maria inget   ndàà li?.
          focus past begin only Maria inf.have good roles
          LO 'It began to be the case that only Mary is getting good roles'

Szabolcsi (2009) argues that in Hungarian and in Italian the subject 'only Mary' occurs in the main clause in the (a) examples but in the complement clause in the (b) examples. That is, on the LO reading the complement of 'begin' is 'only Mary to get good roles'. One piece of evidence is the fact that in Hungarian and in Italian comparable HI and LO readings are available with all control verbs. If this analysis is correct, Hungarian and Italian do not tell us anything about the quantificational status of the raising verb, since the two positions of the operator subject in overt syntax fully account for the HI vs. LO readings. But the overt infinitival subject analysis does not carry over to Dutch, and for all my efforts I have not found evidence that it carries over to Shupamem. How do their LO readings come about?

The overt syntax of Shupamem seems straightforward. This is an SVO language. The verb-initial order occurs when the verb bears the focus-marker *a*. It is most likely that *ndùù Maria* 'only Maria' occupies the same main-clause-subject position in both (14a) and (14b), and the focus-marked verb is preposed in (14b). Now the fact that the (b) order has an unambiguously LO reading might be attributed to the possibility that overt verb-fronting has no semantic effect, but 'only Maria' is covertly lowered into the infinitival clause:

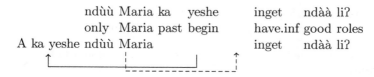

ndùù Maria ka   yeshe   inget   ndàà li?
only Maria past begin   have.inf good roles
A ka yeshe ndùù Maria   inget   ndàà li?

It is rather unusual to assume that the subject covertly lowers if and only if the verb is overtly fronted. Such a situation could at best arise if the intervention of the operator subject between the verb and its trace somehow blocked the verb-trace relation, and thus the subject had to be moved out of the way. But the operator subject has no such harmful effect, at least not generally. In Dutch, for example, the (13b) structure has the verb in "second position", which is somewhat similar to the focused initial position in Shupamem, and it is ambiguous. Thus, the analog of the alleged lowering is not obligatory in Dutch. It is also syntactically unlikely that the trace of the fronted main verb is simply deleted.

It seems natural to attribute the LO reading in (b) to the fact that the verb is overtly fronted. Crucial to the concerns of this section is how verb fronting is interpreted. If the aspectual raising verb were a syntactically opaque operator like $\lozenge$, and the trace of head movement were invariably of the same type α as the head, then head movement could not affect scope. It would be a paradigm case of the type-theoretical way of achieving "semantic reconstruction," cf. the discussion in **§2.3.5**.

(15) $\text{Verb}_\alpha \; \lambda V_\alpha \; [\ldots \text{Subject} \ldots \text{V} \ldots] = [\ldots \text{Subject} \ldots \text{Verb}_\alpha \ldots]$

The only way verb fronting can be semantically significant is if it binds a first-order time argument within the scope of the operator subject.[21] This treatment of the aspectual raising verb can be modeled after Kusumoto's (2005) tense operator PAST, which binds the time argument of the predicate with the mediation of the tense morpheme *past*, a mere free variable. t^* is the time of evaluation. Kusumoto writes the type of times as i.

(16)

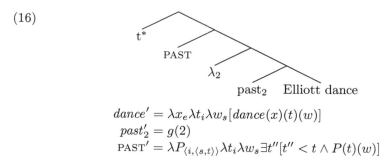

$$dance' = \lambda x_e \lambda t_i \lambda w_s [dance(x)(t)(w)]$$
$$past'_2 = g(2)$$
$$\text{PAST}' = \lambda P_{\langle i,\langle s,t\rangle\rangle} \lambda t_i \lambda w_s \exists t''[t'' < t \wedge P(t)(w)]$$

Our rough approximation of *begin'* has the same type as PAST':

(17) $begin' = \lambda P_{\langle i,\langle s,t\rangle\rangle} \lambda t''_i \lambda w_s \exists t' \exists t'''$
$[t' < t'' < t''' \wedge \neg P(x)(t')(w) \wedge P(x)(t''')(w)]$

With these ingredients, the interpretations of Shupamem (14a) without verb fronting and (14b) with verb fronting will be as follows. For simplicity we ignore worlds, and substitute English lexical items for the Shupamem ones.

(18) $t^*[\text{PAST}'(\lambda t_2[only M'(\lambda x[\underline{past'_2}[begin'(\lambda t[get\ roles'(x)(t)])])])])]$

(19) $t^*[\text{PAST}'(\lambda t_2[\underline{past'_2}[begin'$
$(\lambda t[only M'(\lambda x[t(\lambda t\ [get\ roles'(x)(t)])])])])])]$

To spell out the derivation in terms of actual movement of the tensed verb, one would lift *past₂* and compose it with *begin* to form a mobile unit:

(20) $past_2 \circ begin = \lambda Q[\lambda P[P(t_2)](begin'(Q))] = \lambda Q[begin'(Q)(t_2)]$

Dutch (13b) is ambiguous. Without attempting to disentangle the scope grammar of Dutch we may note that the LO reading might be obtained in a way analogous to Shupamem, see (19), and the HI reading by semantic reconstruction of the tensed verb from C into I. The latter derivation would use a higher-order intermediate trace T, just as was discussed in §2.3.5 for nominal quantifier phrases:

(21) $t^*[\text{PAST}'(\lambda t_2[\lambda Q[begin'(Q)(t_2)](\lambda T[only M'(\lambda x[T(\lambda t$
$[get\ roles'(x)(t)])])])])]$

The natural reason why the verb does not scopally reconstruct in Shupamem (14b) would be that Shupamem verb fronting involves focus, not just plain verb-second.[22]

The moral seems to be that the aspectual raising verb *begin* does not only have quantificational content, its scope behavior also mimics that of nominal quantifiers: it "raises as a quantifier." In doing so it quantifies over a first-order time argument. It also "reconstructs as a quantifier". In doing so it is linked to a higher-order variable whose type is identical to its own.

The ambiguity of English (9), repeated below, might be due to the covert movement of the verb (cf. (19)) or to covert syntactic or semantic reconstruction of the subject *only Mary*:

(22)   In April/from April on only Mary began to get good roles.

At least one consideration favors the covert verb movement analysis. Lasnik (1999) observes that arguments for lowering the matrix subject into the scope of the intensional raising verbs typically involve indefinites, cf. (23), and they do not work in all cases even then.

(23)   A unicorn seems to be approaching.   HI/LO

(24)   Nobody is (absolutely) certain to pass the test.   HI/*LO

(25)   Every coin is 3% likely to land tails.   HI/*LO

Lasnik proposes that there is no quantifier lowering at all; the apparent lowering in (23) follows from special properties of indefinites. Whatever the general force of this argument might be, notice that LO readings of non-indefinites are freely available with the aspectual raising verb *begin*. *Only Mary* is already an example; see also the following hits from Google, which only make sense on the interpretation 'it began to be the case that...':[23]

(26)   Every step began to be a struggle.
        ...it was 2am by this point, but every minute began to count.
        ...that every French solider [*sic*] began to be provided with wine
        in his daily ration.
        Perhaps when every game began to be televised on CBS [...] it
        dulled the interest in the final game.
        Every patient on admission began to be evaluated from head to
        toe for potential skin problems.
        Beginning with Abraham Darby's bridge...in 1779, most bridges
        began to be built of cast and wrought iron.
        ...most saltpeter began to be manufactured in large "niter farms"
        ...in Poland after our independence, all the books began to be
        very angry.
        Because of so much inbreeding the cats began to be born without
        tails.
        ...over 50 percent of my goats began to be born with birth defects.

The claim that the aspectual raising verb quantifies over a first-order time argument rests primarily on the overt movement case of Shupamem. But it is good to know that it also offers an account of the LO readings of English *begin* examples, even if Lasnik is correct and subject lowering is not available.

Are the scope interaction effects replicated with modals and intensional verbs? If Lasnik's (1999) empirical observations are correct, the effects should be severely constrained. Lechner (2007) argues that semantically active covert head movement is indeed involved in the derivation of the so-called split readings below:

(27)   Not every boy can make the team.
        'It is not possible for every boy to make the team'

(28)   No player needs a partner.
        'It is not necessary for there to be a partnered player, i.e. this game can be played alone'

Lechner's analysis has the following LF ingredients: (a) the split of *not every boy* and *no player* into *not ... every boy* and *not ... a player*, (b) head movement of the explicit quantifiers *can* and *need*, binding first-order world arguments, and (c) short reconstruction of *every boy* and *a player* that does not violate the known constraints.

It is not easy to replicate scope interaction between the subject and an intensional raising verb when the subject is not an indefinite. For example, the HI and the LO readings of (29) are true in the same models:

(29)   Only Mary seems to be tall.
        HI 'Only Mary is such that she seems to be tall'
        LO 'It seems that only Mary is tall'

In other words, the fact that *Only Mary seems to be tall* can be used synonymously with *It seems that only Mary is tall* does not prove that the former actually has two readings. Beyond asserted truth-conditions, the presuppositions of the verb might help, but *seem* and *likely* do not have any useful presuppositions. The raising version of the verb *threaten* may provide a test case. I will assume the following rough approximation of its analysis:

(30)   The barn threatens to collapse.
        Asserts: The barn is likely to collapse.
        Presupposes: It is bad (for us) if something collapses.

The diagnostic value of *threaten* comes from consideration of whether the sentence manages to convey that the content of the complement would be bad news. Consider the following examples, where the subject is modified by *only*. (31) has a reasonable HI reading that asserts that the barn is the only thing that is likely to collapse, and presupposes that for something to collapse would be bad news.

(31)   Only the barn threatened to collapse.

If we replace *collapse* with *survive*, as below, the HI reading should become weird and the LO reading reasonable. The HI reading presupposes that it is bad news if something survives. But the LO reading is entirely reasonable in the context of a storm or a flood. It asserts that it is likely that only the strongest building will survive, and it presupposes that it is bad news if only the strongest building survives. We see however that (32) lacks the LO, reasonable reading.

(32)   Only the strongest building threatened to survive the flood.
        HI (weird reading): '...it is bad news if something survives the flood'
        *LO (reasonable reading): '...it is bad news if only the strongest building survives the flood'

On the other hand, in Dutch 'threaten' exhibits an interaction that seems to pattern the same way as (13), although the judgments are more subtle than with 'begin' (J. Groenendijk, p.c.):

(33)   Alleen de schuur dreigde   te bezwijken.
        only   the barn   threatened to collapse
        HI (reasonable): 'The barn was likely to collapse, other buildings were not, and collapse is bad news'

(34)   In mei dreigde   alleen het fort   overeind te blijven.
        in May threatened only   the fortress to survive
        HI (weird): 'In May the fortress was likely to survive, other buildings were not, and survival is bad news'
        LO (reasonable): 'In May it was likely that only the fortress would survive, and for nothing but the fortress to survive is bad news'

This holds out the hope that scope effects of verb-movement can be detected with intensional raising verbs, strengthening the case Lechner builds on modals. At this point I have no idea whether some general difference between English and Dutch accounts for the contrast between (32) and (34), or it is due to some minor lexical difference between the verbs involved.

Raising verbs the way quantifiers are raised is applicable only to operators that can be construed as quantificational. At first blush it cannot endow the fronting of negation with scopal significance. But consider the minimal pairs below:

(35)   a. *Even/any one of you touch the money!
        b. *Even/any one of you don't touch the money!
        c. Don't even/any one of you touch the money!

We see from (35a) that negative polarity items are not automatically licensed in the subject position of an imperative. However, (35c) with fronted *don't* is acceptable. This indicates that the high position of negation is semantically significant: the fronting of *don't* includes the subject in its scope.

Although the view of sentential negation inherited from predicate logic is that it is not a variable-binding operator, using a semantics that attends to events makes a different prediction. If positive sentences are interpreted as existential quantifications over events, negative ones normally involve negative event quantification (Krifka 1989). If so, (35c) can be roughly paraphrased as follows:

(36)   'There should be no event e such that one of you touches the money in e'

If *don't* is a negative quantifier that binds an event variable, then its fronting assigns scope to negation over the subject in English, along the same lines as the fronting of raising verbs has been argued to do in Shupamem.[24]

To summarize, this chapter took a brief look at quantification over domains other than that of traditional individuals, and pointed out a body of literature that extends the standard ideas of generalized quantifiers to these domains. Special attention was paid to the claim, gaining more and more support in recent literature, that natural language quantifies over times and worlds in a syntactically explicit (object-linguistic) manner. The chapter also introduced a new argument that verb-fronting may have scope effects, and that those effects can be accounted for using the same techniques (quantifier raising and reconstruction, however they are formalized) that are well-known from the treatment of the scope of nominal quantifiers.

4

Some empirically significant properties of quantifiers and determiners

An important benefit of generalized quantifier theory is that it enables one to discover and study semantic properties of empirical significance. Some of these properties are useful in expressing descriptive generalizations and in replacing inferior generalizations stated in pre-theoretical terms or with reference to morphology. The best-known examples are the properties involved in the characterization of what noun phrases occur in existential sentences or license certain negative polarity items. Other properties, like conservativity and extension, offer valuable clues to learnability and to the working of the syntax/semantic interface. Yet others are useful building blocks in understanding scope behavior and the ability to be associated with existential closure or exceptive phrases.

Another benefit is that the theory offers a simple insight into how complex quantifiers can be obtained by Boolean operations. This solves an important portion of the compositionality questions arising in the noun phrase domain, although other questions remain, as will be seen in Chapter 5 and in the subsequent chapters.

Finally, in many cases the theory enables us to state the claims in such a way that they are not restricted to quantifiers or to the nominal domain but transcend category boundaries. Monotonicity properties and Boolean combinations are prime examples.

This book strictly follows the terminology that generalized quantifiers are the denotations of full noun phrases like *every dragon* and *more than two dragons*. Expressions like *every* and *more than two* denote semantic determiners. The discussion will proceed in two stages. §4.1 focuses on generalized quantifiers, §4.2 on semantic determiners. The two topics are typically interwoven in the literature, but the linguistically relevant issues they raise are somewhat different. Also, as we shall see later, recent research has revisited the compositional semantics of noun phrases in ways that affect the status of determiners more than that of generalized quantifiers.

4.1 Quantifiers

4.1.1 Boolean compounds

Conjunction, disjunction, and negation are Boolean operations that apply across categories:

(1)   a.   walk or talk, walk and talk, walk but not talk
        b.   above or under, above and under, above but not under
        c.   every dragon and at least one serpent, every dragon or at least one serpent, every dragon but not every serpent

Partee and Rooth (1983/2002) define the set of conjoinable types as those that "end in t", i.e. those that are of the truth value type t or are the types of functions whose ultimate value is of type t. The reason why conjoinable types must be such is that *and* (*but*), *or*, and *not* as applied to subsentential expressions are generalizations of the sentential connectives. The assumption that DPs denote generalized quantifiers, of type $\langle\langle e, t\rangle, t\rangle$ explains how the Boolean compounds in (1c) fit into the picture. Hasse-diagrams can be used to visualize the operations.[25]

Assume that *dragon′* is $\{a, b\}$ and *serpent′* is $\{c, d\}$. The caption of Figure 4.1 spells out the generalized quantifiers (sets of sets-of-individuals) denoted by *every dragon* and by *at least one serpent* in our small universe, and the corresponding areas of the Hasse-diagram are shaded. *And′* intersects the two sets, yielding $\{\{a, b, c\}, \{a, b, d\}, \{a, b, c, d\}\}$. *Every dragon and at least one serpent hissed* is true iff *hissed′* is an element of this set.[26]

Every dragon or at least one serpent′ is the union of the same two sets.

Not every dragon′ is the set of properties that not every dragon has. This is exactly the complement of *every dragon′*. As expected, the constituent-negation of a DP denotes the complement of the generalized quantifier that the DP denotes with respect to the powerset of the universe of discourse. *Not every dragon hissed* is true iff *hissed′* is an element of this set, i.e. not an element of *every dragon′*.

The reader is encouraged to take out pencils and color in Figures 4.2, 4.3, and 4.4 (as well as 4.6 and 4.7 below) for the operations indicated in the captions. (No coloring of library copies, please...)

The Boolean operations intersection, union, and complementation faithfully capture the contents of *and*, *or*, and *not* when applied to expressions that denote generalized quantifiers. But the same intersection and union operations (more generally, their lattice-theoretic counterparts, greatest lower bound and least upper bound) also explicate the contents of quan-

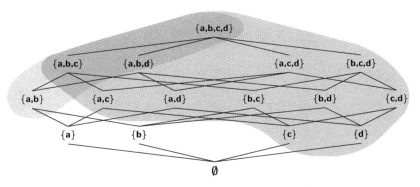

Fig. 4.1 The intersection of two generalized quantifiers
every dragon' = {{*a, b*}, {*a, b, c*}, {*a, b, d*}, {*a, b, c, d*}}
at least one serpent' = {{*c*}, {*d*}, {*a, c*}, {*a, d*}, {*b, c*}, {*b, d*}, {*c, d*},
{*a, b, c*}, {*a, b, d*}, {*a, c, d*}, {*b, c, d*}, {*a, b, c, d*}}
every dragon and at least one serpent' = {{*a, b, c*}, {*a, b, d*}, {*a, b, c, d*}}

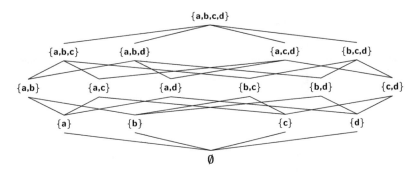

Fig. 4.2 The union of two generalized quantifiers
every dragon' = {{*a, b*}, {*a, b, c*}, {*a, b, d*}, {*a, b, c, d*}}
at least one serpent' = {{*c*}, {*d*}, {*a, c*}, {*a, d*}, {*b, c*}, {*b, d*}, {*c, d*},
{*a, b, c*}, {*a, b, d*}, {*a, c, d*}, {*b, c, d*}, {*a, b, c, d*}}
every dragon or at least one serpent' = {{*c*}, {*d*}, {*a, b*}, {*a, c*}, {*a, d*}, {*b, c*},
{*b, d*}, {*c, d*}, {*a, b, c*}, {*a, b, d*}, {*a, c, d*}, {*b, c, d*}, {*a, b, c, d*}}

tifier expressions whose syntax does not involve connectives, such as *everyone* (or *every dragon*) and *someone* (or *some dragon*).

(The Boolean operations are special cases of more general lattice-theoretic notions: e.g. union is a special case of least upper bound (supremum). The upper bounds of a subset X of some set A are those elements of A that are either greater than or equal to each element of X. The least upper bound, if it exists, is the smallest of these. See SZABOLCSI 1997d: 4 or LANDMAN 1991: 234.)

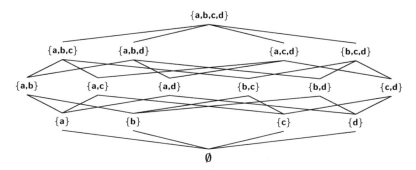

Fig. 4.3 The complement of a generalized quantifier
$every\ dragon' = \{\{a, b\}, \{a, b, c\}, \{a, b, d\}, \{a, b, c, d\}\}$
$not\ every\ dragon' = \{\emptyset, \{a\}, \{b\}, \{c\}, \{d\}, \{a, c\}, \{a, d\}, \{b, c\}, \{b, d\}, \{c, d\},$
$\{a, c, d\}, \{b, c, d\}\}$

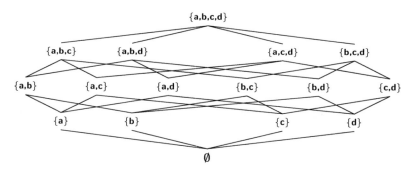

Fig. 4.4 Complement and intersection
$every\ serpent' = \{\{c, d\}, \{a, c, d\}, \{b, c, d\}, \{a, b, c, d\}\}$
$not\ every\ dragon' = \{\emptyset, \{a\}, \{b\}, \{c\}, \{d\}, \{a, c\}, \{a, d\}, \{b, c\}, \{b, d\}, \{c, d\},$
$\{a, c, d\}, \{b, c, d\}\}$
$every\ serpent\ but\ not\ every\ dragon' = \{\{c, d\}, \{a, c, d\}, \{b, c, d\}\}$

Let us first consider the well-known fact that if the universe of discourse is finite and we have names for all its elements, the contents of universally and existentially quantified sentences of first-order logic can be expressed using conjoined and disjoined propositions, as follows.

(2)   If the universe consists of four people, Adam, Bertha, Celine, and Daniel, then

    a. $\forall x[laugh'(x)]$ iff
        $laugh'(a) \wedge laugh'(b) \wedge laugh'(c) \wedge laugh'(d)$
    b. $\exists x[laugh'(x)]$ iff
        $laugh'(a) \vee laugh'(b) \vee laugh'(c) \vee laugh'(d)$

While these equivalences capture the truth conditions of the quantified sentences in the given universe, they do not explicate the contents of universal and existential quantification in general terms. Generalized quantifiers and the Boolean perspective offer such an explication. Informally,

(3)   a.   The set of properties that everyone has is the intersection (greatest lower bound) of the sets of properties that the first-order individuals in the universe have.

        b.   The set of properties that someone has is the union (least upper bound) of the sets of properties that the first-order individuals in the universe have.

This can be easily ascertained starting from our Boolean algebra. Let $\{a\}$ be the singleton set of Adam, $\{b\}$ the singleton set of Bertha, and so on. We have seen that the set of properties Adam has is $\{\{a\}, \{a, b\}, \{a, c\}, \{a, d\}, \{a, b, c\}, \{a, b, d\}, \{a, c, d\}, \{a, b, c, d\}\}$. Intersecting this with the sets of properties of Bertha, Celine, and Daniel one obtains the set whose only element is $\{a, b, c, d\}$, that is, the set $\{\{a, b, c, d\}\}$. (The double curly brackets are important: in terms of shaded Hasse-diagrams, the intersection is the area of the diagram shaded four times, not the element in the area.) This is exactly the set of properties everyone has. Similarly for the set of properties someone has, with unions.

Generalized quantifiers corresponding to first-order individuals (the set of properties Adam has, etc.) are sometimes called Montagovian individuals. Keenan and Faltz (1985), who present a detailed study of Boolean insights into natural language semantics, argue that from a linguistic point of view Montagovian individuals, and not individuals of type e, constitute the universe of discourse. Using that terminology,

(4)   a.   The generalized quantifier *everyone'* is the intersection (greatest lower bound) of the Montagovian individuals.

        b.   The generalized quantifier *someone'* is the union (least upper bound) of the Montagovian individuals.

The reformulation of (2) as (3)–(4) has both logical and linguistic significance. Logically, (3)–(4) are applicable even if the universe is infinite and we do not know everybody's name. The reason is that the finiteness and naming requirements are specifically due to the limitations of propositional and predicate logic. For example, standard propositional logic does not have infinite conjunctions or disjunctions, but taking the greatest lower bound or the least upper bound of infinite sets is definitely possible.[27] Also, now we do not have to list the concrete propositions that jointly cover the same ground as the quantified sentence; we are explicating the universal quantifier itself, irrespective of the particular domain.

The observation that these generalized quantifiers are the products of the same abstract operations that are also realized as connectives (*and* and *or*) has various kinds of empirical linguistic significance. As will be discussed in §12.5, many languages build their existential-quantifier words from morphemes that also express disjunction (and/or their universal-quantifier words from ones that also express conjunction). For example, Japanese *dare-ka* 'someone' and *Taro-ka Akira-ka* 'Taro or Akira' both contain the morpheme *ka*. If such facts prove to be sufficiently systematic, we want them to be accounted for by compositional semantics and not to appear as mere etymological curiosities. We would want to say that the *ka* in *dare-ka* has basically the same meaning as in *Taro-ka Akira-ka*. The theory just outlined supports such an analysis.

The fact that quantifier meanings are given by the operations union, intersection, and complement has consequences for scope. Szabolcsi and Zwarts (1993/1997) propose that computing the semantic effect of a quantifier's scoping over a stretch of the sentence consists in performing the operations associated with the quantifier in the denotation domain of that stretch. The desired scope-taking is therefore incoherent, "unthinkable", if the requisite operations are not available in that denotation domain. For example, the scope of a universal or a negative quantifier cannot be a stretch of the sentence that denotes an element of a mere join semi-lattice (a domain not closed under intersections or complements). An application of this insight is to intervention effects in weak islands.

4.1.2   Monotonicity: increasing, decreasing, and non-monotonic quantifiers

A bird's eye view of negative polarity item licensing will pave the way to a discussion that is of more general interest. The basic observation is that there is a heterogeneous set of words and phrases, *ever, any longer, all that* [*adjective*], *either*, and *sleep a wink* among them, that occur only in a well-delimited kind of environment. For example:

(5)   a.   *This dragon has ever purred.
        b.   *This dragon purred any longer.
        c.   *This dragon is all that friendly.

(6)   a.   I don't think that this dragon has ever purred.
        b.   I don't think that this dragon purred any longer.
        c.   I don't think that this dragon is all that friendly.

(7)   a.   No dragon has ever purred.
        b.   No dragon purred any longer.
        c.   No dragon is all that friendly.

Klima (1964) called the sensitive expressions negative polarity items (NPI) and characterized the good environments in morphological terms, as ones containing an overt negation, i.e. an *n*-word. But reference to surface morphology does not take us very far. Many more expressions that are neither *n*-words nor contain ones trigger (in more current parlance, license) some or all NPIs. An initial list may be this:

(8)   doubt, hardly, every, few, at most two, ...

So perhaps NPI-licensors should be just listed? The following contrast shows that this desperate attempt will not work, either. Should *every*, for example, be listed as a licensor?

(9)   a.   Every dragon that ever swam in this lake got sick.
        b.   *Every dragon that swam in this lake ever got sick.

Fauconnier (1978) and Ladusaw (1980) proposed that NPI-licensors share a semantic property: they are monotonically decreasing (implication reversing, downward entailing) expressions. NPIs want to be in the immediate scope of a monotonically decreasing operator.

Monotonicity properties are entirely independent of syntactic categories and may therefore serve to characterize a heterogeneous batch of operators. (9) ceases to be a problem: closer inspection reveals that *every* is decreasing with respect to its NP-sister but not with respect to the scope of *every NP*, and so the contrast in (9) falls out. Decreasingness also has intuitive appeal: it captures what may have been behind Klima's more limited morphological generalization.

Monotonicity properties pertain to whether a function preserves, reverses, or obliterates the partial ordering that exists in its domain. A partial ordering is a reflexive, transitive, and anti-symmetrical relation; the well-known subset-relation is an example. (The proper-subset relation is a strict partial ordering; it is not anti-symmetrical but asymmetrical.) So imagine a domain of sets, partially ordered by the subset relation: for instance, the set of those who walk and talk, the set of those who just walk, and the set of those who walk or talk, possibly both:

(10)   walk and talk $\subseteq$ walk $\subseteq$ walk or talk

In the extensional spirit of generalized quantifier theory let us specify the membership of these sets as follows:

(11) $\{a, c\} \subseteq \{a, c, d\} \subseteq \{a, b, c, d\}$

Assuming that the set of robots is $\{a, b, c\}$, the noun phrase *more than one robot* denotes the set of those subsets of the universe which contain more than one robot each. The elements of this quantifier are shaded in Figure 4.5.

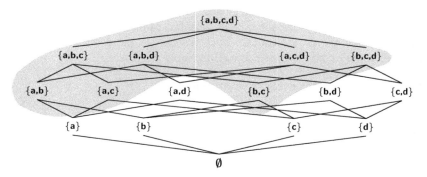

Fig. 4.5 An increasing generalized quantifier
more than one robot' = {{*a, b*}, {*a, c*}, {*b, c*}, {*a, b, c*}, {*a, b, d*}, {*a, c, d*},
{*b, c, d*}, {*a, b, c, d*}}

More than one robot walks and talks is true in this universe, since *walks and talks'*, i.e. {*a, c*} is an element of the quantifier. Observe now that all the supersets of {*a, c*} are also elements of the quantifier; they are {*a, b, c*}, {*a, c, d*}, and {*a, b, c, d*}. Because *walk'* happens to be {*a, c, d*} and *walk or talk'* happens to be {*a, b, c, d*}, this means that whenever *More than one robot walks and talks* is true, so are *More than one robot walks'* and *More than one robot walks or talks'*. These observations diagnose *more than one robot'* as a monotonically increasing (upward entailing, implication preserving) quantifier.[28]

(12)   The generalized quantifier GQ is monotonically increasing iff when-
        ever X is an element of GQ, all supersets of X are elements of
        GQ.

One consequence is that the top element of the powerset, i.e. the whole universe of discourse is always an element of an increasing quantifier.

Let us now consider *at most two robots'* and *exactly two robots'*.

At most two robots' is monotonically decreasing:

(13)   The generalized quantifier GQ is monotonically decreasing iff
        whenever X is an element of GQ, all subsets of X are elements
        of GQ.

For example, {*a, c, d*} is an element of *at most two robots'*, i.e. *At most two robots walk* is true. And sure enough, *At most two robots walk and talk* is also true, {*a, c*} being a subset of {*a, c, d*}. Notice also that the bottom element of the powerset, i.e. the empty set is always an element of a decreasing quantifier.

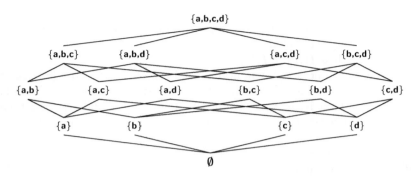

Fig. 4.6 A decreasing generalized quantifier

at most two robots′ = {∅, {*a*}, {*b*}, {*c*}, {*d*}, {*a, b*}, {*a, c*}, {*a, d*} {*b, c*}, {*b, d*},
{*c, d*}, {*a, b, d*}, {*a, c, d*}, {*b, c, d*}}

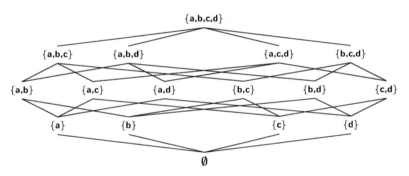

Fig. 4.7 A non-monotonic generalized quantifier

exactly two robots′ = {{*a, b*}, {*a, c*}, {*b, c*}, {*a, b, d*}, {*a, c, d*}, {*b, c, d*}}

In contrast to the previous, *exactly two robots′* is rather disappointing.
If you grab one of its elements, you are not guaranteed either that its
supersets or that its subsets will be elements. Hence no entailments like
the above arise.

(14)   The generalized quantifier GQ is non-monotonic iff it is neither
         increasing nor decreasing.

A general formulation is this:

(15)   a.   A function f is monotonically increasing (with respect to a
                particular argument) iff it preserves the partial ordering in
                its domain. That is, if X, Y are in the domain of f and
                $X \leq Y$, then $f(X) \leq f(Y)$.

b.   A function f is monotonically decreasing (with respect to a particular argument) iff it reverses the partial ordering in its domain. That is, if X, Y are in the domain of f and $X \leq Y$, then $f(X) \geq f(Y)$.

c.   A function f is non-monotonic (with respect to a particular argument) iff it obliterates the partial ordering in its domain. That is, if X, Y are in the domain of f and $X \leq Y$, then neither $f(X) \leq f(Y)$ nor $f(X) \geq f(Y)$ is guaranteed.

To see how this definition works for various kinds of expressions, recall the following simple facts. First, a set can always be traded for its characteristic function (the two are not the same thing, but they are in a one-to-one relation). So a generalized quantifier can be looked upon as a function: the characteristic function of those sets that we called its elements. The quantifier, construed as a characteristic function inspects every subset of the universe, and says yes to it if it is an element and no otherwise. Second (less innocuously), a proposition can be traded for its truth-set: the set of those worlds in which it is true. Therefore a proposition can also be construed as a set, or as the characteristic function thereof. Let us spell out one example using these terms.

(16)   a.   *At most two robots'* is that function f which assigns True to a set X if X has at most two robots in it, and False otherwise.

          b.   If $X \subseteq Y$, then *at most two robots'*$(Y) \subseteq$ *at most two robots'*(X). In other words, every world where *at most two robots'*(Y) = True is a world where *at most two robots'*(X) = True. E.g. given *walk'* $\subseteq$ *walk or talk'*, *At most two robots walk or talk* entails *At most two robots walk*.

          c.   Therefore, *at most two robots'* reverses the subset relation in its domain, i.e. it is monotonically decreasing.

This is one of the first cases where an independently known precise mathematical property was shown to have empirical relevance for a large body of linguistic data that previously defied systematization. It was a break-through in the study of NPIs, although it took many years for semanticists to even start asking why these particular expressions demand the presence of this particular property in their environment, and although it turns out that monotonic decreasingness is not the only property relevant in this domain. Surveying the large literature on polarity licensing is not a goal of this book. We also just note, without going into further details, that there are many other mathematically definable classes of quantifiers that are linguistically relevant (e.g. filters, ideals, principal filters, ultrafilters,...) or philosophically interesting (e.g. what quantifiers are logical; see Keenan 2001; Feferman 1997), and linguistic

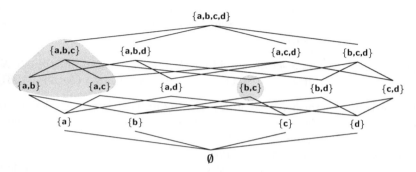

Fig. 4.8 The witnesses of *more than one robot'*
$= \{\{a,b\}, \{a,c\}, \{b,c\}, \{a,b,c\}\}$

applications that manipulate generalized quantifiers in illuminating ways
(see for example the discussion of exceptive constructions in von Fintel
1993; Moltmann 1995; PETERS AND WESTERSTÅHL 2006).

But monotonicity properties have general significance, entirely independently of the NPI-phenomenon. One of their important consequences
has to do with existential quantification over sets, to be discussed in
§4.1.4. For this the notion of a witness set must be introduced first.

4.1.3   Witnesses: the sets quantifiers contribute to interpretation

The set of all its elements is characteristic of a quantifier, but its individual elements are not: they are too heterogeneous. For example, an
element of the GQ denoted by *more than one robot* will contain tigers,
sandwiches, and sonatas besides robots. BARWISE AND COOPER (1981)
define witness sets as elements from which such alien bodies are removed.
It is often useful to say that quantifiers contribute certain sets of individuals to the interpretation of the sentence; see many examples in §4.1.4 and
the treatment of referential variation in §7.2.2. Those sets are typically
the quantifiers' witness sets.

(17)   *W* is a witness set of a GQ iff (i) *W* is an element of the GQ and
        (ii) *W* is a subset of the GQ's "topic set".

Applied to *more than one robot'*, the definition picks out those sets in the
universe that contain more than one robot and no non-robot. Compare
Figure 4.5, the set of elements of *more than one robot'* with Figure 4.8,
the set of its witnesses. All the elements with *d*, which is not a robot, have
been thrown out.[29]

The "topic set" in clause (ii) of definition (17) can be identified in syntactic or in semantic terms. Semantically, the topic set is the smallest set that the GQ lives on:

(18)   GQ lives on a set of individuals L if, for any set of individuals X, $X \in$ GQ iff $X \cap L \in$ GQ.   (BARWISE AND COOPER 1981)

In words: the quantifier lives on L if for any property to be an element of the quantifier is the same as for its intersection with L to be an element of the quantifier. (A smallest live-on set will exist unless the quantifier crucially relies on infinity, e.g. *infinitely many stars*.)

Live-on sets are determined purely from the denotation of the quantifier, irrespective of syntactic analysis. Syntactically the "topic set" is the denotation of the NP that the quantifier phrase's determiner combines with, assuming that such a division can be made. It is called the determiner's restriction, and is discussed in detail in §4.2.2.

Barwise and Cooper state the contrast between increasing and decreasing quantifiers in terms of witnesses as follows. Let W be a witness set of the given GQ and L its "topic set":[30]

(19)   a.   If GQ is monotone increasing,
                 then for any X, $X \in$ GQ iff $\exists W [W \subseteq X]$.
         b.   If GQ is monotone decreasing,
                 then for any X, $X \in$ GQ iff $\exists W [(X \cap L) \subseteq W]$.

§4.1.4 illustrates the significance of (19) with critical issues that arise in the treatment of various quantificational phenomena.

4.1.4   Monotonicity and existential quantification over sets

Monotonicity properties are significant irrespective of the existence of NPIs; they characterize fundamental entailment properties of expressions. One consequence that is important for us is that only the contribution of increasing quantifiers can be formulated in the following form of existential quantification over witness sets. Consider:

(20)   a.   *At least two men walk* = There is a set of men with cardinality at least two such that all its elements walk.
         b.   *At most two men walk* ≠ There is a set of men with cardinality at most two such that all its elements walk.
         c.   *Exactly two men walk* ≠ There is a set of men with cardinality exactly two such that all its elements walk.

Suppose that we look at John and Bill and see that they walk. Then we find out that Ben and Frank walk too. *At least two men walk* remains true in the larger situation, because *at least two men′* is an increasing quantifier, and so whatever it says truthfully about a set is also true of its supersets. On the other hand, both *At most two men walk* and *Exactly two men walk* are false in the larger situation, which is the situation we have to consider. But, unfortunately, the purported paraphrases remain true. In our enlarged situation there are still sets of at most/exactly two men whose elements walk. Therefore sentences involving non-increasing quantifiers can only be rephrased using existential quantification over sets of a given size if a maximality condition is added, i.e. if we guarantee that we are inspecting the largest possible situation. The significance of this problem, which we dub "the maximality problem" is due to the fact that existential quantification over sets is often seen as a desirable tool for formalizing certain meanings. The sets existentially quantified over tend to be witnesses of the GQ, whether or not the authors explicitly say so.

Sometimes the generalization illustrated in (20) offers an insight into why decreasing and non-monotonic quantifiers systematically fail to exhibit a particular behavior. One very well-known example is the extra-wide scope of numerical indefinites, e.g.

(21)   Everyone hates the manager who fired two colleagues of ours.
        'there is a set of two colleagues of ours such that everyone hates
        the manager who fired the members of this set'

It is remarkable that noun phrases denoting decreasing and non-monotonic quantifiers never take extra-wide scope. If extra-wide scope comes about via existential quantification over sets, as the paraphrase in (21) suggests, or in some equivalent way, then this gap becomes understandable: the grammar cannot make this interpretation available to decreasing or non-monotonic quantifiers. In fact, the plural discourse referent analysis in Kamp and Reyle (1993) and the choice-functional analysis in Reinhart (1997), to be discussed in §7.1, are logically equivalent to existential quantification over sorted variables ranging over witness sets. This correctly predicts the restriction to increasing quantifiers. (Monotonicity is not the full story though, because *more students than teachers* denotes an increasing quantifier but does not take extra-wide scope.)

The restriction to increasing quantifiers is also operative in the syntax of Hungarian and receives the same explanation. A striking property of Hungarian is that constituent order in the preverbal field is determined by the semantic class, not by the grammatical function, of the arguments and adjuncts occurring there. The literature distinguishes three regions in the preverbal field; the phrases that can occur in each region must be drawn from a specific inventory. Small samples will be given in Table 8.1 in §8.3. For present purposes it suffices to note that Regions 1 and 2 host only increasing quantifiers, whereas Region 3 is not constrained with respect to monotonicity type. Szabolcsi (1997a) argues that in Regions 1 and 2 quantifiers are interpreted via existential quantification over their witness sets and, in view of the maximality problem, this explains the restriction.

In contrast to the case of NPI licensing, in the cases illustrated above increasingness is the linguistically interesting property, because it enables its bearers to do something that other quantifiers cannot.

Recognizing the maximality problem may guide the choice between alternative analyses. The so-called pair-list (or, family of questions) reading of *wh*-questions presents a puzzle for quantification.

(22)   What does every boy read?
        'for every boy x, what does x read'

May (1985) characterized pair-list readings as ones where the universal quantifier scopes over the *wh*-phrase. The puzzle is how one can quantify into a question, i.e. an expression that does not denote a truth value. Quantification as we know it is not defined for such a case. Both Groenendijk and Stokhof (1984) and Chierchia (1993) solve the puzzle by proposing that in pair-list readings the quantifier does not operate in its usual way; instead, it contributes a set of individuals (a witness), and a regular individual question is then asked about each element, cf. (1) in §**3.1**.

(23)   What did every boy read?   pair-list à la Chierchia (1993)
        $\lambda P \exists W [\text{witness set}(\textit{every boy}')(W) \wedge P(\lambda p \exists f[f \in [W \rightarrow \textit{THING}]]$
        $\exists x[x \in W][\check{} p \wedge p =\hat{} \textit{read}'(f(x))(x)])]$

Relevant in the present context is that the witness set W is introduced using existential quantification. This is all well for examples like (22), but not in the general case. For example, in the complements of verbs like *find out*, *discover*, and *agree* (although not those of *wonder*) almost all quantifiers support pair-list readings. Adding *only* to the matrix makes the pair-list reading of the *at most*-examples smoother:

(24)   I (only) found out what at most two/exactly two/more than two boys / every boy read.
        'for at most two/exactly two/more than two boys / every boy x, I found out what x reads'

(25)   We (only) agreed on what at most two/exactly two/more than two boys / every boy read.
        'for at most two/exactly two/more than two boys / every boy x, we agreed on what x reads'

The story will now be familiar: given that the participating quantifiers include decreasing and non-monotonic ones, these pair-list questions cannot be formalized as 'there exists a set of ... boy(s) such that I found out/we agreed on what each of them reads', and thus the strategy in (23) must be radically revised. See Szabolcsi (1997c); Krifka (2001); and Sharvit (2002) building on Lahiri (2000). The revisions offer improvements in addition to avoiding the maximality problem.

Finally, sometimes the maximality problem is a big nuisance, because one would like to extend the same treatment to quantifiers of all three monotonicity types. One such case is cumulative and branching quantification.[31] Here the increasing cases form the basis of the intuition, as follows (cumulation is discussed in more detail in §8.2.1).

(26) Cumulation ('between them'):
Six mothers gave birth to ten babies.
'There is a set M of six mothers and a set B of ten babies such that every element of M gave birth to an element of B, and every element of B was given birth to by an element of M'

(27) Branching ('completely'):
Six dots are connected to ten stars by lines.
'There is a set D of six dots and a set S of ten stars such that every element of D is connected to every element of S by lines'

However, it is well-known that not only increasing quantifiers participate in such readings; all three monotonicity types as well as mixed patterns are possible. For example:

(28) a. At most six mothers gave birth to more than ten babies between them.
b. Exactly six mothers gave birth to less than ten babies between them.

(29) a. At most six dots are connected completely to more than ten stars by lines.
b. Exactly six dots are connected completely to exactly ten stars by lines.

Sher (1990) is the first to attempt a quantificational schema for cumulation and branching that applies to all quantifier pairs without regard to monotonicity type. She employs existential quantification over sets, and adds a maximality condition that safeguards truth conditions in the non-increasing cases, but has no adverse effect in the increasing case. The reason is that in the increasing case we can pick the largest relevant set to begin with. Here is an application of Sher's schema to (29a), in words:[32]

(30) There is a set X containing at most six dots and a set Y containing more than ten stars such that (i) each dot in X is linked to each star in Y and (ii) the set of all pairs formed from the elements

of X and Y, $X \times Y$ is not part of any bigger $X' \times Y'$ in the dot-links-star relation.

Landman (2004: 33) proposes very much the same solution to the maximality problem with the Adjectival Theory of indefinites. This widely accepted theory, originating probably with Milsark (1977) and Verkuyl (1981), maintains that (contrary to what our discussion above suggested) numeral expressions are not determiners but cardinality adjectives. On this view, *dragon(s)'* does not denote a set of individuals, as in first order logic. Instead, it denotes the set of all dragon-sets. The cardinality adjective *two'* picks out those dragon-sets that have two elements.[33] The problem arises when this is combined with either a null determiner or a closure operation that existentially quantifies over sets whose cardinality is specified by a possibly non-increasing numeral expression (e.g. *at most two*). Landman's Argument Formation operation integrates two sub-operations, existential closure and maximalization.

Although the Sher–Landman strategy takes the bite out of the maximality problem, it raises at least two questions. One is that of compositionality: where is maximalization anchored in the syntax? Another question is how especially theories like Landman's account for the fact that, as we have suggested, non-increasing quantifiers are sometimes handicapped as compared to their increasing brothers. Maximalization built into argument formation does not predict that.

4.2 Determiner denotations

4.2.1 Determiners as relations or two-place functions

Barwise and Cooper (1981) distinguish determiners from quantifiers as follows. Caveat: they use the label NP where generative syntax since the mid-Eighties has been using DP.

(31)   "...semantically ... *more than half* is not acting like a quantifier, but like a determiner. It combines with a set expression to produce a quantifier. On this view, the structure of the quantifier may be represented as below:

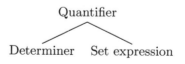

Quantifier

Determiner   Set expression

... we can see that the structure of the logical quantifier corresponds in a precise way to the English noun phrase (NP) as represented in:

most people"

(Barwise and Cooper 1981: 162)

To set the terminology, we refer to expressions like *every, most, more than half, at least two*, and so on as "determiners" and to their denotations as "semantic determiners", or as "determiner denotations". We do not use Det or D to label the expressions, because Det and D are technical terms of particular syntactic theories and therefore what expressions qualify to bear these labels must be decided by their syntactic criteria; for example, as heads of phrases they cannot be as complex as the expression *more than half*. In contrast, Barwise and Cooper identify the determiner by removing the noun from the noun phrase. More on this in Chapter 5.

Determiners denote relations between sets of individuals (noun denotations and predicate denotations) or, equivalently (modulo Currying), functions from noun denotations to noun phrase denotations to sentence denotations.[34] The two perspectives offer somewhat different insights. The relational perspective facilitates the exploration of properties such as symmetry in determiners (Zwarts 1983); the functional perspective is better suited to the purposes of building a compositional grammar and to the study of monotonicity properties. Knowing that the two perspectives are truth-conditionally equivalent enables one to choose that which seems more useful for a given task. (Although indeed they may differ as to presuppositions or implicatures.)

Applied to a noun denotation, the semantic determiner delivers a noun phrase denotation, i.e. a generalized quantifier. So whenever a noun phrase is naturally analyzed as having a determiner as one of its immediate constituents, what kind of generalized quantifier it denotes is a consequence of the nature of that determiner. It is important to emphasize here that the specific properties of determiners with respect to their first (NP) and second (Pred) arguments may be different. The best known example is the case of *every'*, which is decreasing in its noun argument and increasing in its predicate argument. This is notated as $\downarrow$MON$\uparrow$. The relevant entailments are easy to check, and are reflected by the distribution of negative polarity items:

(32) a. Every dragon that ever swam in this lake got sick.
      b. *Every dragon that swam in this lake ever got sick.

We shall see below that other properties like conservativity also pertain to a specific argument of the determiner.

Sometimes it is not self-evident whether the noun phrase has a determiner or what its determiner is. For example, do proper names have determiners? Syntacticians tend to agree that they do. This claim is supported by the appearance of definite and indefinite articles in English when the name is modified by an adjective,

(33)   a.   the young Michael (rebelled against his father)
        b.   an embarrassed Michael (embraced his mother)

and by the fact that in languages like Modern Greek, German, Portuguese, and Hungarian proper names come with definite articles.

What is the determiner–noun division of quantified possessive constructions?

(34)   a.   every girl's mother
        b.   more than one girl's mother

Brody and Szabolcsi (2003) point out that the witness sets of such quantifiers are not simply sets of mothers, but of mothers-of-girls, and that the Hungarian counterparts behave exactly like the counterparts of *every NP* and *more than one NP* in word order and scope relations. These facts suggest that the determiner here is *every/more than one* and its restriction is *girl's mother*; a division to be obtained either in somewhat abstract syntax or in the course of semantic interpretation.

In §**4.2.2** we focus on the determiner's restriction and do not go into much detail with determiners themselves, although classical work by Keenan and by Peters and Westerståhl places them in the center. The reason is that the precise interpretation and compositional treatment of determiners is the part of generalized quantifier theory that has come under the most convincing criticism, as we shall see in Chapter 5 and in the rest of this book. On the other hand, it seems useful to pull together the considerations pertaining to the restriction, because this plays an important role in the compositional semantics no matter how the "determiner" part is analyzed.

4.2.2   The determiner's restriction

4.2.2.1   *Conservativity and extension.* Consider four subsets of the universe of discourse as indicated in the Venn diagrams. In some cases the classical definition of the relation makes reference to nothing but area (ii), the intersection of the two sets (intersective determiners); in other cases, to nothing but area (i), that part of the NP-set that does not overlap with the Pred-set (co-intersective determiners); in yet other cases to both areas (i) and (ii) (proportional determiners).

(35)   (i) NP′ ∩ −Pred′, (ii) NP′ ∩ Pred′, (iii) −NP′ ∩ Pred′,
(iv) −NP′ ∩ −Pred′

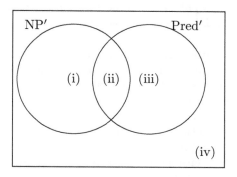

(36)   Some intersective determiners:

$$at\ least\ six' = \{\langle NP', Pred'\rangle : |NP' \cap Pred'| \geq 6\}$$
$$no' = \{\langle NP', Pred'\rangle : |NP' \cap Pred'| = 0\}$$
or equivalently
$$\{\langle NP', Pred'\rangle : NP' \cap Pred' = \emptyset\}$$

(37)   A co-intersective determiner:

$$every' = \{\langle NP', Pred'\rangle : NP' \subseteq Pred'\}$$

(38)   Some proportional determiners:

$$more\ than\ 50\%\ of\ the' = \{\langle NP', Pred'\rangle : |NP' \cap Pred'| > |NP'|/2\}$$
$$most\ of\ the' = \{\langle NP', Pred'\rangle :$$
$$|NP' \cap Pred'| > |NP' \cap -Pred'|\}$$

Although various aspects of the interpretations above have been challenged (see Chapter 5), the observation that natural language determiners do not make reference to areas (iii) and (iv) remains largely uncontested. Indifference to area (iii) is known as conservativity:

(39)   The relation DET is conservative if DET (NP′)(Pred′) is true if and only if DET (NP′)(NP′∩ Pred′) is true.

Indifference to area (iv) is known as extension:

(40)   DET has extension if DET(NP′)(Pred′) remains true if the size of the universe outside changes.

What is the larger significance of these properties?

4.2.2.2   *The significance of conservativity.* Conservativity and extension are significant in connection with language acquisition. The number of all possible semantic determiners is far greater than the number of possible semantic determiners with conservativity and extension.[35] The child's task is simplified if he/she sets out with the innate assumption that whatever relation a determiner may denote comes from this smaller set.

Keenan and Stavi (1986) prove that the three Boolean operations applied to the relations *some'* and *every'*, possibly restricted by extensional adjectives (as in *every blue'*), produce just the set of conservative determiners, and conversely, all conservative determiners can be so produced. The theorem establishes a strong connection between the Boolean structure of this semantic domain and the above-mentioned upper limit on what the child may need to cope with in the course of language acquisition, and in that sense pertains to the intellectual powers of humans. See also the discussion in van Benthem (1986).

Another rationale for conservativity, hinted at in Chierchia (1995) and explicated further in FOX (2002a,b), comes from the other side of the syntax/semantics interface. It is grounded specifically in the copy theory of movement, the standard view in generative syntax since Chomsky (1995). In brief, the view is that movement in syntax, Quantifier Raising included, does not leave traces that resemble variables (as we saw in **§2.3.4**); instead, it copies the moved element in full and independent considerations decide which copy in a chain feeds phonology and which copy feeds semantics. For example:

(41)   every book [you read every book]

The problem is that (41) is not interpretable, at least not correctly. All copies but the highest one must be converted into something semantically appropriate. How should that be done? Much of the descriptive motivation for the copy theory comes from reconstruction, which manifests itself in scope interpretation or in binding condition A/B/C effects (Sternefeld 2001; SPORTICHE 2005, 2006). Reconstruction data suggest that after conversion the lowest copy of an operator-moved phrase retains its NP, but not the scopally relevant determiner. FOX (2002a,b) proposes that the lowest copy be interpreted as a definite description with a bindable variable (indicated by an index). Such a definite can be obtained by syntactic trace conversion or equivalently, following a suggestion by Paul Elbourne, by a semantic rule. The result for (41) will be roughly (42):

(42)   'for every book$_i$, you read that book$_i$'

Fox (2002b: 67) suggests that Trace Conversion is not merely a necessity but it goes a long way to explain why natural language determiners must be conservative. "Trace Conversion yields the right interpretation for chains that are headed by DPs in which D is conservative... Trace

Conversion might play a role in an account of conservativity. Assume that there was a determiner whose denotation D was not conservative... given the copy theory of movement and Trace Conversion, the (characteristic function of the) second argument of D is a partial function defined only for elements that are members of $A(B := \lambda x.B(\text{the } Ax) = (B := \lambda x.(Ax).(Bx))$. It is reasonable to assume that this situation would yield systematic presupposition failure (of the sort we observe in *Most students don't have a car and every student drives his car to school* ...)."

Pursuing this line of reasoning Bhatt and Pancheva (2004) propose that if a determiner is not conservative, its restriction is introduced by Late Insertion to avoid presupposition failure. Their example is the comparative operator *-er*. This is analyzed in Heim (2001) as a non-conservative degree-determiner (a Härtig-quantifier), whose restriction, the comparative clause is obligatorily extraposed. Grosu and Horvath (2006) argue against various empirical aspects of Bhatt and Pancheva's analysis and conclude that we are left with two options. If *-er* is quantificational, then Trace Conversion is at most optional, and Fox's conservativity reasoning is lost; alternatively, Fox's reasoning is upheld but *-er* is not quantificational, following Kennedy (1999).

Sportiche's (2005) Split-DP structure predicts conservativity for determiners in a different way. Sportiche argues, based on selection and reconstruction facts, that argument positions contain NPs, not DPs, and NPs move to get associated with their determiners. This kind of derivation makes NP irrevocably part of the interpretation of the predicate. (More on Split-DP in §**9.4**; see also Johnson 2007.)

4.2.2.3 *The significance of restrictedness: conservativity plus extension.* A different perspective attaches significance not specifically to conservativity but to its combination with extension. The two properties together entail that the determiner's attention is entirely restricted to the set denoted by the common noun phrase (NP). Whatever is going on outside the NP–set is irrelevant to the truth of the claim the determiner makes. The NP–set serves as the determiner's topic set in the intuitive sense. This is interesting, because the relational definition puts the NP–set and the Pred–set on equal footing. Conservativity and extension, together called restrictedness in the linguistic literature, restore the close semantic relationship between the determiner and its syntactic sister. Restrictedness is thus an important fact about the syntax/semantics interface.

It may be noted that conservativity and restrictedness are not always carefully distinguished. Authors often talk about conservativity and give the correct definition, but associate it with an intuition that really presupposes extension.

The restricted character of natural language determiners is the subject matter of many important lines of research. To begin with, recall that Barwise and Cooper (1981) specifically use *most* and *more than half* in stating that these linguistic expressions do not denote quantifiers. Although in Lindström's (1966, 1969) terminology determiner denotations are $\langle 1, 1 \rangle$-type quantifiers (whereas full noun phrase denotations are $\langle 1 \rangle$-type quantifiers), the distinction Barwise and Cooper make serves to emphasize that *most'* and *more than half'* simply cannot be seen as quantifying over the whole universe, and in this respect they are crucially different from quantifiers in first-order logic. This observation can be made precise in two different shapes. The better-known one (Rescher 1962) is that there is no Boolean connective # such that *Most dragons are asleep* is equivalent to $Mx[dragon'(x) \# asleep'(x)]$, where $Mx[\phi]$ is interpreted as 'most things are ϕ'.[36] A stronger claim is that, assuming there are dragons, there is no predicate P such that *most dragons are asleep* is true just in case most things satisfy P (Wiggins 1980, discussed in Szabó 2008). The proof may not be easy, but the basic reason why these meanings are not expressible by quantifying over the whole universe is easy to appreciate: they are concerned with proportions. What proportion of dragons has a particular property is quite independent of what proportion of all things in the universe has a somewhat related property. So, if natural language has proportional semantic determiners at all, then quantifying over a restrictor or topic set is inescapable at least for those. Other determiners, e.g. *every'*, could in principle be said to quantify over the whole universe. But we have just seen that even these blatantly ignore everything outside their NP–sets! So the restricted nature of determiner quantification is not contingent on what is the best analysis of *most* and *more than half* and whether all natural languages possess such expressions; it is merely exploited by proportional determiners.[37]

4.2.2.4   *Is restrictedness specific for determiners? Is it always the sister NP that figures in the restriction?* It is not clear, to begin with, why restrictedness should be specific for determiner quantification. The assumption that restrictedness is not a specialty of determiners is immediately supported by von Fintel's (1994) observation that adverbs of quantification are conservative. For example, the truth of (43) does not depend on cases/times when Fred is not sleepy:

(43)   When Fred is sleepy, Mary is always/never/sometimes/usually alert.

One may say, of course, *always* and its brothers quantify over cases/times/events exactly as *every* and its brothers quantify over individuals, so why the surprise? That is precisely the point: although *every* is a determiner and *always* is not, they operate very similarly.

Next, consider the word *only*, the most famous non-determiner of semantics texts. According to Rooth (1992) the VP–adverb *only* is a universal quantifier whose restriction is a set of focus-alternatives computed
from the interpretation of its sister VP.[38]

(44)   Mary only saw BILL.
         'for every property of Mary in the set that contains seeing Bill
         and its contextually relevant alternatives, that property entails
         seeing Bill'

Much less attention is lavished on (45), which is synonymous with (44).

(45)   Mary saw only BILL.

In (45) the surface syntactic sister of *only* is *Bill*, but *Bill* does not provide the restriction. To obtain the desired interpretation, either *only* or
the complex operator *only Bill* must scope over VP or the whole sentence; then the appropriate restriction will be acquired. Eckardt (2006)
discusses very similar issues writing about German *lauter*, and Vázquez
Rojas (2008) in connection with Mexican Spanish *puros*. English *all* on
its little-known use exemplified in (46) is by and large a counterpart of
lauter and *puros*.

(46)   There were all WOMEN at the bar.
         'The people at the bar were females without exception'

These operators might be ignored in view of the fact that their determin-
erhood is not beyond reasonable doubt.[39] But uncontested determiners
exhibit comparable behavior. Herburger (2000) analyzes a reading of (47)
that is contingent on focus accent on *incompetent*. *Few* is not restricted
by *incompetent cooks*:

(47)   Few INCOMPETENT cooks applied.
         'Few cooks who applied were incompetent'

This last case shows that the ways in which determiners are restricted are
not as simple as it had been thought.

4.2.2.5   *What should be the joint moral of the cases just reviewed?* In
both the adverb and the determiner examples the domain of quantification
(topic set) is smaller than the whole universe, and it is computed from the
interpretation of a designated component of the sentence. When it is not
the denotation of the surface-syntactic sister, the operator is often focus-
sensitive and focus-alternatives make up the domain of quantification.[40]
It is not easy to state an overarching generalization in terms that do not
impose a particular representational strategy by brute force. (One brute
force strategy would be to copy the set of focus-alternatives into a position

analogous to that of the NP-sister of ordinary determiners.) It seems clear however that the fact that determiners are restricted to a grammatically predictable subset of the universe is just a special case; all the operators considered above are so restricted. The restriction being the denotation of the surface-syntactic sister is also just a special case. But then the question that we should answer is not why determiners are restricted by the denotation of their NP-sister. The question that we should answer is why determiners, adverbs, modals, and so on are restricted, and how their restrictions are computed in the general case. Unfortunately, neither Keenan and Stavi's nor Fox's explanation of conservativity naturally extends to the whole class of restricted two-place operators.

4.2.2.6 *Some unusual restrictions.* There are reincarnations of determiners whose relationship to conservativity has not been addressed in the literature:

(48)   a.   What poem does no poet forget? His first poem.
           b.   The poem that no poet forgets is his first poem.

(49)   Four thousand ships passed through the lock.
           'there were 4,000 lock-traversals by ships'

(48) exemplifies functional readings. According to the standard understanding, e.g. Jacobson (1994, 1999), (48a) means, 'what function from individuals to poems is such that no poet forgets the poem that this function assigns to him?' and (48b) means, 'the unique salient function from individuals to poems such that no poet forgets the poem that this function assigns to him is the first-poem-of function'. Jacobson derives the functional reading of *poem* from its basic reading by the application of a type-shifting rule. Although these occurrences of *what* and *the* are not conservative with respect to the run-of-the-mill denotation of *poem*, they are with respect to the derived denotation. (49) exemplifies an event-related reading. On both Krifka's (1990) and Doetjes and Honcoop's (1997) analyses *four thousand* eventually counts event-object pairs. The compositional aspects of these analyses are not clearly developed, so it remains to be seen whether conservativity may be maintained using a methodology similar to Jacobson's treatment of functional readings.

4.2.2.7 *Covert quantifier domain restriction.* The topic set is often even smaller than what the grammatical computation of the restriction assumed above would predict. One kind of case is discussed in Westerståhl (1985). Imagine a summer camp where counselors are assigned to campers based on gender:

(50)   The women look after the women.

(50) can be easily seen to mean that the women among the counselors look after the women among the campers. The first occurrence of *the women* quantifies over a set that is disjoint from the set the second occurrence quantifies over. Because the two domains are different, it clearly will not do to simply shrink the universe of discourse once for all. Westerståhl localizes the specification of what he calls the context set in the interpretation of the determiner, whereas others place it in the NP (see below). We will see in Chapter 12 that the choice between determiner vs. NP continues to be debated and is claimed to vary across languages.

Contextual restriction has become the center of much attention since von Fintel (1994), Roberts (1995), Stanley and Szabó (2000), and Stanley (2000, 2002a,b). Suppose you look in the cupboard and utter (51):

(51)   Every bottle is empty.

You do not mean to claim that all the bottles in the universe are empty, only that the bottles in the cupboard are. (Possibly not even all of those, in case you are looking for oil and there are full bottles of vinegar in the cupboard.) The observation is not new. What grabbed the attention of philosophers and linguists was the claim that such restrictions on the domain of quantification are represented in the syntax. This claim is motivated by two main considerations. The methodological one is that only by representing the contextual restriction in the syntax can compositionality be preserved.

The empirical consideration is that contextual restriction may contain a variable bound by another quantifier in the sentence. One striking example that we will come back to later is (52):

(52)   Every child devoured every apple.

(52) has an unrealistic reading: each apple was consumed more than once (as many times as there were children). This relies on the well-known, fixed interpretation of *every apple*. It also has a realistic reading, the one relevant to us: every child had his/her own set of apples and devoured every element of that set. Stanley and Szabó (2000) represent the realistic reading as follows:

(53)   [every $\langle$child, $i\rangle$]$_j$ devoured every $\langle$apple, $j\rangle$

This notation abbreviates [$\langle$child, $f(i)\rangle$]$_c$, spelled out as [child] $\cap$ $\{x : x \in c(f)(c(i))\}$. Relative to a context c, f is assigned a function from objects to sets, and i is assigned an object. One of the important further questions is exactly how context provides the restriction. Kratzer (2004) argues that it does so using an Austinian topic situation (a space–time location), not by invoking an intensionally defined salient property.

This analysis, especially its syntactic aspect, has been criticized, among others, by Bach (2000), Neale (2000), and Cappelen and Lepore (2001). But it has been inspiring and influential. We come back to it in connection with an attempt to unify the treatments of indefinites and universals in **§7.2.3**.

4.3 Summary

This chapter has looked at some empirically significant properties of generalized quantifiers and semantic determiners. In the former domain we focused on building quantifiers using Boolean operations, on the sets of individuals that quantifiers "talk about": their witnesses, and on monotonicity properties and their general significance. In the latter domain we focused on issues concerning the determiner's restriction that have received much attention in recent years: conservativity, extension, and covert quantifier domain restriction, as well as their significance and the challenges they face. The rest of the book will rely on the findings.

The next two chapters, Chapter 5 and Chapter 6, survey issues that have been considered to be problematic for the generalized-quantifier-theoretic approach, and try to sort out how serious the problems are and how they should reshape the study of quantification.

5

Potential challenges for generalized quantifiers

Generalized quantifier theory (GQ theory, for short) looks like a success story and has become an integral part of most theories of formal semantics. But especially starting with the 1990s many have questioned either its correctness or its relevance. The objections, expressed in the published literature or in professional discussions, are of the form "GQ theory cannot handle ..." or "GQ theory has nothing interesting to say about ...", where the dots are filled by names of empirical phenomena or conceptual issues that do not belong among the classical research topics in GQ theory. The present chapter and the next pull together a range of issues that have figured in such objections, and attempt to evaluate what they tell us about GQ theory. To anticipate the conclusions, some of the objections can be rather easily answered by clarifying certain assumptions or by reminding ourselves of assumptions that may have sunk into oblivion. These definitely do not justify a paradigm shift. Other issues, especially those to be introduced in the next chapter, will be seen to have led to a major transformation of how we think about quantification and scope. The role of generalized quantifiers will be reassessed along the way, but they will not disappear from the picture.

Almost all the issues touched on in these two chapters will come back in Chapters 7 through 12. The reader is asked to bear in mind that the goal here is to briefly consider them as challenges to GQ theory, whereas the goal there will be to scrutinize them in their own right.

5.1 Referential indefinites

Fodor and Sag (1982) observed that indefinites like *a student of mine* exhibit a mixed behavior. In some sentences they scope within their own clause and possibly under some other operator, see (1); in some other sentences they take maximal scope, flouting even syntactic islands, see

(2). Recall that OK indicates that the given reading is available, but there may or may not be other readings that we are not concerned with.

(1)   You haven't talked with a student of mine.
        OK 'You haven't talked with any student of mine'

(2)   Nobody believes the rumor that a (certain) student of mine has been expelled.
        OK 'There is a student of mine such that nobody believes the rumor that he/she has been expelled'

Fodor and Sag suggested that this mixed behavior is due to the fact that indefinites are ambiguous between a quantificational reading, on display in (1), and a referential reading, on display in (2). If this analysis is correct, is it a problem for GQ theory?

Although up till now the discussion has largely followed Barwise and Cooper (1981) in the interpretations of noun phrases and determiners, let us make the obvious point that "GQ theory" is not to be equated with the specific claims of any particular GQ-theoretic article, any more than "generative syntax" is to be equated with a particular article by, say, Chomsky. It is up to the working semanticist to determine, at each stage of the inquiry, what generalized quantifier each noun phrase is best thought to denote. The fact that Barwise and Cooper (1981) did not assign any referential interpretation to indefinites does not mean that "in GQ theory" they have no such interpretation. Barwise and Cooper just made a first stab at the empirical semantic analysis of the expressions they discussed. If indefinites indeed have a referential reading, on that reading they may denote a generalized quantifier much like *Smaug* in (3) of Chapter 2, and the maximal scope properties follow, just as Fodor and Sag argue. Whether the ambiguity analysis is the ideal one is of course a different question, but a question that arises in connection with any ambiguity analysis in any framework. (More on indefinites in Chapter 7.)

5.2 Collective readings

Equating Barwise and Cooper (1981) with "GQ theory" is a fallacy that occurs surprisingly often. For example, it is not uncommon to complain that "GQ theory" does not account for the collective reading of *John and Mary*, as in (3), because it only has a distributive way for interpreting conjunctions, see (4). Simply combining (4) with the predicate *collide* interprets (3) as 'John collided and Mary collided'.

(3)   John and Mary collided.

(4) $\lambda P[P(j) \wedge P(m)]$

In reality the only claim GQ theory as such makes is that *John and Mary* denotes a set of properties. It is silent on what kind of individuals make up the universe and on whether the GQ denoted by *John and Mary* "simply combines" with the predicate. One widely accepted theory of plurality is Link (1983, 1987). Link's claim is that the elements of the universe are either atomic individuals or individual sums; the latter have a part–whole structure. So, alongside the individuals j, m, and b we find the individuals $j \oplus m$, $j \oplus b$, $j \oplus m \oplus b$, and so on, where $\oplus$ is the join operation of lattice theory (SZABOLCSI 1997d: 4 or LANDMAN 1991: 234). To obtain the desired interpretation of (3) one may use the generalized quantifier in (5). This indeed simply combines with the predicate, and it is up to the predicate to apply to the sum as a whole or distributively to its atoms.[41]

(5) $\lambda P[P(j \oplus m)]$

(6) John and Mary sneezed.
$\lambda P[P(j \oplus m)](\lambda x \forall y[atom(x)(y) \rightarrow sneeze'(y)]) =$
$sneeze'(j) \wedge sneeze'(m)$

(7) John and Mary collided.
$\lambda P[P(j \oplus m)](collide') = collide'(j \oplus m)$

Alternatively, conjunction may be taken to be invariably Boolean, so *John and Mary* is interpreted as (4), the intersection of the generalized quantifiers denoted by *John* and by *Mary*. Something like (5) may then be obtained from (4) by a special type-shifter. This is a possibility that Winter (2001) explores, modifying the set of shifters proposed in Partee (1986), see right below. The crucial shifter that Winter employs to obtain collective readings is MIN, which picks out the non-empty unique minimal element of a quantifier if it has one. Van der Does (1992) proposes a different GQ-theoretic treatment of collectivity within a Boolean setting.

So both distributive and collective readings are completely at home in GQ theory; their proper treatment is orthogonal to the assumptions of that theory. (More in Chapters 8 and 9.)

5.3 Type multiplicity

But what if there are empirical arguments to the effect that certain noun phrases, indefinites among them, do not always denote generalized quantifiers? Partee (1986) argues that names, definites, and indefinites are best seen as belonging to not one but three distinct logical types: e (entities), $\langle e, t \rangle$ (sets of individuals, i.e. properties), and $\langle \langle e, t \rangle, t \rangle$ (sets of properties, i.e. generalized quantifiers). Evidence for the first type comes from singular cross-sentential anaphora (see Heim 1982 and Kamp 1981/2002), for the second from predication, and for the third from coordination with unquestionable quantifiers:

(8)   a.   John/the man/a man has arrived. He(anaphoric) looks tired.
       b.   Every/more than one man has arrived. #He(anaphoric) looks tired.

(9)   a.   Mary considers John competent and an authority on unicorns/the authority she should consult.
       b.   *Mary considers John competent and every authority on unicorns.

(10)   I invited a colleague/the president and every/more than one student.

Partee does not relate her data to the Fodor–Sag data, but at least in the domain that she investigates she does not consider indefinites ambiguous. Instead she proposes that so-called type shifters move expressions among the three types. Type shifters are syncategorematic operators whose semantics are sometimes similar to (the logician's approximation of) what some functional elements in some natural languages do. For example, Partee assumes that English indefinites like *an authority* start out as generalized quantifiers, of type $\langle\langle e, t\rangle, t\rangle$ and shift to the property-type $\langle e, t\rangle$ via the BE operator in sentences like (9a); compare *Mary considers John to be an authority*. But she finds it probable that proper names in English start out in type e and shift to $\langle\langle e, t\rangle, t\rangle$ when needed. $\langle\langle e, t\rangle, t\rangle$ is a type that all noun phrases have, as a starter type or by shifting.

In Partee's view the starter types and the available type shifters vary with expressions and with languages. Type shifters are invoked where there does not seem to be syntactic evidence for the presence of a phonetically null element in a phrase whose type/meaning is different from what the overt material would make one expect. Alongside the BE of English we may mention the type shifters of Russian that Partee labels A, THE, and Iota. These are responsible for the fact that although Russian lacks definite or indefinite articles, expressions like *avtoritet* 'authority' function as predicates (type $\langle e, t\rangle$) as well as definite or indefinite arguments (types e and $\langle\langle e, t\rangle, t\rangle$). Chierchia (1998) adds the hypothesis that type shifting is blocked by the presence of an item with identical semantics in the given language. Thus English *authority* does not get to mean 'an authority' or 'the authority'. (More on type shifting in §9.1.)

In the past twenty years type shifting and coercion have been employed in connection with a wide variety of linguistic problems, only a fraction of which have to do with quantification. Concerns about their compositional nature have been raised, e.g. in Dowty (2007) and PYLKKÄNEN (2008).

5.4 Presuppositions and the weak/strong distinction

Whether or not quantificational determiners presuppose the non-emptiness of their restriction has been the subject of much controversy; see the discussion in HEIM AND KRATZER (1998: Chaper 6) of Strawson (1952), de Jong and Verkuyl (1985), Lappin and Reinhart (1988), Diesing (1990), and Reinhart (2006). The crucial issue is argued to be what determiners are classified as quantificational. Milsark (1977) distinguishes between strong and weak determiners as syntactic units. Strong determiners occur in subjects of individual-level predicates (ones that correspond, roughly, to permanent properties) and do not occur in existential *there*-sentences (this is the so-called "definiteness effect"). Milsark proposes that strong determiners are quantifier words, whereas weak determiners are ambiguous between a quantificational and a non-quantificational, cardinality reading. In the former case they have the same distribution as strong determiners. In the latter case they co-occur with *there*, which Milsark analyzes as an existential quantifier. (For attempts to semantically and/or pragmatically characterize the definiteness effect, see Keenan (1987, 2003), Zucchi (1995), and PETERS AND WESTERSTÅHL (2006), among others.)

Turning to the presupposition, it is generally agreed that the sentences in (11) are neither true, nor false (or, are infelicitous) in view of the fact that there are no unicorns.[42]

(11) a. The unicorn(s) will finish breakfast in ten minutes.
      b. Both unicorns will finish breakfast in ten minutes.
      c. Every unicorn will finish breakfast in ten minutes.

On the other hand, people are inclined to judge that (12a) is true and (12b) is false.

(12) a. Every unicorn has exactly one horn.
      b. There are two unicorns in the yard.

Diesing (1990) proposes that all and only determiners on the quantificational reading are presuppositional. This accounts for the presupposition failure in (11) (*the, both,* and *every* are strong determiners) but not for the felicity of (12a) (*every* continues to be strong). Heim and Kratzer argue that (12a) should be construed as a claim about unicorns in those possible worlds where they exist and, given the facts of unicorn mythology, it is indeed true.[43] The ability of (12b) to be felicitously false is due to *two* being interpreted as a cardinality predicate of type $\langle\langle e, t\rangle,\langle e, t\rangle\rangle$. They refer to Partee (1986), Diesing (1992), de Hoop (1992), and Büring (1996) for accounts for the dual behavior of weak determiners.

Already Barwise and Cooper (1981) treat *the, both,* and *neither* as presuppositional determiners. The new analysis of *every, all,* and *most,* etc. merely involves a reclassification.[44] GQ theory definitely does not incorporate and therefore does not explain the fact that all strong determiners or, in Diesing's proposal, all expressions of type $\langle\langle e, t\rangle, \langle\langle e, t\rangle, t\rangle\rangle$ presuppose the non-emptiness of their restriction. But, as far as I can see, neither Diesing, nor Heim and Kratzer derive this fact, either, so why it is true seems an open question.

5.5　Implicatures

Another type of complaint has been that GQ theory misinterprets certain noun phrases. Geurts and Nouwen (2006) observe that *more than three men* and *at least four men* do not mean the same thing, even if replacing one with the other does not affect truth-conditions. One important claim is that *at least/at most* expressions carry epistemic modal implicatures, as in the informal interpretation below:

(13)　　At least four men arrived late.
　　　　'I am certain that four men arrived late and I consider it possible that more did'

In contrast, *more/less than* expressions on their analysis do not reflect on the epistemic state of the speaker.

　　These observations seem correct, but their correctness does not seem to bear on the viability of GQ theory. It is true that in its concrete form GQ theory was designed to pay attention only to truth-conditional distinctions, whereas the critical ingredients of *at least/at most* that Geurts and Nouwen discuss are implicatures. It is also true that being purely truth-conditional or not is a fundamental feature of a theory. But dissatisfaction with the purely truth-conditional treatment of *at least/at most* expressions is really dissatisfaction with the general state of formal semantics at the beginning of the 1980s, when GQ theory was introduced. With the exception of Karttunen and Peters's (1979) pioneering work on *even*, semanticists at that time (and for a long time afterwards) did not pay much mind to Gricean implicatures, whereas twenty years later the descriptive and theoretical issues surrounding implicatures became the center of attention. One of the matters of current debate is whether implicature computation should be a pragmatic supplement to semantics, as in KADMON's (2001) proposal for the treatment of numerals, or it should be part of semantics proper, as in Landman (2000), Chierchia (2006), and related work. But again, these issues appear orthogonal to what GQ theory actually says about quantifiers. GQ theory could be married with implicatures. (More on implicatures in §9.2 and §10.1.)

　　The moral of the cases discussed so far seems to be this. There are important things about noun-phrase semantics that the foundational pieces of GQ-theoretic literature have nothing to say about, or which they simply get descriptively wrong. As the number of such cases grows one indeed has the impression that GQ theory does not help that much with solving the puzzles of current interest. The overall empirical scope of the theory has diminished. But we have yet to see an instance where there is something seriously wrong with it.

There is another type of complaint that may have a chance to make such a case.

5.6   Comparative and superlative determiners vis-à-vis compositionality

Hackl (2000, 2009) makes a number of challenging observations about comparative quantifiers. At this point we single out just two. The first pertains to the contrast below:

(14)   At least two men shook hands.

(15)   #More than one man shook hands.

As has been mentioned above, GQ theory makes the two sentences truth-conditionally equivalent. But the problem here has nothing to do with the modal flavor of (14) that Geurts and Nouwen were interested in; the problem lies with (15). Why is (15) weird? Hackl says that the reason is that it does not mean, 'The number of men who shook hands exceeds one', as GQ theory would have it. Instead, it means approximately this:[45]

(16)   'More men shook hands than how many men shake hands when one man shakes hands'

This paraphrase helps explain the weirdness of (15), because it contains the segment 'one man shakes hands', which is weird in precisely the same way.

Can't we say, just as above, that we are dealing with an accidental descriptive misinterpretation on behalf of GQ-ers? Hackl argues that this misinterpretation is not accidental. It flows from the assumption that the GQ denoted by *more than one man* is built using the semantic determiner denoted by *more than one*, a phrase that GQ theory takes to be an unanalyzed primitive, so to speak. In particular, the comparative is interpreted holistically, without proper attention to its syntax. The argument is that a compositional analysis gets the interpretation right, and GQ theory systematically stops short of being compositional on the determiner level.

The second observation pertains to sentences involving *(the) most* and *(the) fewest*. (Hackl discusses the German counterparts, but the English examples will serve our limited purposes at present.)

(17)   Most (of the) men watched baseball.

It is obvious that the determiner *most* is the superlative of *many* and *more*. But nothing in the standard GQ-theoretic interpretation reflects this fact.

(18) $|man' \cap watched\ baseball'| > |man' \cap -watched\ baseball'|$

This is disturbing enough, but Hackl argues that the absence of a compositional analysis of superlative determiners prevents the GQ theoretic approach from explaining a variety of interesting facts about the interpretations of sentences involving such determiners. One of those facts is that (19) lacks a reading comparable to (18) (in fact, it is ill-formed in English).

(19)   *Fewest (of the) men watched baseball* cannot mean
        $|man' \cap watched\ baseball'| < |man' \cap -watched\ baseball'|$

If (19) is slightly modified, it becomes grammatical, but it still does not carry the missing reading. It only carries a so-called relative (in another terminology, comparative-superlative) reading, not predicted by the GQ analysis (Szabolcsi 1986; Heim 2004):

(20)   The fewest men watched BASEBALL.
        'Fewer men watched baseball than how many men watched any other contextually relevant spectacle'

The most also supports a relative reading, alongside the absolute reading in (18). Comparatives and superlatives are to be discussed in detail in §10.3 and §10.4. Specific details aside, Hackl's general point is this. Because GQ theory does not offer a compositional derivation, it cannot make correct predictions regarding the acceptability and interpretation of determiners. This is a serious matter. Let us see where the error comes from. Is the lack of determiner-level compositionality inherent in GQ theory? Let us retrace our steps.

What this book calls semantic determiners are things in the models: relations between sets. Exactly what expressions denote semantic determiners? Recall Barwise and Cooper (1981: 162), quoted in (31) of Chapter 4. Although Barwise and Cooper put *most*, not *more than half*, under the Det node in their diagram, they clearly commit to *more than half* being a syntactic constituent (they consider the two equivalent). Hackl himself also maintains that the constituent structure of *More than five men walk* is [[*more than five*][*men*]][*walk*]. The difference is that Barwise and Cooper do not investigate the internal structure of the segment *more than five*, whereas Hackl does. He assigns it a comparative clausal structure that contains, among other things, material copied into it at LF and intensional features. That is how the interpretation in (16) is derived.

Incidentally, it is not beyond doubt that *more than half/five* is a constituent; Krifka (1999) and Ionin and Matushansky (2006) propose that it is not. There are other cases where linguists would traditionally not entertain the possibility that a particular string forms a constituent, e.g. *every blue* in *every blue jacket*, but practitioners of GQ theory would insist that these are Dets in the sense of Barwise and Cooper. (This even has mathematical significance for Keenan and Stavi's (1986) reasoning about conservativity.) The question is not so much whether each particular constituent structure is correct; the question is how the decision that *more than five* and *every blue* are Dets comes about, and why the internal structures are not investigated. After all, any sane person knows that these strings are not idioms.

The quote from Barwise and Cooper indicates that they arrive at Dets by reverse engineering. There is much agreement about what expressions are noun phrases. Barwise and Cooper argue that they denote generalized quantifiers. Now Dets are the expressions that combine with nouns to form noun phrases: Dets are noun phrases minus the "head" nouns.

Why does it seem safe to Barwise and Cooper to ignore the internal structure? I believe this has to do with compositionality, and specifically Montague's (1974b) conception of it. Montague defines compositionality in terms of a homomorphic mapping from the algebra of syntax to the algebra of semantics.[46] One corollary of the definition is an analog of the Bracket Erasure Principle of morphology and phonology. Once a complex expression is assembled and its meaning is computed, its internal affairs become entirely invisible ("its internal brackets are erased"). What this means is that if one is sure what an expression means, one is free to ignore its internal structure for purposes external to that expression. Even if you did not ignore it, you could never make reference to it.

How can a follower of this sound strategy go wrong? One possibility is that the expression does not mean exactly what one thought it did. Truth-conditional equivalence or near-equivalence may be deceptive. Hackl effectively argues that both *more than five men* and *most of the men* mean something slightly different than had traditionally been assumed. Subtle meaning-differences can of course be simply intuited, but often they become clear precisely when one works out the compositional derivation. Another possibility is that some of the factors determining the acceptability, or the range of interpretations, of the expression are purely syntactic in nature, so the string actually could not be assembled to carry a particular interpretation. Montague's compositionality scenario works on the premise that there is in fact a legitimate step-by-step derivation of the given ⟨expression, meaning⟩ pair. Such a derivation does not come about by fiat; one must ascertain that it exists.

If Hackl's analysis of comparative quantifiers is correct, then in *More than five men walk* the segment *more than five* can still be seen as denoting a relation between the set of men and the set of walkers – but this relation is computed in a different way than how Barwise and Cooper and many researchers after them imagined. Very informally, just applying the reverse engineering method to Hackl's paraphrase, the relation is this:

(21)   *more than five′* =
        $\{\langle P, Q \rangle : \text{more } P \ Q \text{ than how many } P \ Q \text{ when five } P \ Q\}$

The task for the compositional analysis is to spell out how *more than five* gets to denote (21).

Is it correct that if two Dets in the GQ-theoretic sense are in fact truth-conditionally equivalent, GQ theory cannot in principle account for differences in their behavior? The answer depends on what we mean by "account". Each theory offers particularly illuminating explanations of certain things and not of others. In this sense of "account" it may well be that GQ theory does not account for those differences, i.e. that no great insight stems from its mathematical foundations. But it is not doomed to make incorrect claims. Nothing in the theory says that the compositional derivation of determiners should or could be skipped. Thus, assuming that GQ theory can be enriched with implicatures, modality, etc. and the appropriate compositional effort is put in, in a more modest sense it may well be able to account for the behavior of each determiner.[47]

5.7 De re vs. de dicto, local vs. global

For Montague the proper treatment of quantification did not merely involve assigning a uniform interpretation to noun phrases and showing how it can be used to account for scope ambiguities between quantifiers and negation. Famously, it also involved an account of the de re/de dicto ambiguity in sentences such as (22):

(22)   John seeks a unicorn.
        'There exists a unicorn such that John tries to find it'
        'John stands in an intensional relation with the "idea of" a unicorn'

Montague's solution involves both a possible-world semantics and a particular technology of quantification, beyond what we reviewed in Chapter 2. Whereas possible-world semantics continues to flourish, the scope account of de re/de dicto ambiguities has been by and large quietly abandoned. One reason is that the classical symptoms of the ambiguity are restricted to indefinites; Zimmermann (1993) proposes that (22) should be accounted for by interpreting indefinites as predicates, not as generalized quantifiers; see also Moltmann (1997, 2007). A more generally available ambiguity concerns what world the restriction of the quantifier is interpreted in. Fodor (1970) argued that the quantificational force and the intensional status of certain quantifier phrases can be evaluated independently. Discussing Fodor's "non-specific transparent" reading Keshet (2008) notes that (23) is judged true in a scenario where Mary does not have a specific coat in mind but would not necessarily identify the sort of item she wishes to buy under the description "an inexpensive coat". Mary's only, de dicto desire might be to buy some coat from a particular store whose coats she mistakenly (as we take it) thinks to be outrageously expensive.

(23)   Mary wants to buy an inexpensive coat.

Farkas's (1997a) indexing theory is particularly well-suited to handle what she calls the scope of the descriptive condition (see more in **§7.3**). Keshet (2008) proposes what seems a like-minded solution. Szabó (2009) argues that Fodor's "specific opaque" readings also exist, and defines two types of quantifier raising: one that carries the restrictor of the determiner along and another that does not.[48]

Some of the recent analyses of quantificational expressions have modal or intensional components (Hackl 2000; Nouwen and Geurts 2006); also some analyses for free choice items, polarity items, or other indefinites crucially involve possible worlds and epistemic states (e.g. Dayal 1998; Giannakidou 1998; Yanovich 2005; Jayez and Tovena 2006; Zamparelli 2008). In sum, many but not all important issues in noun phrase quantification can be addressed in a purely extensional semantics.

Of strictly generalized-quantifier-theoretic relevance is the distinction between local vs. global quantifiers (or determiners); see PETERS AND WESTERSTÅHL (2006: Chapter 3) for an introduction and the rest of their book for systematic discussion. A local quantifier is local to a particular universe. A global quantifier is an operator that associates with each model M a local quantifier on M. Basically, a global quantifier is to a local one as the intension of an expression is to its extension in a particular world. Following the linguistically oriented line in GQ theory, the preceding chapters employed the local perspective. Keenan and others regard it as an important fact about quantifiers that they can be studied extensionally. Peters and Westerståhl point out that this will not quite do even in the case of expressions that do not contain non-logical constants such as *dragon* or *treasure*. The reason is that the local perspective does not capture the fact that quantifiers behave identically across models. Even fundamental properties like extension (independence from the size of the universe outside the NP-set and the Pred-set) cannot be stated if we consider just one universe.

5.8   Cross-linguistic variation

Contributions to Bach et al. (1995), MATTHEWSON (2008), and other literature point out that not all languages have quantificational determiners. It is sometimes thought that having a complex system of quantificational determiners is a rare typological characteristic exhibited by some European languages. This latter is certainly not the case. KEENAN (in progress) presents questionnaire-based descriptions of the quantificational devices of Adyghe, Bole, Hungarian, Italian, Malagasy, Mandarin, Russian, Western Armenian, and other languages that demonstrate comparable complexity across language families.

5.9   Interim summary

This chapter has surveyed a range of empirical phenomena and conceptual issues which have been considered problematic for the theory of generalized quantifiers. In most cases we found that they do not constitute serious problems, or that the problems they pose are not specific to this theory. To recap, GQ theory can accommodate so-called referential indefinites, non-distributive readings of plurals and conjunctions, and type multiplicity, and it could adopt the stipulation that the "topic sets" of all GQs are presupposed to be non-empty. Nuances of interpretation that are best described in terms of implicatures pose a greater challenge in that they require a shift away from the basic strictly truth-conditional setup, but almost all descriptive areas in formal semantics have experienced such a shift in recent decades. The proper treatment of de re vs. de dicto ambiguities indeed is an open question. Cross-linguistic studies do not seem to corroborate the suspicion that natural languages only exceptionally have the expressivity GQ theory attributes to them.

Another kind of challenge has come from problems attributed to the absence of fully articulated compositional analyses: the fact that, for example, semantic determiners such as *more than five'* and *(the) most'* are taken to be primitives. I argued that the lack of analysis does not follow from the theory per se, and that the compositional results could be expressed in GQ-theoretic terms. But it seems true that GQ theory offers a better account of sentence-level compositionality than of noun-phrase-level compositionality (with the obvious exception of Boolean compounds of quantifiers). The next chapter introduces a new set of data concerning sentence-level scope behavior that has led to serious reconsideration of the status of determiners.

6

Scope is not uniform and not a primitive

6.1 Different quantifiers, different scopes

In Chapter 2 we discussed the classical notion of scope, stressing its semantic core and the freedom in its grammatical implementation. What we did not ask is how well the predictions of the classical theory (Montague, May, Hendriks, etc.) match up with the data. One feature of the classical theory is that it treats all quantifier phrases alike. Thus, as soon as two expressions are deemed to be quantifier phrases they are predicted to exhibit the same scope behavior. Also, nothing but a stipulation prevents quantifier phrases from scoping out of their clauses, and the stipulation makes all of them clause-bounded. Unfortunately, these predictions are not borne out. The following small sample of data will drive this home.

In (1)–(2) the prepositional object *every show* easily scopes over the subject, but *more than one show* does not:

(1) More than one soprano sings in every show.
   OK 'every show has more than one (potentially different) soprano in it'

(2) Every soprano sings in more than one show.
   #'more than one show has every soprano in it'

In (3)–(4) the direct objects *a famous soprano* and *more than one famous soprano* may scope over the negation, but in (5) *every famous soprano* cannot:

(3) Zdenka did not greet a famous soprano.
   OK 'there is a famous soprano who Zdenka did not greet'

(4)   Zdenka did not greet more than one famous soprano.
        OK 'there is more than one famous soprano who Zdenka did not greet'

(5)   Zdenka did not greet every famous soprano.
        #'every famous soprano is such that Zdenka failed to greet her'

In (6) *a famous soprano* appears to scope out of its clause, even out of an island, but in (7)–(8) *more than one soprano* and *every soprano* do not:

(6)   Two reporters heard the rumor that a famous soprano owns a tiger.
        OK 'there is a famous soprano about whom two reporters heard the rumor that ...'

(7)   Two reporters heard the rumor that more than one famous soprano owns a tiger.
        #'there is more than one famous soprano about whom two reporters heard the rumor that ...'

(8)   Two reporters heard the rumor that every famous soprano owns a tiger.
        #'every famous soprano is such that two reporters heard the rumor that ...'

The latter asymmetry extends to anteceding a pronoun that falls outside the c-command domain of the argument position of the quantifier. In (9) *a great soprano appears* to both scope in the matrix clause and antecede the singular pronoun in the second conjunct, but in (10)–(11) *more than one soprano* and *every great soprano* do not:

(9)   Taro thinks that a great soprano applied and wants to hire her.
        OK 'there is a great soprano who Taro thinks applied and who Taro wants to hire'

(10)   Taro thinks that more than one great soprano applied and wants to hire her. (Hire who?)

(11)   Taro thinks that every great soprano applied and wants to hire her. (Hire who?)

Many of the developments of the past decades have stemmed from contrasts like these. They have led to the conclusion that scope is not a primitive (existential scope, distributive scope, and the scope of the descriptive condition need to be factored out) and not unitary (at least bare indefinites, counting quantifiers, and distributive universals have to be distinguished). Much of the rest of this book will be devoted to fleshing these claims out.

What are the implications for Montague's idea regarding the proper treatment of quantification in ordinary English, (10) of Chapter 2, repeated here as (12)?

(12)   The scope of a quantificational DP, on a given analysis of the sentence, is that part of the sentence which denotes a property that is asserted to be an element of the generalized quantifier denoted by DP on that analysis.

It seems quite likely that (12) will not preserve its direct relevance, among other things because, we argue, there is no such thing as **the** scope of a quantificational DP. On the other hand, when DPs are decomposed into quantificational bits and pieces, those are treated as generalized quantifiers, and the same idea holds for how they take scope. Thus, what definitely remains is (13):

(13)   The scope of a quantifier expression is that part of the sentence that denotes a property that is asserted to be an element of the generalized quantifier denoted by the quantifier expression.

In (13) the term "quantifier expression" is not co-extensive with "quantificational DP (or AdvP, etc.)". Depending on analysis, it may refer to full arguments that appear in surface syntax, but also to other phrases, e.g. comparative clauses as generalized quantifiers over degrees in Heim (2006a), and to much smaller, possibly phonetically silent syntactic units that a compositional analysis finds appropriate to invoke. Likewise, theories that employ type raising rules to account for the range of scope possibilities of quantifier phrases (Bittner, Hendriks, Barker and Shan, etc.) take (13) as a point of departure. Thus the Montagovian idea remains in force, but not as a self-contained account of scope behavior; rather, as a building block of more differentiated and complex accounts.

The observations about scopal diversity are part of a bigger picture. The articles in Szabolcsi (1997b) and much further work demonstrate that whatever quantificational phenomenon one looks at – branching readings, interaction with negation, distributivity vs. collectivity, intervention effects in extraction and negative polarity licensing (viz. weak island effects), event-related readings, pair-list questions, functional readings, donkey sentences, exhaustive focus, and so on – one finds that certain DPs participate and others do not. This suggests that "quantification" involves a variety of distinct mechanisms. Each kind of expression participates in those that suit its syntactic structure and its semantics. Szabolcsi (1997a) proposes the following heuristic principle:

(14)   What range of expressions actually participates in a given process is suggestive of exactly what that process consists in.

(Only suggestive, not indicative, because there may be more than one candidate process that requires the same kind of input expressions.)

The heuristics in (14) contrasts with the more traditional one, according to which all grammatical mechanisms are to be formulated in a fully general fashion and supplemented with filters that prevent them from applying to the "wrong" expressions or discard the result if they did apply. There exists a similar difference between Government-Binding-style syntax on the one hand and lexicalist theories – categorial grammar, HPSG, LFG, Minimalism, etc. – on the other. In its fully developed form GB has one operation: "Affect Alpha" (do anything to anything), whose output is filtered by principles like the Theta-Criterion, the Empty Category Principle, Superiority, and so on. This contrasts with the kind of syntax in which all happenings are driven by the lexical properties of expressions. So for example it is perfectly fine in GB to move a verb to the subject position; structures involving this step will be eventually filtered out. But no such movement ever takes place in a lexicalist theory if neither the verb, nor the inflectional elements that rule over the subject position, nor anything else in the sentence has a need that would be satisfied by such a movement.

Naturally, the reader should not take it on faith that replacing the unitary and primitive notion of scope with a variety of different mechanisms is preferable to filtering out the unwanted results. The value of the new strategy should be judged based on the insights it offers. The chapters to follow lay out some of these insights and point out current and promising directions of research.

6.2 Quantifiers or referring expressions?

One consequence of the diverse behavior and complex analysis of noun phrases is that certain classical questions cease to make sense in their original form. For example, such is the question whether definite descriptions are Russellian quantifiers or Strawsonian referring expressions:

(15)   The serpent hissed.
    a. $\exists x \, \forall y [(serpent'(y) \leftrightarrow y = x) \wedge hissed'(x)]$
    b. $hissed'(\iota x[serpent'(x)])$

It may well be that one of the formulae is a better paraphrase of the sentence *The serpent hissed* than the other. But that will hardly settle the quantifier vs. referring expression issue. First, it does not seem to be the case that noun phrases in general squarely fall into one or the other of two such classes; so the question as to which of the two *the serpent* belongs to is ill-founded. More generally, there is no good answer to the question as to exactly what expressions *the serpent* would mimic if it were a quantifier. Second, the bits and pieces that the compositional analysis of various noun-phrase types calls for bear little resemblance to the bits and pieces that the logic employed especially in (15a) offers. More generally, there does not seem to be a unique logical or structural characteristic that separates quantifiers and referring expressions. Therefore, whereas the observations that scholars have made in the course of attempting to settle the dispute remain interesting and challenging, the classical question itself looks like a product of linguistic innocence.

The philosopher Michael Glanzberg reaches a convergent conclusion in a case study of the expression *both*. He writes:

(16)   "We often think about quantifiers via intuitions about kinds of thoughts. Certain terms are naturally used to express singular thoughts, and appear to do so by contributing objects to the thoughts expressed. Other terms are naturally used to express general thoughts, and appear to do so by contributing higher-order properties to the thoughts expressed. Viewed this way, the main condition on whether a term is a quantifier or not is whether its semantic value is an object or a higher-order property. At least, these provide necessary conditions ... We also often think about quantifiers in terms of a range linguistic features, including semantic value, presupposition, scope, binding, syntactic distribution, and many others ... *[B]oth* appears quantificational by some linguistic standards, and yet appears object-denoting by standards based on intuitions about the kinds of thoughts it expresses. It can appear this way, I shall argue, because the notion of quantification in natural language is in fact the intersection of a number of features, which do not always group together in the same ways, and do not always group together precisely in accord with our intuitions about expressing singular and general thoughts. *Both* has some important properties related to presupposition and to having objects as semantic values that allow it to contribute objects to thoughts. These are not present in some other canonical quantifiers. Yet *both* still has scope features that are present in other canonical quantifiers. Thus, *both* can be construed as contributing objects to thoughts, while at the same time displaying some important features of quantification." (Glanzberg 2008: 208)

6.3   How to obtain reliable scope data

Scope judgments are held to be notoriously difficult. Part of the difficulty may be an artifact of the classical theory: if one expects all quantifiers to behave uniformly, it is bewildering to find that they do not. Another reason may be that scope independent readings blur the picture; see Hintikka and Sandu (1997), Schein (1993), and Landman (2000). But it is indeed important to proceed carefully when obtaining judgments, now that we see that the diversity of scope behaviors may have theoretical significance. The goal of this section is to provide some guidance for the working semanticist regarding how to obtain reliable scope data.

Where there is a potential ambiguity, one of the readings is typically easy. This tends to be the one where the scopal order of quantifiers and other operators matches their left-to-right order or surface c-command hierarchy. This is called linear or direct scope. What is often difficult to tell is whether inverse scopal orders are possible. To investigate this it is useful to shut out the easy reading and, to borrow Ruys's (1992) slogan, to let the difficult one shine. For example, the easy, subject-wide scope readings of the sentences below are implausible in view of encyclopedic knowledge. A single pink vase cannot grace every table (at the same time); a single guard cannot be posted in front of every building (at the same time):

(17)   a.   A pink vase graced every table.
              OK 'every table was graced by a (different) pink vase'
        b.   A guard is posted in front of every building.
              OK 'every building has a (different) guard posted in front of it'

The fact that the sentences nevertheless make perfect sense indicates that the object wide scope readings are fine. At the same time, the fact that the variants below are less natural or even nonsensical confirms that the method still has some discriminating power. It does not allow all quantifier phrases to take inverse scope; rather, it shows that *every NP* is a much better inverse-scope-taker than *all of the NP* or *none of the NP*.

(18)   a.#?A pink vase graced all / none of the tables (at 5 o'clock).
        b.#?A guard is posted in front of all / none of the buildings (at 5 o'clock).

Unfortunately, the easy reading can only be shut out if the difficult reading can be true without it. If the difficult reading entails the easy one, there is no shutting it out. In that case one tries to exploit some linguistic phenomenon, for example cross-sentential anaphora, that is contingent on a reading that the grammar produces, not just on what is entailed to be true. In (19), an example attributed to B. Partee, *it* cannot refer to the unique missing marble, although its existence can be inferred from the first sentence.

(19)   I dropped ten marbles and found only nine of them. # It must
        be under the sofa.

In this spirit, suppose we want to find out whether *two NP* and *two
or more NP* are capable of taking inverse scope over *every NP* – but here
the inverse readings entail the easy, linear ones. (If there is a particular
x that is related to every y, then for every y we can find an x that is
related to it.) To construct a test case, let us imagine two schools. In the
parent-friendly school a teacher is fired if any parent complains. In the
teacher-friendly school a teacher is fired only if every parent complains.
The following is reported:

(20)   Every parent complained about two teachers. They were fired.

(21)   Every parent complained about two or more teachers. They were
        fired.

Can this be the teacher-friendly school? Speakers usually find it easy
to judge that only (20) may describe an incident in the teacher-friendly
school. Notice that the answer depends solely on whether *they* in the
second sentence can be understood to refer to those teachers who every
parent complained about (the precondition of firing in the teacher-friendly
school). This in turn depends solely on whether the first sentence allows
the reading 'there were two (two or more) teachers such that every parent
complained about them'.

In sum, this scenario tests just the scope judgment that we are interested in; but the involvement of anaphora and a non-metalinguistic
question make the task easier and more natural than it is to judge paraphrases or truth-values. An additional reason why the use of such indirect
methods is preferable is that work in all areas of processing suggests that
speakers create underspecified representations and only get to the bottom of what has been said if a specific task forces them to (KOLLER AND
NIEHREN 1999; SANFORD AND STUART 2002; FERREIRA AND PATSON
2007).[49] But then one does not want to turn the task into an IQ-test;
anaphora resolution is an appropriate linguistic task.

Test cases of the above sort may be used to sharpen one's introspective
judgments as well as to design controlled experiments where participants
respond by answering questions like, "Can we be in the teacher-friendly
school?" Kurzman and MacDonald (1993) asked speakers to judge continuations to assess the role of grammatical factors in scope interpretation. A
significantly more labor-intensive but perhaps more reliable technique is
to measure self-paced reading times. In reading-time studies participants
are not asked to judge truth-values or to answer questions, just to read
sentences or texts at their own pace. Reading times are measured region
by region. The assumption is that participants slow down where the text

becomes difficult to process or difficult to integrate with what has already been processed. For example, (20)–(21) might be recast in ways indicated below. When the first sentence has no inverse reading, the second sentence is confusing and participants would take longer to read it.

(22)   Every parent complained about two teachers.
         These two teachers were fired.
         Since every parent complained about them, they had to be fired.

(23)   Every parent complained about two or more teachers.
         These two or more teachers were fired.
         Since every parent complained about them, they had to be fired.

Tunstall (1998) and Villalta (2003) conducted extensive reading-time experiments pertaining to preferred readings in sentences involving the distributive quantifiers *each* and *every*.

Reading-time experiments do not track how scope interpretation interacts with prosody. Jackendoff (1972), Büring (1997), and Krifka (1998) discuss how pitch contours manipulate information structure vis-à-vis negation: Jackendoff's "A" and "B" accents in sentences of the type *Every horse didn't jump across the fence*. Jackson (2006) identifies a distinct effect in sentences with two quantifiers: the use of lengthening to support the preferred scope reading. In Jackson's experiments sentences contained *a(n) NP* in combination with *every NP* or *a few NP*. Each sentence was accompanied by two pictures, which represented two potential scope readings. Participants were instructed to read the sentence in such a way as to convey one of the readings; they were told that other people will listen to the recordings and try to guess which of the readings they meant to convey. Subjects increased the duration of the indefinite to support its wide scope reading. It is important to see however that both the "B accent" and the increase in duration highlight certain readings but are not strictly necessary to elicit them.

For more on the processing of quantifiers, see PYLKKÄNEN AND MCEL-REE (2006). We also draw attention to the huge psychological literature pertaining to reasoning with quantifiers (Johnson-Laird 1983; Johnson-Laird and Byrne 1991; Rips 1994; Braine and O'Brian 1998). Geurts and van der Slik (2005) is a pioneering attempt to use monotonicity patterns to predict the accuracy with which people judge inferences involving sentences with two quantifiers. Chemla (2008) tests the predictions of different theories of presuppositions against examples of the sort *Each/None of these ten students quit smoking* versus *Two of these ten students quit smoking*, and finds that only the sentences with positive/negative universals presuppose that all ten students used to smoke.

7

Existential scope versus distributive scope

This chapter argues that both indefinites and universals call for a distinction between existential scope and distributive scope. After motivating the distinction it focuses on existential scope; matters of distributivity are taken up in the next chapter.

Picking up the thread from §5.1 we start with the well-known case of indefinites, motivate the existential vs. distributive scope distinction, and explore the choice-functional implementation in some detail. We then go on to argue that *every NP*-type universals warrant the same distinction, and make several steps towards unifying their treatment with that of indefinites.

7.1 Indefinites

7.1.1 No such thing as "the scope" of an indefinite

The well-known claim (e.g. May 1977) that quantifier scope is clause-bounded is based on examples like the following:

(1) A colleague believes that every paper of mine contains an error.
'for every paper of mine there is a potentially different colleague who believes that it contains an error'

As was mentioned in §5.1, Fodor and Sag (1981) noticed that the scope of singular indefinites is not clause-bounded, see (2); it even escapes islands for movement, such as a Complex DP Island, see (3):

(2) Each colleague believes that a paper of mine contains an error.
OK 'there is a paper of mine such that each colleague believes it contains an error'

(3)   Each colleague overheard the rumor that a paper of mine contains
        an error.
        OK 'there is a paper of mine such that each colleague overheard
        the rumor that it contains an error'

In fact, they proposed that if an indefinite escapes an island it takes
maximal scope. (3) lacks the so-called intermediate reading below:

(4)   Each colleague overheard the rumor that a paper of mine contains
        an error.
        # 'for each colleague there is a paper of mine such that he/she
        overheard the rumor that it contains an error'

Given maximal scope and the fact that this reading is best available
with specific indefinites,[50] i.e. ones modified by a partitive (*a student
of mine*), by a relative clause (*a director that I know*), or by *some* or
certain (*some book, a certain book*), Fodor and Sag proposed that such
indefinites are referential. The maximal scope of a referring expression
does not come about by scope assignment; it is simply a valid inference.
Compare: *Everyone thinks that I haven't met John* entails that there is
an individual whom everyone thinks I have not met.

Farkas (1981) countered this by observing that intermediate readings
are possible; see Ludlow and Neale (1991) and Abusch (1994) for further
discussion.

(5)   Each student has to hunt down every paper which shows that some
        condition proposed by Chomsky is wrong.
        OK 'each student > some condition > every paper'

So we have the first observation: the scope of indefinites is "upward unbounded" – but it does not have to be maximal. The second observation
is based on a datum in Ruys (1992) and Reinhart (1997). (6) now involves
a plural, rather than singular, indefinite: *three relatives*:

(6)   If three relatives of mine die, I will inherit a house.

(6) means either that (a) if the number of my dead relatives reaches three,
I inherit a house (whichever relatives of mine pass away), or that (b) there
are three particular relatives such that if they all die, I inherit a grand
total of one house. It cannot mean that (c) there are three relatives of
mine such that the passing of each leaves me with a house (a total of three
houses).

So, what **is** the scope of *three relatives* in (6)? Already on the acceptable (b) reading *three relatives* is taking extra-clausal scope. But
clause-internal scope relations teach us that a wide-scoping plural indefinite should be able to make another indefinite dependent, to wit:

(7)   Three relatives of mine left me a house.
        OK 'there are three relatives of mine such that each left me a separate house'

We simply cannot talk about (6) using the traditional scope vocabulary. *Three relatives* shows one diagnostic of wide scope: its referent is chosen independently of the condition expressed by the *if*-clause; its existential import is at the level of the main clause. But it fails to exhibit another equally respected diagnostic: it does not make an indefinite falling within its scope (in the above sense) dependent. The only way to resolve the conflict is to say that the two diagnostics are in fact diagnostics of two different things. Informally, let us call the first existential scope, and the second distributive scope, and wait for the theoretical proposals to give them precise content.

(8)   Existential vs. distributive scope
        Indefinites have two distinct kinds of scope. Their existential scope is unbounded. Their distributive scope is clause-bounded.

7.1.2   Existential closure of a choice function variable

Reinhart (1997) makes two important proposals to account for the above data. One is to appeal to the structure-building rule of existential closure. Using existential closure, as opposed to Quantifier Raising, is motivated by the island-free nature of the indefinite's scope. The other proposal is that existential closure applies to a choice-function variable, as opposed to an individual variable. A choice function picks out an element of any set that it applies to. E.g. the choice function f_1 may be such that it picks Spot from the set of dogs, Tokyo from the set of capitals, and my laptop from the set of objects currently on my desk. Another choice function will differ from f_1 in at least one of its picks. E.g. $f_1(dog') = $ Spot and $f_2(dog') = $ King. If numerals are treated as cardinality adjectives (Verkuyl 1981; Landman 2004), then *dogs* will denote the set of all subsets (i.e. the powerset) of dogs, and *two'* will restrict them to those that have two elements. Then, it may be that $f_1(two'(dogs')) = \{$Spot, King$\}$ and $f_2(two'(dogs')) = \{$Spot, Spike$\}$.

To connect different strands of research, notice that the values of the choice functions employed in the interpretation of indefinites are nothing else than witness sets of the generalized quantifiers denoted by those indefinites. This is especially transparent in the case of indefinites like *two dogs*. When viewed as denoting a generalized quantifier, its witness sets contain two dogs and no non-dogs. As explained right above, these are exactly the values of $f(two'(dogs'))$. Therefore the witness-set and choice-functional analyses of indefinites are to a great extent equivalent. Minimal

witnesses also correspond to KAMP AND REYLE's (1993) discourse referents that are introduced into the current DRS or into a superordinate
one, as opposed to a subordinate DRS via "box-splitting".

The intermediate reading of (5) will be explicated roughly as follows:

(9) $\forall x[student'(x) \rightarrow \exists f \forall y[(paper'(y) \wedge$
        $shows\ to\ be\ wrong'(f(condition'))(y)) \rightarrow hunt\ down'(y)(x)]]$

In words: For every student x there is a choice function f such that for
every y that is a paper and shows the element that f picks from the set
of conditions [proposed by Chomsky] to be wrong, x hunts down y. Here
conditions vary only with students, not with papers.

Why choice functions, as opposed to individual variables? Choice functions have become so widely used in the past decade that one hardly
stops to think about the motivation any more. Choice functions were first
employed to interpret specific indefinites and to help model notions like
'another' by von Heusinger (1992); Hilbert's epsilon-operator that he uses
is nothing else than a choice function. In his work existential quantification over choice functions serves to derive non-specific indefinites from
specific ones, so to speak. Reinhart (1997) offers a very different kind of
motivation. She shows that quantifying over individual variables makes
it difficult to let specific indefinites take arbitrarily wide existential scope
and to ensure at the same time that the existential quantifier does not
get separated from the restriction of the indefinite. As originally observed
by Heim (1982), that those two stick together is crucial for sentences in
which the surface position of the indefinite is in a syntactic domain that
gets interpreted as the antecedent clause of material implication, the classical interpretation of an *if*-clause and of the restriction of the determiner
every. Consider (11) as an interpretation of (10).

(10)   If we invite a certain philosopher, Max will be offended.

(11) $\exists x[(philosopher'(x) \wedge invite'(x)(we')) \rightarrow offended'(m)]$

(11) does not say, 'there is a philosopher such that if we invite him, Max
will be offended'. Because the existential quantifier scopes out of the *if*-
clause on its own, (11) says, 'there is an individual such that if he is a
philosopher and we invite him, Max will be offended'. Given that the falsity of p suffices to make $p \rightarrow q$ true, the existence of an individual who
is not a philosopher or whom we do not invite makes (11) true; but these
do not make (10) true. So the restriction $philosopher'(x)$ cannot be lower
than existential closure. But what drags it up there? If the indefinite were
a traditional existentially quantified phrase and its scope were assigned by
QR, QR would, but recall that QR is not island-free (it is even restricted
to its own tensed clause). Moreover, argues Reinhart, such an interpreta-

tion would make plural indefinites distributive outside their own clause – incorrectly: recall (6), repeated below:

(12)   If three relatives of mine die, I will inherit a house.

So, Reinhart concludes that a new device is needed for the combination of properties of extra-wide scoping indefinites. Choice functions are appropriate, because they allow us to leave the NP-part in-situ and still get the truth conditions right. Along the lines of (9), the choice-functional interpretation of (10) is this:[51]

(13) $\exists f[invite'(f(philosopher'))(we')) \rightarrow offended'(m)]$

In words: 'there is a choice function f such that if we invite the individual whom f picks from the set of philosophers, Max will be offended'. This is basically equivalent to 'there is a philosopher such that if we invite him, Max will be offended'. The hedge is due to the fact that the two formulations potentially diverge when the NP-set is empty; see Reinhart (1997) and a good solution in Winter (1997: 434–437).[52]

This is a suggestive but not quite conclusive argument in favor of choice functions.[53]

(i) It is not beyond reasonable doubt that *if*-clauses and the restriction of *every* are to be interpreted as antecedents of material implication. Regarding *if*-clauses, see KRATZER (1991a,b) and von Fintel and Iatridou (2002); the latter propose to interpret conditionals using strict implication. Regarding *every*, recall that determiners are now thought to be restricted by their NP-sisters and even to presuppose the non-emptiness of their restrictions.

(ii) If material implications were retained, the choice-functional analysis would not help the fact that the existence of a non-invited philosopher also makes (11) and (13) true.

(iii) It is not quite correct that a refashioned, island-free QR would necessarily make incorrect distributive predictions for (6). It would, if it followed Barwise and Cooper's (1981) interpretation of indefinites like *three relatives*. But collective readings need to be accommodated anyway, and we already mentioned in §5.2 that generalized quantifier theory might very well incorporate, say, Linkean plural individuals.

(iv) The inseparability of existential scope and the property denoted by the NP can be ensured in other ways: by quantifying over variables restricted to witness sets (Szabolcsi 1997a) or by expressing quantifier phrase denotations in a modal propositional logic where the NP-property plays the role of the accessibility relation (Ben-Shalom 1996).

(v) Schwarzschild (2002) argues that the illusion of indefinites with special properties arises when there happens to be just one single relevant entity in the discourse context.

But there have been interesting further arguments in support of choice functions. One is Reinhart's own suggestion that the choice-function variable that directly applies to NP or NumP denotations (*philosopher'* and *three relatives of mine'*, respectively) has the same type as a determiner.[54] It is thus advantageous for a compositional analysis of indefinites as DPs. Another argument, somewhat paradoxically, constitutes a partial revision of Reinhart's proposal. Prior to discussing this, let us consider a residual issue.

In §6.1 it was observed that singular indefinites whose existential scope is not confined to the finite clause are also capable of anteceding singular pronouns outside their c-command domain, as in (9) of that section. This property of indefinites has been in the focus of Discourse Representation Theory (see KAMP AND REYLE 1993 for the most extensive version) and Amsterdam-style dynamic semantics, introduced in Groenendijk and Stokhof (1990, 1991). A distinctive property of the latter theory is that it retains the classical view that singular indefinites existentially quantify over individuals, but enables them to extend their binding abilities over the incoming discourse. We have no space to review these theories in detail, but see some discussion of context change potentials in §2.3.6. What is remarkable in the context of the present section is that Reinhart and Winter, who are committed to the choice-functional treatment of wide-scope indefinites, remain silent about how those indefinites support non-c-commanded anaphora and thus they solve only half the problem. The simplest example is (14):

(14)   A dog strolled in. It barked.

The issue is how to provide a linguistic (as opposed to simply inferred) antecedent for the pronoun *it* in a way that ensures that the correct choice function is used and that it is applied to the correct set. Von Heusinger (2004) offers a dynamic update semantics account that interprets *it* as 'the thing'. This ensures that the correct choice function is picked up, but that function is applied to the set *thing'*, not to the set *dog'*. This causes various problems known from the literature on pronouns as definite descriptions; see Elbourne (2005) for recent discussion. Brennan (2008) combines von Heusinger's account with Elbourne's NP-ellipsis account of pronouns.

7.1.3   Skolemized choice functions

Kratzer (1998) argues against intermediate-scope existential quantification over choice functions. She suggests that intermediate readings are only felicitous when there is a contextually salient way of picking elements of the NP-set of the indefinite and pairing them with the individuals that the wider-scoping quantifier ranges over. In the case of (5), repeated below, this would be the way conditions proposed by Chomsky are paired with students.

(5)   Each student has to hunt down every paper which shows that some condition proposed by Chomsky is wrong.
       OK 'each student > some condition > every paper'

Many examples with intermediate readings in the literature even contain a pronoun within the indefinite's NP that is linked to the wider-scoping quantifier, e.g.

(15)   Each professor rewarded every student who read a certain book that he wrote.
       OK 'each prof$_i$ > a certain book he$_i$ wrote > every student'

Therefore, Kratzer proposes to use choice functions with an optional individual-variable argument (Skolemized choice functions) to interpret non-maximal scoping indefinites. On her view the choice function itself is always contextually given, much like the reference of Fodor and Sag's maximal-scope indefinites. The presence of the variable captures the possible dependence on some quantifier of how the choice function picks elements from the indefinite's NP-set. (5) will now be explicated as (16). The relevant change from Reinhartian (9) is in the underlined part. The x variable of f is bound by $\forall x$, and $\exists f$ has disappeared; if it were to be spelled out, it would be assigned widest scope. (16a) retains material implication for the sake of comparison with (9); (16b) uses restricted quantification, which is closer to Kratzer's own intentions.

(9) $\forall x[student'(x) \rightarrow \exists f \forall y[(paper'(y) \wedge \text{ shows to be}$
       $wrong'(f(condition'))(y)) \rightarrow \text{hunt } down'(y)(x)]]$

(16)   a. $\forall x[student'(x) \rightarrow \forall y[(paper'(y) \wedge \text{ shows to be}$
            $wrong'(\underline{f(x)(condition')})(y)) \rightarrow \text{hunt } down'(y)(x)]]$
       b. $\forall x[student'(x)]\forall y[(paper'(y) \wedge \text{ shows to be}$
            $wrong'(\underline{f(x)(condition')})(y))][\text{hunt } down'(y)(x)]$

To introduce a bit of terminology, Skolemized choice functions are Skolem functions that have both set and individual arguments (or parameters).[55] A Skolem function eliminates an existential quantifier. If the existential was not within the scope of a universal, the Skolem function is a constant, of zero arity. E.g. Skolemizing $\exists x \forall y[P(x)(y)]$ we get $\forall y[P(f)(y)]$. If the existential was within the scope of one or more universals, the Skolem function bears the indices of those universals as arguments/parameters: by Skolemizing $\forall y \exists x[P(x)(y)]$ we get $\forall y[P(f(y))(y)]$. The fact that our Skolem functions are also choice functions is an independent feature: not all Skolem functions have a set argument, as we have just seen.

Skolem functions have been employed in the treatment of various related phenomena. Steedman (2000, 2009) treats scope alternation and donkey anaphora using Skolem functions. Winter (2004) makes a connection between the wide existential scope of indefinites and functional readings of copular sentences, analyzed in Jacobson (1994):

(17)   The (only) woman that every man loves is his mother.
        'the (only) function in the set $\{f : f$ maps every man to a woman he loves$\}$ is the function that maps every man to his mother'

Winter unifies Kratzer's and Jacobson's approaches in terms of Skolem functions of arbitrary arity.

Schlenker (1998, 2006a) observes a reading that cannot be expressed without Skolemization:

(18)   [Context: Every student in my syntax class has one weak point: John doesn't understand Case Theory, Mary Binding Theory, etc. Before the final I say:]
        If each student makes progress in some/a certain area, nobody will flunk the exam.

The intended interpretation is that there is a certain distribution of weaknesses such that if each student makes progress in his/her own weak field, nobody will flunk. This is straightforwardly expressed by asserting that there is a Skolemized choice function (the "main weakness-of" function) such that each student should make progress in the area this function assigns to him/her; but it is not expressible by asserting that for each student there is a field that he/she should make progress in. The latter formalization would allow a student to escape flunking by making progress in an arbitrary field that is not his/her weakness.[56]

The prospects of Skolemization clinch the argument for choice functions, because Skolemized choice functions have greater expressive power than quantification over individuals, and apparently the additional expressive power is necessary.

So, can existential closure of choice functions be dispensed with? Chierchia (2001) argues that it cannot. He points out that a problem arises when the indefinite is within the scope of a decreasing quantifier. The positive version of his example is in all relevant respects identical to Farkas's (5). The novelty lies with the negative version, (20).

(19)   Every linguist has studied every solution that some problem might have.

(20)   Not every linguist has studied every solution that some problem
         might have.

If (19) is interpreted using a contextually given Skolemized choice function
à la Kratzer, as in (21), then (20) will be interpreted as just its negation,
as in (22):

(21) $\forall x[linguist'(x) \rightarrow \forall z[solution\ to'(f(x)(problem'))(z) \rightarrow studied'(z)(x)]]$

(22) $\neg\forall x[linguist'(x) \rightarrow \forall z[solution\ to'(f(x)(problem'))(z) \rightarrow studied'(z)(x)]]$

Chierchia tests (22) in a revised shape, adding widest-scope existential
closure, following Matthewson (1999), who proposed that interpretation
be directly in the form of (23):

(23) $\exists f\neg\forall x[linguist'(x) \rightarrow \forall z[solution\ to'(f(x)(problem'))(z) \rightarrow studied'(z)(x)]]$

In words, 'there is a way to pair up linguists and problems so that not
every linguist studied every solution to the problem he/she is paired with'.

Chierchia observes that (23) is extremely easy to make true, while (20)
is not. For example, if I take a function that pairs every linguist with a
problem in particle physics, we can be quite sure that (23) will be true.
But this does not make (20) true. On the relevant reading, (20) means
this:

(24) $\neg\forall x[linguist'(x) \rightarrow \exists f\forall z[solution\ to'(f(x)(problem'))(z) \rightarrow studied'(z)(x)]]$

In words, 'it is not the case that for every linguist there is a way of
choosing a problem such that the linguist studied every solution to the
problem so chosen'. (24) contains intermediate existential closure of the
choice function variable f and no Skolemization – as in Reinhart (1997)
and Winter (1997).

Chierchia conducts a detailed study of the syntactic and semantic distribution of problem cases, and concludes that both the Reinhart (1997)–
Winter (1997) strategy and Kratzer (1998) strategy are necessary (Chierchia 2001: 81):

(25)   a.   Indefinites, when interpreted as choice functions, always have
               a hidden parameter.
         b.   Existential closure is restricted to (the top and) the immedi-
               ate scope of a decreasing operator.

Regarding (25a) note that Chierchia follows Reinhart (1997) and Kratzer (1998) in reserving the choice-functional interpretation for extra-wide-scoping uses of indefinites and maintaining the quantificational interpretation for narrow-scoping ones. (In contrast, Winter 1997, 2000, 2004 assumes that potentially extra-wide-scoping indefinites are always choice-functional; see **§9.1**.) He attributes certain interpretive limitations, not discussed here, to weak-crossover involving the choice function's hidden parameter, and considers various theoretical options to derive the effect that the choice function must be existentially closed within the immediate scope of a decreasing (or generally, non-increasing) quantifier.[57]

Kratzer (2003) disagrees with Chierchia's reasoning; she rejects that going from (22) to (23) is within the spirit of her account.

(26)   "I do not see the problem. The contextualist account of wide-scope indefinites says that (4) [*Not every student$_x$ read every paper that some$_x$ professor wrote*] can only get an 'intermediate scope' reading for the indefinite DP in contexts where *some* can successfully refer to a method pairing all relevant students with a unique professor. For out-of-the-blue utterances, a function pairing every student with their favorite professor in the field of papers to be read (or something like that) can be easily accommodated. What happens if we ask subjects to judge (4) against the background of particular contexts? Let's try this one: Suppose we are told that every student but John read every single paper by Chomsky, but just one paper by Montague, and John read every single paper by Montague, but just one paper by Chomsky. Given this scenario, (4) seems intuitively false on the intended 'intermediate scope' reading. This judgment is quite compatible with the referential analysis. For reasons we may never fully understand, the context provided most readily evokes a function that connects John to Montague, and other students to Chomsky ... Be this as it may, in contrast to Matthewson's account of wide-scope indefinites, which existentially binds the choice function variable at the highest level, the referential analysis is not automatically threatened by the mere existence of verifying values for the choice function variable in (4). For (4) to be a threat for the contextualist account of wide-scope indefinites, a good case has to be made that problematic values are in fact plausible values in realistic contexts." (Kratzer 2003: 4–5)

The issue Chierchia points out is a difficult one and it seems unsettled in the literature. There is a sentiment that it would be preferable if only Kratzer's strategy were needed, see e.g. Breheny (2003) and Yanovich (2005, 2008, 2009), but a satisfactory response to the full range of Chierchia's observations has not yet been produced. Others (e.g. Schlenker 2006a) follow Matthewson (1999) in assuming wide scope existential quantification, modulo Chierchia's criticism.

The plot thickens, though, because we have seen that the intended meaning of (18) is strictly Skolem-functional. But then the non-increasing version, (27), cannot be rescued along the lines Chierchia considered.

(27)   [Context: Every student in my syntax class has one weak point: John doesn't understand Case Theory, Mary Binding Theory, etc. Before the final I say:]
        If not every student makes progress in a certain area, somebody will flunk the exam.

Schlenker (2006a) suggests that the correct interpretation of (27) is obtained by wide scope existential quantification over what he calls "natural functions"; he proposes to extend the same solution to an overgeneration problem pointed out in Schwarz (2004). The notion of a natural function is familiar although not well-defined (and one wonders how well it could be defined): it refers to a mapping that is somehow homogeneous. Invoking natural functions has a somewhat similar effect as Kratzer's contextualist analysis, but Schlenker's position still differs from Kratzer's in that it does not assume that the context supplies a unique choice function for the interpretation of the indefinite.

Z. Szabó (p.c.) suggests that the critical reading of example (20) that Chierchia uses to motivate intermediate existential closure may be the denial (metalinguistic negation, to use Horn's term, as opposed to plain negation) of (19). This would restrict the phenomenon to the immediate scope of negation, although it remains to be seen how it would extend to cases with other decreasing or non-monotonic quantifiers. Mascarenhas (2009) independently proposes that the contextual givenness of the choice function should be understood as presupposition of the existence of a contextually relevant choice function, rather than the actual choice function necessarily being part of the common ground. The existential presupposition can be locally accommodated in the immediate scope of a non-increasing operator. The choice function escapes the scope of the non-increasing operator if it is anaphoric to a pairing that is in fact part of the common ground. Although local accommodation can be seen as subsuming denial, the converse does not hold, and so this proposal has a wider coverage than Szabó's.[58] Some solution along these lines could help eliminate the undesirable disjunctiveness of existentially closed vs. not closed choice functions.

The developments are reminiscent of von Heusinger's (1992) epsilon-operator approach, on which specific indefinites are basic and existentially quantified ones are derivative.

Finally, contextually salient choice functions have to be slightly different from their simple existentially-closed relatives. Recall that a choice function looks at each subset of the universe (give or take the empty set) and picks an element of it. What can make such an "omnivorous" function contextually salient? I suppose it would be necessary for the context to make salient a particular element of each subset of the universe: books, mountains, water molecules, prime numbers, and so on. But when we talk about *a certain book*, all we mean is that the context supplies a salient book, or a way to pair students with books in the case of Skolemization, and do not assume the availability of salient mountains or water molecules. Therefore, salient choice functions should be restricted to a single set-argument; or, the set should be used as a parameter in the definition of the function.

7.2   Universals of the *every NP*-type

7.2.1   Existential vs. distributive scope in universals

The previous section started from the assumption that the scope behavior of indefinites is substantially different from that of universals, in particular those of the *every NP*-type. But is it? Indefinites are characterized by three relevant properties: (a) their existential scope is potentially unbounded, i.e. their "reference" can be kept independent of any structurally higher operator in the sentence, but of course (b) they can be referentially dependent on a higher operator, and (c) their distributive scope is clause-bounded. A moment of reflection shows that *every NP* has the same properties.

Potentially unbounded existential scope characterizes *every NP* on its run-of-the-mill interpretation if its restrictor-set is non-empty. Compare:

(28)   Nobody believes the rumor that every student of mine will be expelled.
OK 'there is a set of students of mine (in fact, the set of all my students) such that nobody believes the rumor that they will be expelled'

On this interpretation *every NP* has a unique minimal element, the set of all my students (it denotes a principal filter). Its existential import is just like that of a plural definite.

But *every NP* also has a varying, non-principal-filter interpretation, as was pointed out in (52) of §**4.2.2**. This possibility was first observed in Kuroda (1982).

(29)   Every child tasted every apple.
(i) OK 'there is a set of apples such that every child tasted each

of its members'
(ii) OK 'every child had his/her own apples and tasted each of them'

And finally, *every NP* has clause-bounded distributive scope. This is no news: the news was that indefinites share this property.

The observations concerning the parallel behavior of indefinites and such universals were made, cumulatively and more or less independently, by Beghelli, Ben-Shalom, and Szabolcsi (1997), Beghelli and Stowell (1997), Farkas (1997a), and Szabolcsi (1997a), among others. They can be summarized as follows:

(30)   Parallels between *every NP* and *two NP*:
Both support distributive readings, but only within their own clauses.
Both can be referentially dependent or, even clause-externally, referentially independent.

7.2.2   Inducing and exhibiting referential variation

Why did it initially seem that *every NP* has clause-bounded scope but unmodified indefinites (*some NP*, *two NP*) have unbounded scope? The reason is that different questions were asked in diagnosing their scope behavior. In connection with universals the traditional question was, Within what domain can they make other expressions referentially dependent? This is a question about distributive scope. In connection with indefinites, the traditional question was, Within what domains can they remain referentially independent of other operators? This is a question about existential scope.

To take a closer look at the ability of an expression to induce referential dependency in another, consider the following diagram that depicts a situation where the S > O reading of *Every man saw some dog* is true (assume that there are altogether three men). The notion of a witness set will be useful in talking about it. As was discussed in §4.1.3, a witness of a generalized quantifier (GQ) is a set of individuals that is an element of the GQ and is also a subset of the determiner's restriction set (BARWISE AND COOPER 1981). Any set of individuals that contains at least one dog and no non-dogs is a witness of the GQ denoted by *some dog*. The unique witness of *every man'* is the set of men (on its well-known, non-varying reading). The unique witness of *no man'* is the empty set. See Beghelli, Ben-Shalom, and Szabolcsi (1997) for the discussion of referential variation involving increasing quantifiers in these terms; Beghelli and colleagues suggest that non-increasing quantifiers operate in a different way.

Figure (31) shows a witness set of the wide scope quantifier *every man'*. Each element of this witness is connected by the *see'*-relation to some witness or other of the narrow scope quantifier *some dog'*.

(31)   Scope and witness sets

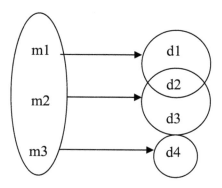

A quantifier phrase can induce referential variation only if it has a minimal witness with more than one element – otherwise there is nothing to vary with; it can exhibit referential variation only if it has more than one witness – otherwise it has no way to vary. The indefinite traditionally considered in the literature was singular *some NP'*, whose minimal witnesses are singletons, and thus cannot induce referential variation. On the other hand, the fixed-reference universals that linguistic literature traditionally considered have unique witnesses, and thus cannot exhibit variation. These choices, probably influenced by first order logic, may explain why only one aspect of each used to be recognized. Attention to plural indefinites and variable-reference universals, as in (29)(ii) thus plays an important role in forcing the conclusion that both indefinites and universals have potentially unbounded existential scope (import) and clause-bounded distributive scope (ability to induce variation).

7.2.3   Indefinites and universals unified?

The observation that the existential versus distributive scope distinction extends to universals like *every NP* may allow for a unification of the context dependence of indefinite interpretation as in Kratzer (1998) with quantifier domain restriction as in Stanley and Szabó (2000). Stanley and Szabó argue that the domain of quantifiers is always contextually restricted, that this restriction may contain a variable linked to another quantifier, and that this restriction is specifically located in the NP, not the determiner. Recall (52) of §**4.2.2**, interpreted by Stanley and Szabó as (53), both repeated here:

(32)   Every child devoured every apple.

(33)   [every ⟨child, i⟩]$_j$ devoured every ⟨apple, j⟩

The similarity with indefinites is captured if *every NP* is interpreted using a possibly Skolemized choice function applied to the denotation of NP. As was assumed for indefinites, the denotation of NP is the powerset of the noun-set. $f(Pow(child'))$ picks out a contextually salient subset of children, just as ⟨child, i⟩ does when i remains unbound, and $f(x)(Pow(apple'))$ picks out a subset of apples that a contextually salient Skolem function pairs with elements of the set that the variable x ranges over, just as ⟨ apple, j⟩ does when j is bound by the index of the subject. (This does not yet account for the distributivity of *every*; we take that up in the next chapter.)

So, the question arises: matters of distributivity aside, what is the difference between *every NP'* and *some NPs'*? Going back to Stanley and Szabó's basic example, what is the difference between uttering (34) and (35) when you look in the cupboard and see that all the three oil bottles in there are empty, although the two vinegar bottles are full?[59]

(34)   Some bottles are empty.

(35)   Every bottle is empty.

Both sentences can be uttered truthfully in this same situation. Which of the two is going to be uttered depends on whether the oil bottles have a privileged status for the conversational partners, or at least the speaker – is it the case that we need oil and not other substances that are kept in bottles? So the difference will have to be in how the verifying choice functions are obtained in the two cases. In the case of (34) we will assume existential quantification over (individuals or) choice functions, as proposed in Reinhart (1997), Matthewson (1999), Chierchia (2001), and Schlenker (2006a) for the range of cases discussed in the previous section. Therefore various different choice functions may verify the sentence containing the indefinite, although they possibly have to be "natural" ones. In the case of (35), we will assume that the context supplies the choice function (i.e. the domain restriction), so the hearer simply has to know what that choice function is. This is essentially the contextualist position Kratzer (1998) takes in connection with specific indefinites – we are proposing it for *every NP* instead.[60]

Whether the device should be called domain restriction or a choice function, exactly how does the context uniquely determine the current domain for universal quantification? Kratzer (2004) employs the Austinian notion of a topic situation; for comments, see McConnell-Ginet (2005).

The above unification of universals with indefinites is similar in spirit to the unification of definites with indefinites in Heim (1982), following in some respects Lewis (1975) and Evans (1980). In that case the earlier received wisdom had been that indefinites are existential quantifiers, whereas definites are either Russellian unicity-quantifiers or Strawsonian individual-referring expressions. Heim proposed to analyze both as a formula containing a free variable: $dog(x)$. She stated the remaining difference in terms of the Novelty versus Familiarity Conditions: indefinites must introduce a fresh discourse referent (file card), whereas definites add information to a familiar one.

The unification of indefinites and *every*-phrases in terms of existential scope was first proposed in Farkas (1997a) and Szabolcsi (1997a); unification of the domain-restrictional and choice-functional views was first explored in von Fintel (1999b).

To summarize, on this view indefinites and universals exhibit significant similarities in their existential scope properties: how far up they may be referentially independent and how they become referentially dependent on other quantifiers. They differ as to how the choice function involved in their interpretation is picked. Indefinites and universals also exhibit significant similarities in their distributive scope properties: they only induce variation within their own clause. They differ as to the source and the precise nature of their distributivity, as will be discussed in the next chapter.

Definites, especially plural definites (*the dogs*) share some properties with indefinites and some with *every*-phrases, which is expected if the phenomenology of each of these phrase-types results from the combination of several "smaller" properties.

We come back to the internal structure of *every NP* and its cross-linguistic counterparts in Chapter 12.

7.3   Do all "quantifier phrases" have the same dual scope behavior?

First of all, not all "indefinites" (*a(n) NP, some NP, a certain NP, n NP*, and their partitive versions) and not all "universals" (*every NP, each NP, all NP, all (of) the NP*, etc.) have identical existential and distributive properties. The "intra-indefinite" and "intra-universal" differences have not been the subject of appropriate descriptive research, so explicit or implicit overgeneralizations are prevalent in the literature and quite possibly in this book. Some of the differences among indefinites are addressed in Liu (1997) for English and Mandarin; Kratzer (1998);

Becker (1999); Schwarz (2004); Ionin (2006) for English; Gutiérrez-Rexach (2001); Alonso-Ovalle and Menéndez-Benito (2002); Martí (2008); von Heusinger (2008) for Spanish and Brazilian Portuguese; Kornfilt and von Heusinger (2008) for Turkish; von Heusinger and Klein (2008) for Uzbek; von Heusinger and Onea (2008) for Romanian; and Yanovich (2005) for Russian. Following Carlson (1977), van Geenhoven (1998), and others, bare plurals are never included among the "indefinites" (with the possible exception of languages that do not have overt articles). The generic, free-choice, and negative polarity item readings of indefinites are not addressed in this book.

Then, modified numeral QPs such as *two or more buildings* do not seem to have divergent existential and distributive scopes, at least not in English.

(36)   Every fireman thought that two or more buildings were unsafe.
       #'there are two or more buildings such that every fireman thought that they were unsafe'

Likewise, distributive scope is not always clause-bounded: *each NP* supplies solid counterexamples:

(37)   A timeline poster should list the different ages/periods (Triassic, Jurassic, etc.) and some of the dinosaurs or other animals/bacteria that lived in each. (Google)
       OK 'for each period, some of the dinosaurs that lived in it'

(38)   Determine whether every number in the list is even or odd.
       ? 'for every number, determine whether it is even or odd'

(39)   Determine whether each number in the list is even or odd.
       OK 'for each number, determine whether it is even or odd'

Finally, Fodor (1970) and Farkas (1997a) observe that there is a third kind of scope to reckon with; Farkas calls it the scope of the descriptive condition (cf. **§5.7**). The denotation of NP in both *every NP* and *two NP* may be indexed to the world of the speaker or to that of a superordinate subject:

(40)   Some boy imagined that every violinist had one arm.
       (i) OK 'a boy imagined of every actual violinist that he/she had one arm'
       (ii) OK 'a boy thought up an all-one-armed-violinists world'

(41)   Some boy imagined that two violinists had one arm.
       (i) OK 'a boy imagined of two actual violinist that he/she had one arm'
       (ii) OK 'a boy thought up a world with two one-armed violinists'

It is important to notice that the scope of the descriptive condition cannot be equated with existential scope. This is shown by upward monotonic *two or more NP* and downward monotonic *no NP*. Neither has unbounded existential scope, but their descriptive conditions can be indexed with the world of the speaker or of a superordinate subject. In the former case both (42) and (43) talk about actual violinists.

(42)   Some boy imagined that two or more violinists had one arm.
        OK 'Some boy imagined that two or more individuals who, according to the speaker, are violinists in the actual world had one arm'

(43)   Some boy imagined that no violinist had one arm.
        OK 'Some boy imagined that no individuals who, according to the speaker, are violinists in the actual world had one arm'

The scope of the descriptive condition will not be discussed further here. Farkas's proposal offers a non-quantifying alternative to Montague's (1974) treatment of some de re vs. de dicto ambiguities. (See §**5.7**.)

7.4 Summary

This chapter argued that the notion of "the scope" of a DP is in many cases descriptively inadequate and has to be factored into at least two components that we called existential scope and distributive scope. The position we have taken, with Beghelli and Stowell (1997) and Farkas (1997a) on English, Szabolcsi (1997a) on Hungarian, and work building on these (Lin 1998; Matthewson 2001) is stronger than the position taken in much of the literature that follows Kamp and Reyle (1993) and Reinhart (1997). We do not only make the existential and distributive scope distinction in the case of indefinites (and definites, to which the arguments seem to carry over) but also in the case of *every NP*-type universals. We do not group the latter together with the so-called counting quantifiers such as *two or more NP, less than five NP*, etc. The motivation for not lumping these together comes in part from the data described in §**6.1**, and is further discussed in Chapters 10 and 11. On the other hand, we are not aware of reasons to make the existential versus distributive scope distinction for *each NP* and for counting quantifiers. *Most (of the) NP* and *the most NP* are very much understudied from this perspective.

The "existential scope" of a DP is the domain over which it has existential import (referential independence), whether or not this is due to explicit existential quantification or to an inference, as in the case of contextually salient choice functions. The next chapter analyzes "distributive scope", which likewise turns out to have different sources in different kinds of DPs.

8

Distributivity and scope

The goal of this chapter is to discuss how distributive readings come about in a rather wide variety of phrases.[61] §8.1 starts out with an introduction to the collective vs. distributive distinction, with special reference to events. §8.2 considers plural definites and indefinites, including those modified by *all* or *both*, and conjunctions with stressed or unstressed *and*. §8.3 scrutinizes distributive singulars like *every NP*, *each NP*, and *many a NP*. It is argued that in both the plural and the singular cases the source of distributivity is an operator external to the DP (modulo some poorly understood quantifiers).

§8.4 considers another facet of distributivity: NP-pluralization. It zooms in on anti-quantifiers, from binominal *each* in English to reduplicated numerals in Telugu, and argues that they all are instances of distribution involving a set of events as the sorting key.

Finally, §8.5 raises the question, largely open as of date, as to the division of labor between Skolemization and event-key distribution as sources of referential dependency.

8.1 Background notions: sorting keys, distributed shares, and events

Barwise and Cooper (1981) define all semantic determiners as relations between sets of atomic individuals. Here distributivity is not a separate aspect of the interpretation of quantifiers: all quantifiers are construed as distributive, and the domain of their distributivity automatically coincides with their scope. As was pointed out in Chapter 5 however there is nothing "anti-GQ-theoretic" in assuming that individuals are not atomic but may have a part-whole structure, or in replacing individuals with sets in the domain. So, collective readings can be added with minimal modification. Distributive scope might still remain co-extensive with "the scope" of a traditionally distributive quantifier. Some noun phrases (e.g. *two men*) might be seen as ambiguous between a collective and a quantificational-distributive construal.

The foregoing discussion has called for a more radical modification. The basic empirical argument for distinguishing between existential scope and distributive scope has been that both unmodified indefinites (*a NP*, *some NP*, *a certain NP*, *n NP*) and *every*-phrases have potentially unbounded existential import, whereas their ability to make other expressions referentially dependent is typically confined to the tensed clause they belong to. This section considers how these expressions and some of their kin acquire their distributive interpretations.

The picture so far is this. (1) below represents the common core of sentences of the form *Q man/men lifted Q chair(s)*, where each *Q* may be any of *the*, *some*, and *every*. The NP-part of the (in)definite or universal combines with a choice function, and the $f(NP')$ so obtained can be left in its original argument position.

(1) $lift'(f(chairs'))(f(men'))$

The existential scope of the noun phrase is obtained either by existential closure of f or is inferred from f being contextually given. (1) as it stands yields a collective reading, or a naïve approximation thereof, where a plurality/group/set of men lifts a plurality/group/set of chairs in one fell swoop: a single chair-lifting takes place. Distributivity must come from some separate operator that is capable of working from this kind of input.

It is virtually impossible to discuss distributivity matters without taking a stand in philosophical and terminological debates about plurals that are orthogonal to the concerns of this book. Some theories will treat the denotation of phrases like *(the) (two) men* as sets of individuals, some as sums of individuals (i-sums, plural individuals), and some as predicates; see the discussion in Link (1983), Landman (1994, 2000), and Schein (1993). These are practically equivalent for our purposes, so we use these terminologies almost interchangeably, even adding the neutral label "plurality" for convenience.

The set and the individual sum construals are very similar to each other. Picking up the thread from **§5.2**, in both cases the domain is a partially ordered set closed under union and without a bottom element: a join semi-lattice.[62] Imagine a tiny domain with no other men than Arthur and Ford. Expressions such as *Arthur and Ford, the men, two men*, and *the two men* can be construed as denoting the set $\{a, f\}$ or the i-sum $a \oplus f$. On the first construal the individual a is not in the domain, but the singleton set $\{a\}$ is. On the second construal a is in the domain, and it is one of the atoms of the i-sum $a \oplus f$. As said above, this is not an ambiguity, just two alternative and wide-spread formalizations.

(2)

a. $\{a, f\}$ b. $a \oplus f$

$\{a\}$ $\{f\}$ a f

The distributive operator is a universal quantifier that establishes a relation between the sorting key and the distributed share (Choe's 1985 terminology). On the distributive interpretation of *Two men lifted three chairs* the sorting key is a plurality provided by $f(two\ men')$, construed either as $\{a, f\}$ or as $a \oplus f$, and the distributive operator associates something with each element/atom of that plurality. On the traditional view the distributed share is provided by a DP, so each man will be associated with a set, or i-sum, of three chairs. See also §7.2.2. Theories of scope typically resort to such "un-event-ful" representations to this day.

In the literature on distributivity, the by now standard view is that distribution is always mediated by events. The reasons for including events in the linguistic ontology are many-fold, starting with Davidson (1967) and gaining much support from the study of aspect and argument structure; see RAMCHAND (2007) for an overview. The strongest argument to the effect that specifically distributivity must involve events comes from complex examples that combine cumulative readings with a distributive dependency (see e.g. (9) below); it was put forth in Schein (1993) and adopted in Landman (1994) and Kratzer (2003), among others. We simply take this result for granted. Revising the above in this spirit, each man will be associated with one or more atomic chair-lifting events. In the neo-Davidsonian tradition thematic roles mediate among predicates and their traditional arguments. So, each man will be associated with chair-lifting events that he is the agent of. Atomic events have a unique agent, unique theme, and so on. Note that this unique agent or theme need not be a singleton set or an atom. On the distributive reading of *Two men lifted three chairs* each atomic lifting event may involve just one chair (in which case each man is the agent of three different events), or three chairs (in which case each man is the agent of just one event and he lifts the chairs in a stack), or perhaps one or more of the men is associated with two events, one in which he lifted a single chair and another in which he lifted two in a stack. The domain of events may also be construed as forming a join semi-lattice; this way non-atomic events and non-atomic bearers of thematic roles can be obtained.

Schein (1993) argues that all first-order quantifiers have an event quantifier within their immediate scope. As a first approximation these would be existential quantifiers. But, because of maximality problems in non-increasing contexts and in order to exclude unwanted subevents, Schein uses second-order definite descriptions of whatever events of the relevant sort there are, and allows just one existential event-quantifier per sentence: the main quantifier that corresponds to the possibly composite event that the sentence as a whole describes. This existential event-quantifier is underlyingly clause-initial and QR raises quantifiers to positions superior to it. Other authors tend to retain existential quantification in the scope of first-order quantifiers and either ignore the concomitant problems or deal with them in some different way.

Below are Schein's analyses of a few examples (Schein 1993: 314–318). Because Schein uses a complex formalism that we cannot introduce here, only the prose versions are quoted; the reader is encouraged to consult the original. *There* is understood as definite event-anaphora.

(3) Sum of plurals
     Some students shared twenty-three pizzas.
     'There are some events of sharing such that some students are sharers in events that completely overlap those events, and in completely overlapping events twenty-three pizzas are shared'

(4) Distributivity
     Every student ate a pizza.
     'Every student is such that whatever he did as an eater, if anything, is such that there are some events in which a pizza is eaten'

(5) Distributivity and a decreasing quantifier
     Every student ate no pizza.
     'Every student is such that whatever he did as an eater, if anything, is such that no pizza is such that whatever happened to it there, if anything, [is] an eating'

(6) Semi-distributivity
     Few composers collaborated.
     'Few composers are such that whatever they and some other composers did as collaborators, if anything, is such that there is a collaboration'

(7) Event dependence
     No more than then students (ever) work on three problems.
     'Whenever there is a working on three problems, no more than ten students participate'

(8) Cumulative quantification
     No more than two detectives solved no more than three crimes.
     'No more than two detectives solved crimes, and there no more than three crimes were solved'

(9)   Cumulation combined with a distributive dependency
        No more than two detectives (each) solved two crimes, for no more
        than five agencies.
        'No more than two detectives each solved two crimes for agen-
        cies, and whatever events there were of detectives each solving two
        crimes were solving for no more than five agencies'

Schein's work as well as Lasersohn's (1995), Landman's (1994), and
Kratzer's (2003) have firmly established that reference to events is crucial
in the semantics of plurality. It is remarkable though that even leading
neo-Davidsonians like Kratzer do not incorporate events into the discussion of all semantic phenomena; compare for example her work on choice
functions and on Hamblin-quantifiers (no events) with her practically simultaneous work on argument structure (all about events). One reason
for not framing all analyses in terms of event semantics may be that certain theoretical issues in event semantics are unresolved and therefore the
theory does not extend easily to arbitrary new domains. Another reason
may be the tendency in the formal semantics literature to compartmen-
talize, even beyond what might be an unavoidable simplification in each
given case. In any case, this book generally invokes events only when the
literature under review crucially does so.

8.2   Distributive readings with plural (in)definites

8.2.1   Distributivity and cumulativity

Various aspects of the interpretation of numeral indefinites will be discussed in §9.2; this section is specifically concerned with distributivity.

The considerations in §8.1 begin to apply as soon as we know, on independent grounds, where the distributive operator, a first-order universal
quantifier, is located. Does it come with the noun phrase, or the predicate,
or something else? In the case of plural (in)definites, the first question is
whether they are ambiguous between a collective and a distributive construal; e.g. whether plurals like *the men* have a silent **each** [*of*] associated
with them. (10) shows that collective and distributive predicates can be
coordinated when the subject is a definite or indefinite plural. This suggests that *(the) six men* is not ambiguous. Distributivity in (11), indicated
by **each**, is a property of the second predicate.

(10)   (The) Six friends watched a movie together and had a glass of
        wine.

(11) $\lambda P[watched\ a\ movie\ together'(P)$
        $\wedge\ had\ a\ glass\ of\ wine\ \textbf{each}'(P)]\ (f(six'(friends')))\ =$

$$= watched \ a \ movie \ together'(f(six'(friends')))$$
$$\wedge \ had \ a \ glass \ of \ wine \ \mathbf{each}'(f(six'(friends')))$$

Each can be a silent operator, or an overt one: floating *each* or binominal *each*. Its core contribution can be spelled out as follows (more on the overt items in the next section):

(12)   a.   with P and Q variables over sets of atomic individuals:
$$\lambda P \lambda Q \forall x [P(x) \rightarrow Q(x)]$$
    b.   with P an atomic or plural individual and Q a set of individuals:
$$\lambda P \lambda Q \forall x [(atom(x) \wedge x \leq P) \rightarrow Q(x)]$$

The first conjunct of (10), which contains the word *together* and requires a subject that denotes a non-singleton set or a non-atomic individual applies to the denotation of *(the) six friends* directly. On the other hand, the second conjunct says that every element/atom in the denotation of *(the) six friends* had a glass of wine.

As Reinhart already noted, this strategy immediately predicts that distributive scope is unaffected by how high the choice function is existentially closed. Distributivity kicks in when a predicate combines with an argument. There is simply no way for the extra-clausal locus of existential closure to play any role.

Let us add, because it will be important below, that distributive predication applied to a plurality carries a homogeneity presupposition ('all or none'). (13) is a presupposition failure if Trillian will visit some of her friends but not others.

(13)   Trillian will (not) visit her friends.

See Löbner (1998) and Beck (2001) for plurals, and Szabolcsi and Haddican (2004) for conjunctions.

Clause-internally, which argument slots of a lexical or syntactically assembled predicate can be modified by **each**? There are at least four possible determining factors. One, the lexical-conceptual meaning of the predicate may delimit the options. For example, *be tall* is distributive, *be numerous* is collective, and *be heavy* can be either (Dowty 1987; Winter 2001). Two, predicates may establish a certain hierarchy among their arguments. For example, it could be that the subject can make the direct object referentially dependent, but not vice versa. Three, further syntactic aspects, among others occurrence in particular operator positions may affect distributive interpretation. Four, processing limitations may be at work.

The role of lexical semantics will not be commented on further. Regarding the other factors, Gil (1982), Ruys (1992), Liu (1997), Beghelli

(1997) and Kratzer (1998) are in agreement as to the basic observation: plurals do not readily take "inverse distributive scope". It should be noted immediately that there is no logical necessity in this: see Lasersohn (1998). In one of the very few detailed empirical studies of distributivity data Beghelli (1997: 365) finds that (in English), when both the sorting key and the distributed share are non-partitive indefinites, the following hierarchy is observed. (Beghelli calls distributivity due to silent **each** "pseudo-distributivity".)

(14)   Subject > Indirect object/Adjunct > Direct object

For example, in (15) the following are predicted to be natural: quadruplets of news agencies vary with journalists but not with accidents; triplets of accidents vary with journalists and/or news agencies; and pairs of journalists do not vary at all.

(15)   Two journalists reported three accidents to four news agencies.

On the other hand, Beghelli finds that if the non-subject sorting key argument is presuppositional (e.g. partitive), then it can go against the hierarchy in (14), although it cannot make the subject dependent; and if the distributed share is presuppositional, then only the subject can make it dependent. So in addition to the readings observed for (15), the 'quadruplets of news agencies vary with accidents' reading becomes available in (16), though not the 'pairs of journalists vary with accidents' reading, and the previously available 'triplets of accidents vary with news agencies' reading is lost:

(16)   Two journalists reported three of the accidents to four news agencies.

If these observations are by and large correct, the conclusion is that both grammatical function and presuppositionality play a role. The latter factor may be purely interpretive, or it may be grammaticized. In line with Beghelli and Stowell (1997), Beghelli (1997) assumes that the Logical Form representation of English sentences contains a set of designated operator positions, and presuppositional indefinites move to a specific position. The attachment of the silent operator **each** is dependent both on grammatical function and on operator position. Why presuppositionality plays a role is not well understood.

Reinhart (2006: 110–123) proposes a processing account of some of the observed limitations. One of the general ideas that she explores in this book is that in many areas where constraining factors have been thought to be purely syntactic or semantic, the explanation lies in the processing load that the given task requires. The child acquiring his/her mother tongue as well as the adult processor may be unable to cope with that load. A telltale sign of processing load problems is chance frequency in the performance of experimental subjects (as opposed to, say, a 20% or 70% error rate). Reinhart discusses (17) on the inverse distributive reading. Her theory allows QR (covert scope shifting in the terminology of Fox 2000) of the indefinite within its own clause, and this is what she assumes for (17).

(17)   Two flags are hanging in front of three buildings.
        'three buildings, six flags'

Whether such a covertly shifted reading is available depends, in the spirit of Interface Economy (Fox 2000), on whether it is necessary in order to express a particular, typically truth conditional, content. To determine that, the processor must compute a reference-set of ⟨ derivation, interpretation ⟩ pairs. Reinhart argues that in this case, as opposed to the case of *A flag was hanging in front of every building*, the reference set is simply too big. She considers five pairs – we will see that Landman offers eight. The culprit is the variety of distributive–collective combinations available. This is a very important line of research, but it is not clear whether it predicts the fine-grained data reviewed above, and whether it extends to many other cases of missing inverse readings. For example, we have seen that *Every soprano sings in more/fewer than five shows* lacks an inverse reading, but the size of the reference-set cannot be the explanation. The reason is that this sentence lacks the collective readings that boost the size of the reference-set in (17).

Important further data and insight might come from languages with relatively "free" constituent order: do they allow for linear order to override the hierarchy in (14)? In such languages leftward scrambling, shift, or topicalization may be conditioned on the presuppositional character of the argument, so that overt syntactic structure resembles Beghelli and Stowell's LF for English. The data are not very well researched from the perspective of distributivity.

Up till now we have equated the distributive interpretation of a DP with one where it induces referential dependency in others, calling for a multiplicity of objects or at least events. Schein and Landman cut the cake differently. Landman (2000) interprets *two dogs* initially as a sum (a plural individual with two dogs as its atomic parts). This can be shifted to a group. A group is a sum whose internal structure is invisible and thus it only receives a collective interpretation. But the unshifted sum itself can be introduced in two ways, both of them distributive. If the operation he dubs "scopal quantifying-in" is used, the sum-expression can induce referential dependency. In contrast, a distributive but scopeless (in-situ) sum does not induce dependency in a co-argument. Landman implements Schein's (1993) crucial observation that distributive but scopeless plural co-arguments yield a cumulative reading. That cumulative readings can be captured in this way is a benefit of neo-Davidsonian event-semantics. In that theory the properties of an event are specified in a series of conjoined propositions, and the arguments of the predicate appear in separate conjuncts: hence their scopal independence. Distributivity is anchored in the interpretation of the thematic roles *Agent and *Theme. An example from Landman:[63]

(18)   Three boys invited four girls
        (sum subject in-situ + sum object in-situ)

$$\exists e \in {}^*\text{INVITE} : \quad \exists x \in {}^*\text{BOY} : |x| = 3 \wedge {}^*Agent(e) = x \ \wedge$$
$$\exists y \in {}^*\text{GIRL} : |y| = 4 \ \wedge {}^*Theme(e) = y$$

where *INVITE is an event-semi-lattice with INVITE providing its set of atoms (similarly for the entity-semi-lattice *BOY), and ${}^*Agent(e) = x$ iff $\forall z \in atoms(x) : \exists e \in \text{INVITE} : Agent(e) = z$ (similarly for *Theme).

Thus (18) says that there is a sum of inviting events e, a sum of three boys x and a sum of four girls y such that every atomic part of x is the Agent of an atomic part of e, and every atomic part of y is the Theme of an atomic part of e. This is the cumulative reading 'three boys invited four girls between them'.

Landman assigns eight distinct derivations to a sentence like (18): four where both arguments are either groups or sums in-situ (scopeless readings, no dependency) and four where at least one of the two arguments is a sum scopally quantified in (scopal readings with dependencies). This system offers more options than those envisaged earlier. Whether or not Beghelli's (1997) description is correct down to the last detail, the generally acknowledged restrictions indicate that Landman overgenerates by freely allowing scopal quantifying-in. Another issue is whether arguments that are not scopally quantified in are simply in some default argument position (as the Davidsonian conjunctive account seems to predict). To my knowledge the syntactic configurations that yield cumulative readings have not been carefully studied in any language. The semantics of plurals deserves a volume of its own; this section has merely attempted to indicate some ways in which it bears on general issues of quantification.

8.2.2   *All, both,* stressed *AND,* and some cross-linguistic counterparts

We round out the discussion of distributivity with observations pertaining to DP-adjoined *all, both,* and conjunctions.

Plural definites and *all (of) the NP* basically pattern with plural indefinites. For example, as subjects they can be either collective or distributive, but as direct objects they do not readily induce dependency in the subject:

(19)   The men lifted up a table. / All (of) the men lifted up a table.
        OK 'together, one table'
        OK 'individually, possibly different tables'

(20)   A journalist reported the events. / A journalist reported all (of) the events.
        OK 'the same journalist'
        #'journalists vary with events'

On the other hand, *all*+bare plural has essentially the same range of readings as bare plurals, not as definite plurals, as discussed in some detail in Matthewson (2001).

(21)   a.   Desks are brown.
        b.   All desks are brown.
        c.   #All pages in this book were torn.
        d.   All the pages in this book were torn.

According to Matthewson, a similar though subtler contrast obtains between *most NP* vs. *most of the NP*.

If *all (of) the NP* is not a distributive quantifier, what is the contribution of *all*? Brisson (2003) takes Schwarzschild's (1996) semantics for definite plurals as a point of departure. Schwarzschild does not treat sentences with plurals as structurally ambiguous between distributive, cumulative, and collective readings. Instead, he assumes that their interpretation makes reference to a context-sensitive cover of the domain, and the ambiguity derives from what cover is picked up. A cover is a set of possibly overlapping subsets (whereas a partition excludes overlaps); the predicate is applied to the elements of a contextually relevant cover. An ill-fitting cover of *the boys'* is one where some of the boys are lumped together with non-boys in a cell of the cover. We know from Dowty (1987) that definite plurals allow exceptions, e.g.

(22)   The boys are asleep.
        'Enough of the boys are asleep for sleeping to be attributed to the whole group'

Brisson (1998, 2003) proposes that *all* eliminates exceptions by removing ill-fitting covers from consideration. This makes an independently induced distributive reading true. The analysis makes it natural for *all (of) the boys* to have the same distributivity behavior as *the boys*: *all* merely strengthens that reading; it does not bring it about. Whether the same analysis extends to *both (of the) NP* is not clear. Consider (23a):

(23)   a.   My parents are tall.
       b.   Both (of) my parents are tall.

What exceptions does the truth of (23a) tolerate that *both* eliminates in (23b)?

A somewhat different analysis might be that *all* and *both* manipulate the presupposed vs. asserted nature of homogeneity. Earlier in this section we mentioned that distributive predication applied to pluralities carries a homogeneity presupposition, cf. (13). *All* and *both* may signal that it does not go without saying (is not presupposed) that the members of the plurality are uniform in possessing the property under discussion; instead, it is remarkable (asserted) that they uniformly possess it. This analysis is supported by their interaction with negation: whereas *John did not see the girls* entails that John saw none of the girls, *John did not see all/both of the girls* does not.

For some speakers *both (of) the NP* is more strictly distributive than *all (of) the NP*, but Livitz (2009) observes that for others the contrasts by and large replicate those with *all*. See more on *both* in Winter (2000); Glanzberg (2008); Leu (2008).

(24)   a.   #   All (of) these people are a good team.
       b.   OK   All (of) these people hate each other.

(25)   a.   #   #   Both (of) these people are a good team.
       b.   #   OK Both (of) these people hate each other.

There is cross-linguistic variation in the behavior of the "dictionary equivalents" of these expressions. For example, colloquial Dutch *beide NP* 'lit. both NP' as well as *de beide NP* 'lit. the both NP' can be distributive or collective (Landman 2004 and H. van Riemsdijk, p.c.). In contrast, Swiss German *bäidi mäitli* is distributive, whereas *di bäidä mäitli* is ambiguous (Leu 2008 and H. van Riemsdijk, p.c.):

(26)   Bäidi   mäitli hend es piär trunkä.
       both.agr girls   have a beer drunk
       'Both girls had a beer (her own beer)'

(27)   Di   bäidä mäitli hend es piär trunkä.
       the.agr both girls   have a beer drunk
       'The two girls had a beer (shared or not)'

Szabolcsi and Haddican (2004) observe that conjunctions with unstressed *and* behave much like definite plurals with respect to collective vs. distributive readings, as is predictable from their basic semantics. But, surprisingly, those with stressed *AND* are strictly distributive:

(28)   a.   OK Mary and Bill are a good team.

b.   OK Mary and Bill hate each other.

(29)   a. #Mary AND Bill are a good team.
       b. #Mary AND Bill hate each other.

Why are these collective readings absent? The analysis follows Winter in deriving collective readings from a Boolean input using the type-shifting operation MIN, cf. **§5.2**; Szabolcsi and Haddican propose that stress on the connective bleeds MIN. Thus *Mary AND Bill* retains its $\lambda P[P(m) \wedge P(b)]$ interpretation. The reason why stress bleeds MIN is that the role of focus is to invoke alternatives, but whereas Boolean meet has Boolean join as an alternative, semi-lattice join has none; so focus could not fulfil its role after the shift. See the paper for further semantic contrasts between stressed *AND* versus unstressed *and* in English, among other things the interaction with negation.[64]

The distributive inverse scope taking abilities of *both NP* and conjunctions with stressed *AND* are somewhere between those of *all (of) the NP* and *every NP*:

(30)   a.   A flag was hanging from both windows.
            'flags vary with windows'
       b.   A flag was hanging from the first floor window AND the attic window.
            'flags vary with windows'

(31)   a.   A boy borrowed both books.
            ?? 'boys vary with books'
       b.   A boy borrowed "Jurassic Park" AND "The Jungle Book".
            ?? 'boys vary with books'

Szabolcsi and Haddican observe that in Russian, Italian, and Hungarian among other languages the counterparts of the connective *and* can at best receive corrective stress. The properties of English stressed *AND* are replicated, instead, by the paired connectives 'and (also) ..., and (also) ...' in such languages. The examples below are from Russian.

(32)   Sergej i   Marija kupili   jabloko.
       Sergej and Maria bought apple.acc
       'Sergej and Maria bought an apple (together or separately)'

(33)   *Sergej i[stress] Marija kupili   jabloko.
       Sergej AND   Maria bought apple.acc

(34)   I   Sergej, i   Marija kupili   jabloko.
       and Sergej and Maria bought.pl apple.acc
       OK 'Both Sergej and Maria bought an apple (separate apples)'
       # 'Sergej and Maria bought an apple together'

A closer study of the English and the cross-linguistic data in (19) through (34) would be useful for separating the core properties of plural (in)definites from the more or less accidental ones. The subtle variation cautions against lightheartedly borrowing judgments from one language into another.

8.3 Distributive singular quantifiers

The main topic of this section is *every NP*, with some remarks on *each NP*, *many a NP*, and some cross-linguistic data. The next section will take up floating quantifiers and so-called anti-quantifiers.

Every NP differs from *five NP* in two main respects. Within its own clause it is always distributive (or almost always, see below) and a very good distributive inverse scope taker. (As was observed by J. Higginbotham in the 1980s, the quantifier word *everyone* differs from *every NP* in that it participates in collective readings. The reason is not known, but this outlier should not confuse the picture.)

To test collective readings it is advisable to employ punctual accomplishment verbs such as *lift up*, as opposed to *lift*, which has an activity reading. *Every boy lifted the table* is fine on the reading 'Every boy participated in (the effort directed at) lifting the table' – but participation happily distributes to the elements of the set.

(35)   Every boy lifted up the table.
        'individually, one after the other'
        #'collectively, together'

(36)   #Every boy watched a movie together.

(37)   Some boy or other has read every book.
        OK 'boys vary with books'

On the other hand, we have argued that *every NP* shares a number of properties with *n NP*. To recap, both have unbounded existential scope but lack clause-external distributive scope, and their dependence on context and on other quantifiers probably warrants a similar Skolemized choice-functional treatment.

Beghelli (1997), Beghelli and Stowell (1997), and Szabolcsi (1997a) propose a "have your cake and eat it too" treatment for *every NP*. *Every NP* is interpreted as $f(Pow(NP'))$, where f is a choice function possibly with one or more Skolem parameters (see **§7.2.3**), but *every NP* differs from *n NP* in how it acquires its tensed-clause-internal distributivity. *Every NP* carries a [dist] feature that sends it to the specifier position of a particular functional projection, whose head Dist is semantically speaking nothing else than a distributive operator, i.e. a universal quantifier. The role of *every NP* is to supply the sorting key for Dist: the set of boys picked out by f. The distributed share of Dist is supplied by its complement ShareP: events or individuals.

(38)

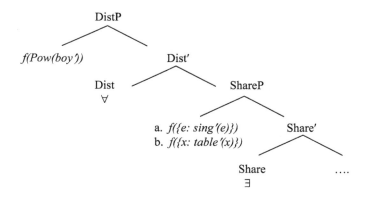

(39)   Every boy sang.
        'for every member of the contextually relevant set of boys there
        is a singing event [that he is the agent of]'

(40)   Every boy lifted up a table.
        'for every member of the contextually relevant set of boys there
        is a table [that he lifted up]'

The specialty of the analysis is that universal quantification over the elements of the boy-set is not performed by an operator coming from the lexical meaning of *every*, nor is it the contribution of the predicate that *every NP* combines with. It is the contribution of a functional head, i.e. a consequence of *every NP*'s occurring in a particular syntactic position. The only lexical anchor is the [dist] feature that sends *every NP* to that position, similarly to how the [*wh*] feature is thought to send *who* to the Specifier of an interrogative CP in English. In what follows we look at the ingredients of this analysis one by one.

8.3.1   The claim that *every NP* supplies just the domain of quantification but not the distributive operator was made in Chierchia (1993) in connection with the pair-list readings of questions. Recall that quantifying into questions is a problem, because questions are not of type t. Chierchia among others proposes to solve the difficulty by attributing a special behavior to universals in that context; see the formalization in (23) in §4.1.4. Apart from localizing the distributive operator in Dist, Beghelli and Stowell's proposal can be seen as saying that what Chierchia regards as a special behavior shows the universal's true colors.[65]

8.3.2 The claim that *every* is not a determiner in the GQ-theoretic sense but, rather, an uninterpretable "agreement marker", and distributivity is contributed by an abstract operator, converges with the reassessment of some other traditional determiners in Reinhart (1997) and Kratzer (2005). Reinhart does not attribute any semantic significance to *a(n)* and *some* – they do not even denote choice functions on her analysis. Building in part on Shimoyama (2001) and Kratzer and Shimoyama (2002), Kratzer (2005) puts forth the programmatic idea that the treatment of various items traditionally thought to denote relations between sets should be modeled after Ladusaw (1992) on negative concord. Ladusaw argues that in Romance and in non-standard English negation is expressed by an abstract, phonetically null sentential operator, and all the elements traditionally thought to express negation are just morphological markers that indicate that the item must be within the scope of the abstract negation. To use Kratzer's example from non-standard German, the three bold-faced elements below are mere negative concord markers:

(41)   Ich hab' **keinem** Mensch **kein** Wort **nicht** gesagt.
       I   have no-dat person no   word not   said
       'I didn't say anything to anybody'

Landman's (2004) and Lechner's (2007) analyses of split readings such as (42) also postulate that *no* is not a classical negative determiner:

(42)   You need no husband.
       'You don't need a husband'

(But see Penka and Zeijlstra 2005 for the argument that split-scope readings, negative concord, and the licensing of negative polarity items are three different phenomena, each taking place in a different component of grammar.) In addition to negative concord, Kratzer makes a case for interrogative concord (based on intervention effects discussed in Beck 1996), and for an existential-concord-marker analysis of German *irgend-*, as below, with an abstract operator scoping under the modal:

(43)   Du musst irgendwem   irgendwas   schenken.
       you must irgend-one-dat irgend-thing give
       'You must give something or other to somebody or other as a gift'

As Kratzer observes, the analyses of universals in Beghelli and Stowell's (1997) for English, Lin's (1998) for Mandarin, and Matthewson's (2001) for St'át'imcets (Lillooet Salish) are all in this same spirit in that each of these works assume that distributivity is ensured by a sentence-level operator that is separate from what is perceived as the "universal DP". More discussion of this type of analysis of universals will follow in Chapter 12.[66]

(44)   Měi-ge   xuéshēng *(dōu) mǎi-le   shū.
        every-classifier student   **dou** buy-perf book
        'Every student bought a book'   Lin (1998: 219)

(45)   tákem [i   smelhmúlhats-a]
        all   det.pl woman(pl)-det
        'all the women'   Matthewson (2001: 146)

8.3.3   The specific assumption that *every NP* acquires its distributive interpretation in a designated syntactic position is also one supported by cross-linguistic comparisons. Beghelli and Stowell (1997) mention that in KiLega (Kinyalolo 1990) and in Palestinian Arabic (Khalaily 1995) the counterparts of *every NP* move to a special position in overt syntax. We are in a better position to recap the argument concerning Hungarian in Szabolcsi (1997a). It has been observed by many researchers since the early 1980s, Hunyadi, Kenesei, Kiss, and Szabolcsi among them, that quantifier phrases in Hungarian have their own designated positions in the preverbal field; see Table 8.1.

The observation relevant in the present context is that whenever a phrase occurs in Region 2, its interpretation is distributive.[67] Whether a DP occurs in Region 2 or 3 is easily diagnosed by the preverbal vs. postverbal placement of particles like *fel* 'up', predicate nominals, locative PPs, and infinitival complements, somewhat similarly to subject–auxiliary inversion being a diagnostic of a clause-initial operator in English. The only possible position of *minden NP* 'every NP' is in Region 2:

(46)   Minden gyerek fel-emelte / *emelte fel az asztalt.
        every   child   up-lifted / *lifted up the table.acc
        'Every child lifted up the table (#together)'

Can the Hungarian data be used to show that distributivity does not reside in the lexical semantics of the determiner, but is due to the fact that the DP occurs in a particular position, where it associates with an abstract operator, as Beghelli and Stowell claim? An item especially interesting in this connection is *több, mint hat NP* 'more than six NP'. It may occur either in Region 2 or in Region 3. There are concomitant differences in its interpretation. Important to us is the fact that in Region 2 *több, mint hat NP* 'more than six NP' is unambiguously distributive and has potentially unbounded existential scope – just like *minden NP* 'every NP'. In Region 3 however neither of these observations hold: *több, mint hat NP* 'more than six NP' behaves like English counting quantifiers. The distributivity contrast is illustrated below. Compare (48) with Schein's (1993) event-dependency example in §8.2.[68]

Table 8.1 *Quantifier classes in Hungarian*

Region 1	Region 2	Region 3	Verb ...
Kati	*Kati is*	*csak Kati*	
'Kate'	'Kate too'	'only Kate'	
a(z) NP	*minden NP*	*kevés NP*	
'the NP'	'every NP'	'few NP'	
hat NP	*több, mint hat NP*	*pontosan hat NP*	
'six NP'	'more than six NP'	'exactly six NP'	
a legtöbb NP	*sok NP*	*több, mint hat NP*	
'most of the NP'	'many NP'	'more than six NP'	
etc.	etc.	etc.	

(47) In Region 2: only distributive
Több, mint hat gyerek felemelte az asztalt.
more than six child up.lifted the table.acc
'More than six children each / #together lifted up the table'

(48) In Region 3: collective or distributive
Több, mint hat gyerek emelte fel az asztalt.
more than six child lifted up the table.acc
'There was a table-lifting event whose collective or individual agent(s) was/were children, and the number of children involved is greater than six'

Szabolcsi (1997a) and Brody and Szabolcsi (2003) analyze Region 2 in analogy to Beghelli and Stowell's Specifier of DistP.

Thus, what we see is that both *minden NP* and *több, mint hat NP* in (47) are comparable to the indeterminate pronoun bases discussed in Kratzer (2005) in that a certain aspect of their interpretation is determined by their association with a particular sentential operator.

8.3.4 Dist requires its complement ShareP to supply distributed shares. Like Schein (1993) and Landman (2000), in (38) Beghelli and Stowell place event-quantifiers within the scope of distributive operators; but unlike the former, they do not restrict distributed shares to events. The motivation for this comes from the interaction of *every NP* with negation. It is well known that direct object *every NP* is trapped within the scope of sentential negation:

(49) John didn't read every book.
#'every > not'

But it is in fact not always trapped there:

(50)   A boy didn't read every book.
        OK 'every > a > not'

Following Krifka (1989) and others Beghelli and Stowell assume that sentential negation is always the negation of the existence of an event of the relevant kind. Thus in both (49) and (50) *not* has the existential closure of the event variable within its immediate scope. In both (49) and (50) *every book* ought to move to the Specifier of DistP to scope over negation. In (49) this results in the interpretation 'for every book, no event is such that John read the book in it'. But on this construal Dist has no distributed share. (50) is possible because, if *a boy* occurs in Spec of ShareP it scopes over the negative event quantification and at the same time provides a distributed share for Dist. The interpretation is 'for every book, there is a boy such that no event is such that the boy read the book in it'.

Both (49) and (50) allow another reading, where *every book* is within the scope of negation. To allow for this Beghelli and Stowell say that movement of *every NP* to Spec of DistP is optional. When it remains within the scope of negation, *every NP* is not distributive. What distinguishes *each NP* from *every NP* is that the former obligatorily moves to Spec of DistP; hence the following contrast (unless negation is focused, indicating response to an accusation, i.e. denial or metalinguistic negation):[69]

(51)   a.   John didn't read every book.
              'not > every'
        b.   John didn't read each book.
              # 'not > each'

The strength of the argument in favor of distributivity unmediated by event quantification depends, in part, on how unacceptable it is for *every NP* and *each NP* to scope immediately above negation. Speakers of English tend to agree that such a reading requires focus prosody; but it is not clear how Beghelli and Stowell would obtain the reading in the presence of focus on the universal.[70]

As was mentioned in **§8.1**, Schein (1993) places a definite description ("whatever events there are") in the scope of a decreasing operator. See Schein (1993: 316) for the formal details:

(52)   Every student ate no pizza.
        'Every student is such that whatever he did as an eater, if anything, is such that no pizza is such that whatever happened to it there, if anything [is] an eating'

This analysis gives us the missing reading to the extent it is available, but it does not predict that without focus on *every* the 'none' reading of (49) is infelicitous.

8.3.5 In sum, according to this analysis the distributive readings of the plural and singular DPs discussed above are similar in that the distributive operator is external to the DP. They differ in the specific source of distributivity (silent **each** vs. Dist). Do these claims offer a unified explanation of why the "distributive scope" of the DP is clause-bounded in both cases? Yes, in the sense that if the DP were to be covertly moved it could not drag along the distributive operator, since the latter is not part of the DP. But no, in the sense that it is not quite clear why all these DPs lack the ability to associate with a distributive operator in a higher clause. The analyses have to be tightened to show whether clause-boundedness in the two cases is a coincidence.

Specifically, the particular position of DistP in the hierarchy of operator and argument positions of English explains, according to Beghelli and Stowell, that *every NP* is such a successful inverse scope taker. But why *every NP* cannot successive-cyclically move to associate with a Dist outside its finite clause is not clear, as observed in Surányi (2003). See Cecchetto (2004) for a recent proposal for the clause-boundedness of QR in terms of phase syntax.

Each NP easily takes distributive scope outside its tensed clause, even outside a relative clause island:

(53)   A timeline poster should list the different ages/periods (Triassic, Jurassic, etc.) and some of the dinosaurs or other animals/bacteria that lived in each. (Google)
        'for each period, some of the dinosaurs that lived in it'

May (1985) suggests that *each NP* is focused, and attributes its ability to take scope as above to focusing, which is not clause-bounded. It is not clear how this view might combine with Beghelli and Stowell's. Perhaps the distributive operator is part of the lexical semantics of *each*, in contrast to *every*. The fact that *each*, like *every*, is reluctant to scope directly above negation could still follow from its distributive operator needing a distributed share.

8.3.6 Following Gil (1995), Beghelli and Stowell (1997) observe that the [dist] quantifiers *every NP* and *each NP* are both grammatically singular, in contrast to *all the NP* and its kin.[71] They regard singular number as a critical property of distributive quantifiers, as it probably forces distribution over singletons (or, atoms).

The behavior of *many a NP* underscores the role of singular number (at least in English). *Many a NP* is clearly distributive:

(54)   Many boys lifted up the table together.

(55)   #Many a boy lifted up the table together.

On the other hand, speakers' judgments vary greatly regarding inverse distributive readings with *many a NP*. Some judge all three interpretations below possible, some only (56).

(56)   Flags were hanging from many a building.
        'flags vary with buildings'

(57)   A flag was hanging from many a building.
        % 'flags vary with buildings'

(58)   Some boy or other has read many a book.
        % 'boys vary with books'

The variation in judgments seems to go against the assumption that any grammatically singular quantifier phrase acquires its distributivity by moving to the Specifier of DistP. Even though *many a NP* is stilted and speakers do not have a lot of exposure to it, if the grammar automatically forced it to behave like *every NP*, speakers could have solid intuitions about it, as has been claimed in the famous case of parasitic gaps.

How the construction *every n children* relates to *every child* is not well-researched. One is tempted to say that *every n children* quantifies over a domain of sets/sums of cardinality *n*, just as *every child* quantifies over a domain of singletons or atoms. But whereas all speakers accept (59), the judgments are varied regarding (60).

(59)   a.   OK   One chaperon is admitted free for every five children.
        b.   OK   Every group of five children huddled.

(60)   a.   #   OK   OK   Every five children carried a pole.
        b.   #   OK   ?   Every five children formed a circle.
        c.   #   OK?   ???   Every five children huddled.

B. Schein (p.c.) and Y. Winter (p.c.) suggest that contextualization is at stake: they judge that all the above examples are acceptable provided it is understood how to cover the children with fives. In realis contexts, there must be some understood partition of them. In modal or counterfactual contexts, the understood cover may be complete in including every and any five children, with the result that every child belongs to many fives (see Schein 1993: 101–107).

Linking the two constructions Schein (2009: Chapter 3) discusses *many a natural number* vs. *many a one or more natural numbers* vs. *many natural numbers. Every five children* would fall into the second class, parsing it in effect as 'all a five children'.

8.4 Floating quantifiers, anti-quantifiers, and dependent plurals

8.4.1 Floating quantifiers: an overview

Floating (or, floated) quantifiers are exemplified by (61). One big question is how these sentences are related to those in (62). In this text the term "floating quantifier" is used as a neutral descriptive label.

(61)   The boys have all/both/each finished their breakfasts.

(62)   All/both/each of the boys has/have finished his/their breakfast(s).

An illuminating review and evaluation of the state of the art can be found in BOBALJIK (2001), and this subsection draws heavily from it. Much of the literature is based on French, where *tout(es)* 'all' and *chacun* 'each' alternate between the two positions (but see also Hebrew, Arabic, German, Japanese, Korean, etc.).

A widely assumed analysis of quantifier float is the stranding one. According to this the quantifier starts out in DP-initial position. The DP moves in small steps to its surface position. The quantifier may move along all the way, as in (62) or it may be stranded in any of the pre-surface positions, effectively tracking the journey of the DP (Sportiche 1988; Shlonsky 1991). There have been two main reasons for proposing that (61) is derived from the same source as (62). First, pairs of such sentences are felt to have the same meaning, especially in their quantificational aspects. Second, in languages where determiners and modifiers agree with the noun in case, number and gender, floating quantifiers agree in the same way as those attached to the DP.

Influential as it has been, this analysis is known to face many syntactic problems. In addition, the "sameness of meaning" claim is not beyond doubt. One semantically relevant difference is that when the quantifier is DP-initial, the DP is optionally or obligatorily partitive (*each *(of) the boys, all (of) the boys*), in contrast to the floating version (*the boys ... each, *of the boys ... all*). Another is that floating quantifiers scope in their surface position, in contrast especially to wide-scope-loving *each (of the) NP*. The in-situ scoping of floating *each* is highlighted when an in-situ scope is infelicitous:

(63)   a.   Gore and Bush should each be 50% likely to beat the other.
        b.   #Gore and Bush should be 50% likely to each beat the other.

(64)   a.   Someone said that [each of the men won the race].
            OK 'for each man, someone said that he won the race'
        b.   #Someone said that [the men have each won the race].
            # 'for each man, someone said that he won the race'

Finally, floating quantifiers may quantify over things DP-initial ones do
not:

(65)   Les enfants prendront chacun un ballon l'un   après
        the children will.take each   a ball   the.one after
        l'autre.
        the.other
        'The children each will take a ball one after the other'

(66)   ?*Chacun des   enfants prendra un ballon l'un   après
          each   of.the children will.take a ball   the.one after
          l'autre.
          the.other
          'Each of the children will take a ball one after the other'

(67)   a.   Bears, tigers and lions are all scary.
             'None of these kinds is an exception'
        b.   All bears, tigers and lions are scary.
             # 'None of these kinds is an exception'

These interpretive differences may be by-products of how a single initial
structure develops during the two derivations, but they have not actually
been shown to be. More importantly, Bobaljik emphasizes that it is not
clear what one should make of the sameness of meaning when it appears
to hold. Sameness of meaning may be a reason to trace different surface
structures to the same underlying structure only if there is no other way
to account for it.

   The alternative analysis capitalizes on the fact that floating quantifiers occur in adverbial positions (Dowty and Brodie 1984; Doetjes 1992,
1997; Junker 1995; Brisson 2003 – these works are among the sources of
the semantic observations as well). Specifically Junker (1995) and Doetjes (1997) relate their analyses of floating quantifiers to other analyses
of adverbial quantification and of binominal *each*. The adverbial analysis
avoids many of the pitfalls of the stranding one, but Bobaljik believes
that it does not make the right predictions about cross-linguistic variation. His conclusion is that much has been learned, but the issue of the
correct analysis of quantifier float is still open. See also the more semantically inclined analyses in Kang (2002); Kobuchi-Philip (2003); Nakanishi
(2004).

8.4.2 Binominal *each* and other anti-quantifiers

Binominal *each* (Postal 1974; Choe 1987; Safir and Stowell 1988; M. Zimmermann 2002a,b) has been dubbed an anti-quantifier, because it expresses the quantificational force on the distributed share, not on the
sorting key or on the predicate. When both floating and binominal *each*

are available, the truth conditions of the sentences containing them are much the same. The host of binominal *each* is italicized in (68b):

(68) a. The boys have each eaten one apple.   floating *each*
          'each of the boys has eaten one apple'
      b. The boys have eaten *one apple* each.   binominal *each*
          'each of the boys has eaten one apple'

But the distribution of binominal *each* is much more restricted. Compare:

(69) a. The boys have each agreed to stop fighting.
      b. #The boys have agreed to stop fighting each.

(70) a. The boys have each seen this film/most of the films/every film.
      b. The boys have seen #this film each/#most of the films each/#every film each.

(71) a. The boys have each seen six films/more/less than six films.
      b. The boys have seen six films each/more/less than six films each.

Floating *each* is indifferent to the nature of the dependent nominal argument; it does not even require one. This is understandable if it specifically uses events as its distributed shares. Binominal *each* on the other hand only attaches to certain nominals. At first blush it appears that they are the same as those that occur in existential *there* and relational *have* contexts (Milsark 1977; Partee 2004): *this NP, most of the NP, every NP* – bad; *six NP, more/less than six NP* – good. But, as Sutton (1993) observes, the sets of weak DPs and hosts of binominal *each* only overlap, they do not coincide. Existential sentences without a coda are used to sharpen the contrast:

(72) a. #There are more than 50% of the films.
      b. The boys have seen more than 50% of the films each.

(73) a. #There are few of the films.
      b. The boys have seen few of the films each.

(74) a. There are good films.
      b. #The boys have seen good films each.

(75) a. There is/are no problem(s).
      b. #The boys have no problem(s) each.

(76) a. There is a problem.
      b. ??The boys have a problem each.
          (compare: OK one problem each)

Sutton's descriptive generalization is that the hosts of binominal *each* must be "counting quantifiers". This explains both the fact that certain strong determiners are allowed and the fact that not all weak ones are. The class of counting quantifiers has received more and more attention in the past decade. Sutton (1993) was probably the first to isolate this class, or property, as empirically relevant. (She offers no explanation though as to why the counting property is needed in the binominal *each* construction; we come back to this below.) As Sutton herself observes, the "counting" property cannot be demarcated in truth-conditional terms. The following two sentences have the same truth-conditions, but *more than 50% of the films* hosts binominal *each*, whereas *most of the films* does not:

(77)   a.   The boys have seen most of the films (# each).
          b.   The boys have seen more than 50% of the films (each).

At the moment we keep the notion of a counting quantifier informal, as does Sutton; we return to the class in §**10.5**.

Regarding the sorting key, the received wisdom is that it must be provided by a definite or indefinite plural (as in the examples above); see M. Zimmermann (2002a,b). If this were so, it would mesh nicely with data and analyses relating to other constructions. Therefore it came as a surprise that the native speakers I consulted overwhelmingly accepted examples like (78), and some even accepted (79):[72]

(78)   Every boy had one apple each.

(79)   % Each boy had one apple each.

Naturally occurring examples of *every NP, each NP* in combination with host+*each* are not difficult to find:

(80)   a.   Every Australian donated one sequin each to supply ON-J with enough for her and her back-up singers.
              `dethroner.com/2007/04/27/`
              `clips-chronology-of-olivia-newton-johns-hair/`
          b.   These three bands made a tripling single together, Mikkai, where every band had one song each.
              `www.jame-world.com/us/database-artist.php?id=706`
          c.   Every patient received one subcutaneous infection each of the synthetic and the animal preparation, . . .
              `www.pubmedcentral.nih.gov/`
              `articlerender.fcgi?artid=1630127`
          d.   Every square costs one Cent each at the beginning – but the price doubles at each transaction.
              `ricegraineffect.wordpress.com/`

(81)   a.   Give each student one worksheet each. They should circle "prediction" on the page.
`ed.fnal.gov/trc_new/sciencelines_online/`
`winter96_97/classroom_activities.html`
 b.   There must be less than five players, and each of the four will chose one symbol each (eg. hearts, spade, etc).
`rachel-with-the-fang.blogspot.com/2009/01/`
`new-year-day-sleepoverd.html`

The observed classes of distributed shares and sorting keys are echoed by a comparable (I argue) construction not countenanced in English: distributed-share numeral reduplication, as in Telugu (Balusu 2005), Hungarian, and other languages. To the extent I am aware they are also replicated by constructions involving the Japanese distributive suffix *-zutsu* and the Korean distributive suffix *-ssik* that have a rich literature, among others Choe (1987); Gil (1990, 1995); Oh (2001); Kobuchi-Philip (2003); Miyamoto (2006); and by the Quechua *-nka* suffix (Faller and Hastings 2008); but the Slavic *po*-construction does not necessarily require a counting quantifier (Pereltsvaig 2008a,b).[73]

Below I will focus on Telugu because, as far as I can see, it carries the widest range of meanings. It is plausible that the well-known anti-quantifier constructions should be approached from the Telugu perspective and obtained as special cases. The road to Telugu numeral reduplication leads through the semantics of plural nouns, typically studied in the shape of existential bare plurals.

8.4.3   Plurals – dependent plurals among them

The common-sense position is that *children* means 'more than one child', but various authors in recent literature have converged on the view that morphological plurals are truth-conditionally number-neutral, i.e. that *children* means 'one child or more' (Sauerland, Andersen, and Yatsushiro 2005; Zweig 2005b, 2008, 2009; Spector 2007). Two of the many arguments for this position are the behavior of plurals in decreasing contexts, see (82), and the phenomenon of dependent plurals, see (83)–(84).

(82)   I didn't buy neckties.
#'I did not buy more than one necktie [I can have bought one]'
'I did not buy either one or more than one necktie'

(83)   Unicycles have wheels.   (Chomsky 1977)
'Each unicycle has one wheel; in total they have more than one'

(84)   My friends have big heads.
'My friends each have a big head; in total they have more than one'

There is agreement that the multiplicity inference from the positive *I bought neckties* 'I bought more than one necktie' is due to an implicature, although authors vary as to how they obtain the implicature. What is crucial to us is that only the proposal in Zweig (2005b, 2008, 2009) extends to dependent plurals, so below we only consider this theory.

The standard view of dependent plurals (see, among others, de Mey 1981 and Roberts 1990 for English, Bosveld-de Smet 1998 and de Swart 2006 for French) is that they constitute a subcase of cumulation, however cumulation is analyzed. Zweig shows that determiners like *most, all,* and (in some configurations) *every* support dependent plurals, as in the (b) examples, although they do not participate in cumulative readings with numeral indefinites in the same configurations; see the (a) examples:

(85)   a.   Most students read thirty papers $\not\Rightarrow$
              Most students read at least one paper and a total of thirty papers is read by students
        b.   Most students read papers $\Rightarrow$
              Most students read a paper and a total of more than one paper is read by them

(86)   a.   All the students read thirty papers $\not\Rightarrow$
              All the students read at least one paper and a total of thirty papers is read by students
        b.   All the students read papers $\Rightarrow$
              All the students read a paper and a total of more than one paper is read by them

(87)   a.   Three trains leave every day to Leiden from this station $\not\Rightarrow$
              At least one train leaves every day, and a total of three trains is involved
        b.   Trains leave every day to Leiden from this station $\Rightarrow$
              At least one train leaves per day, and a total of more than one train is involved

The cumulative *every day* example comes from de Mey (1981). Zweig adds that although subject *every NP* does not support a dependent plural in English, direct object *every NP* does, similarly to *every day* in (87b):

(88)   a.   Every boy flew kites.
              #'one kite per boy'
        b.   Boys flew every kite.
              OK 'one boy per kite'

The gist of Zweig's proposal is that dependent plurals involve asymmetric distributive readings. Sentences like *The students/most students read papers* assert that each of the relevant students read at least one paper. The second part of the inferences above, "more than one overall" is an implicature. In other words, the dependent plural cannot be used if the speaker is cooperative and is aware that all the students read the same paper. The implicature can be canceled under the usual circumstances:

(89)   The suspects live in big cities, maybe even in the same big city.

See Zweig (2008, 2009) for a detailed argumentation and a compositional semantics.

8.4.4 Numeral reduplication as NumP pluralization

With Zweig's analysis of plurals in mind we turn to distributive numeral reduplication in Telugu, a Dravidian language (Balusu 2005). To approach the data from the perspective of English, the examples are similar to sentences with binominal *each*, with the difference that the numeral component of the distributed share indefinite is reduplicated and there is no morpheme like *each* attached to it.

(90)   ii   pilla-lu renDu renDu kootu-lu-ni   cuus-ee-ru
        these kid.pl two   two   monkey.pl.acc see.past.3pl
        lit. 'these kids saw two two monkeys'

One reading of (90) is comparable to the only reading of *These kids saw two monkeys each*; Balusu calls this the "participant-key" reading as a first approximation. But (90) has two further readings, where the distributed key is the temporal or spatial aspect of a non-atomic seeing event, chunked up in some contextually defined way. Balusu calls these "temporal-key" and "spatial-key" readings:

(91)   a.   These kids each saw two monkeys.   Participant-key
        b.   These kids saw two monkeys in each interval. Temporal-key
        c.   These kids saw two monkeys in each location. Spatial-key

Replacing *ii pillalu* 'these kids' with *prati pillavaaDu* 'every kid' yields the same three readings. There are no subject–object asymmetries: the reduplicated numeral may be the subject and the plural or universal the direct object. A clause may contain more than one reduplicated numeral. If the sentence does not contain a plural or universal, it receives only a temporal-key and a spatial-key interpretation; for example:

(92)   renDu renDu kootu-lu egir-i-niyyi
        two   two   monkey.pl jump.past.3pl
        lit. 'two two monkeys jumped'

(93)   a. #Participant-key reading
        b. Two monkeys jumped in each time interval.   Temporal-key
        c. Two monkeys jumped in each location.   Spatial-key

Balusu's analysis has two main components. One is that numeral redu-plication is NumP (Number Phrase) pluralization. Just as many languages reduplicate a whole noun or part of a noun to mark plurality, Telugu and other languages, Hungarian among them, use numeral reduplication to indicate the plurality of a larger phrase:

(94)   a. anak   'child'   (Malay)
            anak anak   plural of 'child'
        b. renDu kootulu   'two monkeys'   (Telugu)
            renDu renDu kootulu   plural of 'two monkeys'

(The morphological realizations of N(P) and NumP pluralization are in-dependent within a language: in contrast to Malay, both Telugu and Hun-garian have banal suffixes for plural nouns.)

Another ingredient of the analysis is that a pluralized NumP always has a distributive operator associated with it and serves as the operator's distributed share. In the case of temporal and spatial key readings in (90) and (92) it is obvious that the sorting key is a silent event (aspect). Likewise, the temporal-key reading of (95) is easy. It goes something like this: 'for every child x there is an event e such that for every temporal chunk e' of e, x saw two monkeys in e' ... '.

(95)   prati pilla-vaaDu renDu renDu kootu-lu-ni   cuus-ee-ru
        every kid   two   two   monkey.pl.acc see.past.3pl
        lit. 'every kid saw two two monkeys'

(96)   a. Every kid saw two monkeys each.   Participant-key
        b. Every kid saw two monkeys in each interval. Temporal-key
        c. Every kid saw two monkeys in each location. Spatial-key

How do participant-key readings come about? In (90) the plural sub-ject 'these kids' could be the sorting key. But, as Balusu points out, in sentences like (95) with a distributive universal subject, extending the same analysis to participant-key readings would generate double, i.e. vac-uous, distribution. You can only distribute pairs of monkeys over children once. The reader will notice that the exact same problem arises in con-nection with our newly discovered piece of English data, (78):

(97)   Every boy had one apple each.

Balusu's proposal for Telugu is that participant-key readings are spe-cial cases of event-key readings. The contextually given chunking of the event that serves as the sorting key is always a partition of the event into a set of subevents that do not overlap and jointly exhaust the event. The so-called participant key reading emerges when we have a trivial, one-cell partition, $\pi(e) = \{e\}$, where all the monkey-sightings that the given kid was an agent of are lumped together. So, we have, 'for every child x there is an event e such that for every chunk e' of e (where $e = e'$), x saw two monkeys in e' ...'. Going back to definite plurals such as 'these kids', Balusu proposes that when the predication applied to the plural is collective or cumulative and the event-partition is non-trivial (has multiple cells), we obtain temporal and spatial key readings. When the predication is distributive and the event partition contains a single cell, we get the (illusion of the) participant-key reading. Finally, the distributive predication plus non-trivial event partition combination yields readings that are parallel with those observed with universals, and these latter possibilities are indeed observed.

Finally, Balusu observes that Telugu distributive numeral reduplication exhibits the same "more than one overall" requirement that Zweig (2005b) attributes to plural nouns, including dependent plurals, in English. If the speaker knows that all the children saw the same pair of monkeys, or that the same pair of monkeys jumped over and over again, use of the reduplication construction is not felicitous. That is to say, Telugu reduplicated numeral expressions are dependent plural Numeral Phrases.

The "more than one overall" requirement also explains why (98) has only temporal and spatial key readings:

(98)   Raamu renDu renDu kootu-lu-ni   cuus-ee-Du
        Ram   two   two   monkey.pl.acc see.past.3sg
        'On each occasion/at each location Ram saw two monkeys'

(98) crucially differs from (95), with 'every kid' in the place of 'Ram'. If each kid saw just two monkeys, it is possible for them to have seen more than two in total; but if Ram saw just two monkeys, the requirement cannot be satisfied. Therefore (95) does not require monkey-pairs to co-vary with occasions or locations in order to satisfy the "more than one overall" requirement, but (98) does.

8.4.5 All NP/NumP pluralization is event-key distribution

Let us take stock. In Telugu distributive numeral reduplication the (superficial) sorting key expression can be an (in)definite plural or a distributive quantifier, and the distributed share is provided by a numeral indefinite, i.e. counting phrase; the same holds for binominal *each* in English. But the Telugu examples had event-key readings: both obvious ones and, if Balusu is correct, ones masquerading as participant-key ones; in contrast,

English binominal *each* has only participant-key readings. So perhaps the two constructions are still quite different.

Japanese, Korean, and Hungarian will walk the extra mile between them. Japanese and Korean have distributive suffixes (rather like binominal *each*) and do have obvious event-key readings. Hungarian, on the other hand, has reduplicated numerals but (at least superficially) only participant-key readings, below:[74]

(99)   A   gyerekek két-két majmot   láttak.
        the children two-two monkey.acc saw.3pl
        'The children saw two monkeys each'

(100)   Minden/Valamennyi gyerek két-két majmot   látott.
        every/each   child two-two monkey.acc saw.3sg
        'Every/each child saw two monkeys each'

What we see is that anti-quantifier morphemes are not restricted to apparent participant-key readings (*each* is, Korean *ssik* and Japanese *zutsu* are not), and neither does numeral reduplication necessarily carry obvious temporal and spatial key readings (in Telugu it does, in Hungarian it does not). The morpho-syntax does not predict the range of readings. It appears that Telugu is the most generous with readings, so perhaps it should be taken as the base-line, and the more restricted cases should be obtained as special cases. The lack of temporal and spatial key readings in English and Hungarian could be obtained by stipulating that in these languages the partition must be trivial (one cell). Telugu is also the most suggestive in that it points to dependent plurality as the semantic umbrella under which all of these cases should fit. Zweig (2008, 2009), formalized in terms of Landman's (2000) event semantics, may prove useful as a framework. Finally, the numeral reduplication perspective begins to make sense of Sutton's (1993) generalization that binominal *each* in English attaches specifically to counting quantifiers. Syntactically or semantically counting quantifiers form a natural class with Numeral Phrases.

In sum, it seems attractive to hypothesize that all the anti-quantifier constructions reviewed in this section, including those with binominal *each*, are to be analyzed along the lines of Telugu, as instances of event-key distribution, even when superficially they only have participant-key readings.

Balusu (2005) does not offer a compositional derivation for NumP reduplication, and a question that naturally arises is why some languages specifically use reduplication to signify plurality. It is not clear whether an intuitively interesting answer will be forthcoming. In a series of papers (Marantz 1982 through WILTSHIRE AND MARANTZ 2000) Marantz proposes that the phonology of reduplication (copying) is independent of the role of the reduplicating morpheme in the syntax and semantics, so there would be no explanation of any correlation between reduplication and a particular semantic function. The same might hold at the phrasal level.

The claim that what seem like participant-key readings are in fact event-key readings that involve a trivial event-partition is of course compatible with the existence of other anti-quantifiers that do require nontrivial event-partitions. To single out adverbial elements formed from numerals, such are English *in twos* and *two by two*, Hungarian *kett-es-é-vel* 'two-adj-poss-with', and Basque *bi-na-ka* 'two-distr-adv'.

The case of Basque is interesting because, as Pereltsvaig (2008b) points out, the distributive suffix *-na* by itself works much like binominal *each* in English. So at first blush it appears that noun-modifier numeral-*na* specializes for participant-key readings and adverbial numeral-*na-ka* for event-key readings. It turns out however that *bina sarrera* 'two-*na* ticket' can take a distributive universal (with determiner *bakoitzak* 'each') as its superficial sorting key:

(101)   Irabazle bakoitzak bina   sarrera eskuratuko ditu.
         winner   each.erg   two-na ticket   receive.fut aux
         'Each winner will receive two tickets'

Therefore the same vacuous-distribution argument that showed that Telugu, English, and Hungarian participant-key readings must be event-key readings in disguise carries over to Basque.[75]

All in all, the anti-quantifier data consistently support the idea that distributivity is mediated by events.

8.5 Referential dependency: event semantics vis-à-vis Skolemization

The literature surveyed in §7.1.3 explores a particular way of creating referential dependencies: Skolemization. Applied to (102a) this strategy would yield something along the lines of (102b):

(102)   a.   Every dragon spotted some adventurer.
         b.   for every dragon x, x spotted $f(x)$(adventurer)

In words, every dragon spotted the adventurer that a particular choice function f assigns to it. The literature surveyed in the present chapter would establish the dependency with the intervention of event quantification:

(103)   a.   Every dragon spotted some adventurer.
         b.   'for every dragon x there is a spotting event e such that x is the agent of e and an adventurer is the theme of e'

How do the two methods compare with respect to utility? We have seen that Skolemized choice functions are more expressive than plain narrow-scope existential quantification over choice functions (or individuals) and are thus an indispensable addition. At the same time, if Skolemization is tied to choice functions, then it is limited to expressions whose general behavior justifies the choice-functional treatment – expressions that have at least potentially unbounded existential import. This means that the distributive readings of (104) and (105) do not fall within the purview of Skolemization as considered there:

(104)   The dragons were heavy (individually).

(105)   The dragons spotted more than three adventurers (each).

Distribution with the mediation of events was seen to be crucial when it did not at the same time give rise to referential dependency (as in cumulation, cf. Schein 1993). It is also crucial in NumP and NP pluralization (Balusu 2005; Zweig 2008, 2009). So this technique cannot be dispensed with, either.

Do these tools ever combine? Bare numeral indefinites, such as *two subjects* resemble *certain*-indefinites in that they easily take extra-wide scope. Now consider Schlenker's "main weakness-of" example (18) in §**7.1.3** in a modified situation where I know that each of my students has weaknesses in two subjects, though in different ones. It appears that numeral reduplication in Hungarian is entirely natural in this situation; it does not force an "improve in two arbitrary subjects" reading:

(106)   Ha minden diák   javít   két-két tárgyból,
         if   every   student improves two-two subject.from
         akkor senki nem bukik meg.
         then nobody not fails perf
         'If every student improves in two subjects [each], then nobody
         will fail'

This example requires both Skolemization and event-dependent existential closure. Skolemization is required by the truth-conditions, just as was argued for (18). Event-dependency is required in order to compositionally derive those truth-conditions in the presence of a reduplicated numeral.

An important question calling for future research is how these different means of creating referential dependencies cover the descriptive spectrum, and how they combine in a single principled theory of the syntax/semantics interface.

9

Bare numeral indefinites

Two previous chapters have already discussed aspects of the semantics of unmodified numeral indefinites that they share with other plurals: Chapter 7 focused on existential scope and Chapter 8 on distributive scope. The present chapter turns to aspects that specifically have to do with the presence of the bare numeral. Modified numeral expressions have overall different properties and are discussed in the next chapter.

§9.1 starts by situating numerical quantifiers in the broad landscape of DP types and their internal structures. §9.2 surveys the issues surrounding the 'at least' vs. 'exactly' interpretations. The next two sections are both concerned with the cardinal vs. individual readings of numeral phrases. §9.3 traces this ambiguity to two quantificational layers in numeral phrases (the so-called "split scope" analysis) and presents the ambiguity as a scope ambiguity vis-à-vis modal operators; §9.4 draws attention to the morpho-syntactic correlates of these interpretations, as reflected in gender/number agreement in French and Russian. It also introduces the split DP hypothesis, according to which D and NP do not start out as a DP constituent in syntax. (For an overview of the syntax of quantified phrases with an emphasis on Germanic and Romance, see CARDINALETTI AND GIUSTI 2006.)

9.1 The flexible DP hypothesis

Reinhart (1997) and Winter (2000, 2001) spell out the relation between the choice-functional analysis and the internal structure of DP. Specifically Winter assumes that the expressions traditionally classified as determiners occur in DPs in three different locations, and proposes the flexible DP hypothesis.

(1)   The flexible DP hypothesis:
       The NP-level is rigidly predicative. The DP-level is rigidly quan-
       tificational. The D′-level is flexible between the two semantic cat-
       egories.

(2)   Initially predicative DP. Choice-functional shift applied to D′ can
       turn it into a generalized quantifier

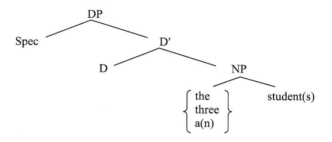

(3)   Initially generalized quantifier DP. Minimum-operator shift ap-
       plied to D′ can turn it into a predicate

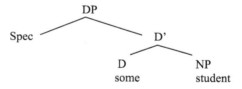

(4)   Purely quantificational DP

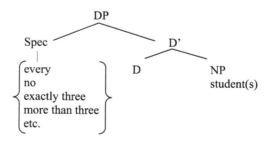

(2) and (3) are flexible DPs. Descriptively they differ from purely quantificational ones in that they can take extra-wide existential scope and combine with strictly collective predicates such as *be a good team*, and to a lesser extent in their grammaticality in predicative position. The first two properties are the hallmarks of choice-functional DPs in Reinhart (1997) and its companion paper Winter (1997). Winter assumes that *some* denotes a choice function, and that additionally a type-shifter is available with the same interpretation. Winter's choice functions do not simply choose an element of the set they apply to; they deliver a generalized quantifier: the set of properties of that element. It is in this sense that *some student'* as well as $f_{CH}(the\ student')$, $f_{CH}(three\ students')$, and $f_{CH}(a\ student')$ are quantifiers; the choice functions are existentially closed in a separate step. The type-shifter that works in the opposite direction (MIN) picks a minimal element of a generalized quantifier and thus maps it to a set; hence the ability of initially non-predicative flexible DPs to occur in predicative position. Winter demonstrates that his two shifters cover all the critical grounds that Partee's (1986) richer system does (see **§5.3**). To wit, his choice-functional shifter also accomplishes the job of type-lifting in coordinations like *Mary and every student*, and the sequential application of the minimum operator and the choice-functional shifter makes it possible to obtain a collective interpretation for *John and Mary* while starting from a Boolean conjunction (intersection of the sets of John's properties and Mary's properties). An important advantage of this idea is that it treats the connective *and* invariably as an intersection (meet) operator, whereas the Link–Landman approach must treat it as the join operator in the domain of individuals (cf. $\oplus$ in **§5.2** and **§8.1**).

It is interesting to note that Winter's solutions are fully generalized-quantifier-theoretic, but he re-evaluates the roles of various items that classical generalized quantifier theory treats as semantic determiners. In his view the singular definite and indefinite articles as well as numerals modify sets with cardinality information. This underscores the fact that generalized quantifier theory as applied to full-DP denotations has good uses irrespective of exactly how the so-called determiners are analyzed.

It is a parsimonious feature of Winter's theory that it does not assign both a choice-functional and a quantificational interpretation to plain indefinites (*a(n) NP, some NP, three NP*). Associating such a structural ambiguity with their specific and non-specific uses appears stipulative; I am not aware of tangible compositional arguments. But Winter's uniform choice-functional interpretation has to be supplemented with an operative notion of specificity, and its relation to distributivity mediated by events needs to be clarified; cf. **§8.5**.

In Winter's theory *some'*, *every'*, *no'*, and the denotations of modified numerals retain their status as semantic determiners. In the preceding chapter we have seen reasons to go further in abandoning the classical categorization. For example, it was suggested that *some, every,* and *no* are merely "concord markers" that indicate what DP-external operators the DPs are linked to. We subjected DPs containing *every* to particular scrutiny and suggested that they are in some respects rather similar to indefinites, and their interpretation may well involve a choice function. Winter's main concern is with the flexible DPs and has little new to say about the purely quantificational ones. Moreover the flexible DP hypothesis offers a very syntactic account of why *every, no,* and modified numerals do not take extra-wide scope, do not combine with *be a good team,* and do not work as predicates: because they occur in Spec of DP, they are outside the reach of the type-shifters that might enable them to do such things. This by itself does not seem satisfactory. Modified numerals reasonably end up in Spec of DP, seeing that they are syntactically too complex to be heads, i.e. D. But since heads are often multi-morphemic, it seems like a somewhat accidental fact that the meanings of modified numerals are expressed in a way that is not only morphologically but syntactically complex. Conversely, it seems too lucky that the only semantic determiner that denotes a choice function (*some*) consists of a single word and can thus inhabit D. But, alas, we lack a more illuminating account of why *three* and *at least three* differ as to Winter's criteria, to mention one of the more baffling cases.

9.2 How many is *two*?

How many dogs do you have if you have two dogs? Exactly two? At least two? Either one, depending on the context? Let us start by fixing the terms of the debate. The interpretation of the numeral *two* is one thing and the interpretations of sentences that contain predicates or noun phrases of the form *two dogs* are another. The superficial reading of the generalized-quantifier-theoretic definition may create some confusion. The standard definition is this:

(5) $two' = \{\langle P, Q \rangle : |P \cap Q| \geq 2\}$

In words, *two* denotes the set of pairs of properties whose intersections have 2 or more elements. Notice though that this is not the semantic definition of the numeral *two* that would be a building block of sentences like *At most two dogs are barking,* or *The two dogs are barking,* or *Two and two is four.* This is the definition of the GQ-theoretic determiner *two* that occurs in *Two dogs are barking* and, perhaps, depending on your theory of predication, *Those are two dogs.* That is to say, (5) incorporates both cardinality and existential import. When P and Q are instantiated as *dog'* and *bark',* the result is equivalent to the first order formula,

(6) $\exists x \exists y [x \neq y \wedge dog'(x) \wedge dog'(y) \wedge bark'(x) \wedge bark'(y)]$

(5) does not directly tell us what the numeral *two* would mean, i.e. what the cardinality information is. In the literature it is unfortunately not always crystal clear whether authors are discussing the interpretation of the numeral or that of a particular noun phrase in a particular sentence or sentence type.

Partee (1986) and Winter (2001) survey a body of data that will be easy to account for if the numeral's contribution is 'exactly two'. One such piece of data is that *two dogs* on its predicative and collective readings means 'exactly two dogs':

(7)   Those are two dogs.
       (false if the speaker is pointing at three dogs)

(8)   Two dogs pulled the sled to the barn.
       (false if the collective agent of the event consisted of three dogs, or of two dogs and a sheep)

The same holds for cumulative readings, as observed in Scha (1981):[76]

(9)   Five Dutch companies produced two thousand computers between them.

In cross-sentential anaphora, the plural pronoun or definite description will refer to just the two hungry dogs the first sentence is thought to be about, even though the first sentence can be true if there are altogether more than two dogs hungry.

(10)   Two dogs were hungry. They barked.
       The dogs barked.
       The two dogs barked.

In sum, if the 'exactly' reading features in all the above contexts, then the possibility of having an 'at least n' interpretation is confined to full noun phrases (as opposed to numerals), and specifically to those that occur as arguments of distributive predication. How are these effects derived?

Partee (1986), Winter (2000, 2001), and others, e.g. KAMP AND REYLE (1993), Kadmon (1993), and Krifka (1999) assume that *two* as a numeral says that the cardinality of the plurality (set or individual sum) denoted by the NP it modifies is exactly two. (This analysis only insists that numerals are cardinality modifiers; it is neutral as to whether they are adjectives or, as Ionin and Matushansky 2006 argue, nouns.)

(11)

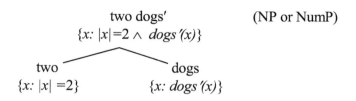

In predicative position (11) occurs as is, so *Those are two dogs* means that the plurality pointed at has the dogs-property and its cardinality is exactly two.

For sentences that contain an argumental DP of the shape *two dogs* these authors may or may not additionally assume the existence of a determiner *two*, homonymous with the numeral; but let us set this possibility aside and explore what happens if there is only one word *two*, as in (11). When the NP or NumP *two dogs* becomes part of a DP argument, existential closure will apply to (11), directly or with the mediation of a choice function.[77]

First consider the case where the predicate is collective:

(12)   Two dogs (together) pulled the sled to the barn.
        'there was a plurality of exactly two dogs that was the collective agent of some sled-relocation event'

Existential quantification here has no effect on the 'exactly two' interpretation. Suppose there was a sled-relocation event $e[3d]$ whose collective agent was three dogs. The occurrence of $e[3d]$ does not make (12) true; nor does it make (12) false. 'There was a collective agent of three . . .' does not entail 'There was a collective agent of two . . .'; these propositions are independent.[78]

The situation is different when the NP or NumP *two dogs* is part of the DP argument of a distributive predicate.

(13)   Two dogs are hungry.
        'there is a plurality consisting of exactly two dogs such that each of its members is hungry' (more precisely: 'there is a plurality of exactly two dogs such that for each member there is an event of hungriness that it is the theme of')

First notice that the involvement of a plurality of exactly two dogs in the computation of (13) plays a role in connection with anaphora; cf. (10). KAMP AND REYLE (1993) assign to (13) a discourse representation structure (DRS) that contains a plural referent X whose cardinality is exactly two, whose elements are dogs, and whose elements are hungry. This X will serve as an antecedent for *they* or *the two dogs*.[79]

To determine truth or falsity, Kamp and Reyle embed the DRS in a model; this corresponds to existential closure applied to X, a plurality of exactly two hungry dogs. But now existential closure has the effect that will already be familiar from §4.1.4. Coupled with distributive predication it voids the upper bound on the number of hungry dogs. As before, suppose there is a plurality of three dogs that satisfies the predicate. The predicate distributes to the individual members of the pluralities (each dog has its own hungriness-event), so 'There are three individual dogs that are hungry' entails 'There are two individual dogs that are hungry'. In sum, (13) is true if there are two or more hungry dogs.

This is the classical compositional procedure to obtain an 'at least' interpretation for DPs of the form *two dogs* as arguments of distributive predicates. (We may think of the generalized-quantifier-theoretic determiner *two* in (5) as something that obtains the same result in one fell swoop, without deriving it compositionally and without saying anything about predicative and collective uses of the string *two dogs*.) As it stands (13) does not predict that such sentences ever convey that there are exactly two dogs with the relevant property. If such cases exist, they must contain some phonetically null operator on top of what has already been taken into account, or the 'exactly' interpretation must be a pragmatic inference, a neo-Gricean scalar implicature.

Following HORN (1972, 2004), LEVINSON (1983), and others, KADMON (1993, 2001) fleshes out the pragmatic argument, which can be quickly summarized as follows. The meanings of numerals form a so-called Horn-scale, i.e. they are linguistically recognized as alternatives ordered with respect to strength. The literal meaning of *Two dogs are hungry* is as in (13). Suppose someone utters this sentence and in the utterance situation (i) it is relevant exactly how many dogs are hungry, (ii) the hearer believes that the speaker knows the facts, and (iii) the hearer believes that the speaker is cooperative (gives as much information as is relevant). Then the hearer is entitled to infer that two dogs and not more are hungry. Because if the stronger claim *Three dogs are hungry* were true, then (under the assumptions we just made) the speaker would have said so. This view is supported by two kinds of considerations. The first involves constructing situations where not all of (i) through (iii) hold and showing that the hearer would not make the 'not more than two' inference. The second is that the hearer does not make such an inference when *Two dogs are hungry* occurs in a monotonically decreasing context, as is shown by the infelicity of the continuations indicated when *two* is not focused:

(14)   a.   It is not the case that two dogs are hungry.
             infelicitous continuation: Three are.
             felicitous continuation: Only one is.
        b.   If two dogs are hungry, we need more meat.
             infelicitous continuation: If three dogs are hungry, we may or
             may not need more meat.
             felicitous continuation: If three dogs are hungry, we need
             more meat too.

The reason why here the hearer does not infer that not more than two
dogs are hungry is that decreasing contexts reverse the implicational scale.
(At least) three dogs are hungry makes a stronger claim than *(At least)
two dogs are hungry*, but *It is not the case that (at least) three dogs are
hungry* is not stronger – it is in fact weaker – than *It is not the case
that (at least) two dogs are hungry*. So neo-Gricean reasoning does not
generate an implicature.

To summarize, the view outlined offers a compositional account of the
'exactly' versus 'at least' literal interpretations of phrases like *two dogs* in
predicative, collective argument, and distributive argument positions and,
supplemented with neo-Gricean pragmatic strengthening, it also makes
predictions as to when non-literal 'exactly' inferences arise.

In the past decade the neo-Gricean component of this view has been
called into question (the other components reviewed above often remain
unaddressed in the revisions). Some of the reasons are specific to numerals.
One comes from language acquisition studies. Papafragou and Musolino
have found, in a series of papers, their (2003) among them, that children
do not treat the implicatures of *some* and numerals in the same way.
Children initially interpret (the cross-linguistic counterparts of) *some* as
'some and possibly all', not computing the 'but not all' implicature. This
is in line with the general observation that in pragmatic matters they
do not yet perform like adult speakers and with the observation that
processing a sentence with the 'but not all' implicature is more costly even
in adults (Bott and Noveck 2004). But children do not initially interpret
two dogs as 'two and possibly more'; they quickly zoom in on the 'two and
not more' interpretation. This suggests that the 'exactly' interpretation
of numeral indefinites is not a pragmatic matter. Other reasons pertain
to specific problems with when and how the various interpretations arise.
Carston (1998) observes the existence of 'at most n' readings in decreasing
contexts,

(15)   If you have two children, you do not qualify for tax exemptions.

and argues that numerals, or numeral indefinites, are underspecified for
the 'at least n', 'exactly n', and an 'at most n' distinction. In contrast,

Geurts (2006) recognizes an ambiguity. He starts out from a DP interpreted as 'exactly n NP'. Such a DP can be lowered into a predicative NP retaining the 'exactly n' reading. This however can be turned into a quantifier again by an existential shift which (as we have seen with Partee, Winter, Kamp and Reyle, etc.) yields an 'at least n' interpretation. Breheny (2008) takes the radical position that numeral indefinites only have an 'exactly n' literal meaning; the attested 'at most n' and 'at least n' readings are obtained by combining this with pragmatic reasoning and background knowledge (for example, knowledge about how particular tax exemptions work).

CHIERCHIA, FOX, AND SPECTOR (2008) approach the issue from the perspective of the program of grammaticalizing scalar implicatures, following Landman (2000) and Chierchia (2006). Landman and Chierchia propose that the calculation of implicatures takes place as part of the recursive component of the grammar, rather than following it (although see Sauerland 2004 for new arguments supporting the globalist position). The main motivation comes from the behavior of implicatures within the scopes of various operators, which we do not review here. Suffice it to say that on this view scalar implicatures in general (not only those associated with numerals) result from a phonetically null counterpart of the operator *only* known from Rooth's (1992) semantics of focus. In Rooth's proposal *only(p)* means that of the contextually relevant alternatives to the proposition p (where the set of alternatives contains p itself) the ones that are stronger than p are not true. Applying this to the problem of numeral indefinites, they themselves have an 'at least n NP' reading, but they are automatically associated with the covert exhaustivity operator (notated as O). Different readings are obtained depending on where O is inserted. This method replicates the results of the ambiguity-view, but also generates crucial further readings. Spector (2008) considers three alternative positions for O; he credits the idea of (16b) to D. Fox:

(16)   a.   Every student has to solve O(two problems).
                'Every student has to solve exactly two problems'
        b.   Every student O(has to solve two problems).
                'Every student has to solve two problems, is allowed to solve more, and no student has to solve three problems or more'
        c. O(Every student has to solve two problems).
                'Every student has to solve two problems or more, and not every student has to solve three problems or more'

The fact that the phonetically null exhaustivizer O is inspired by Rooth's semantics for *only* raises the question whether 'exactly' readings correlate with focus in any way. One logical possibility is that O is a focus-sensitive operator and therefore associates with focus. If so, then we expect either (i) that the availability of 'exactly' readings is clearly delimited by focus placement, or (ii) that 'exactly' readings come about in two different ways: relying on O when association with focus is present, and in a neo-Gricean manner when it is not. Bear in mind that this hypothesis does not predict that focused numerals always come with an 'exactly' reading. The hypothesis is not, "if focus, then exhaustivity"; rather, "if exhaustivizer O, then focus".[80]

It may be interesting to take a brief look at Hungarian in this connection. Hungarian is a language that has been claimed since the early 1980s to have a surface syntactic position in which phrases carry an exhaustive interpretation (Region 3, in terms of Table 8.1). The early view was that the language has an overt syntactic movement rule whose sole purpose is to focus the moved constituent. In an important break with this view Horvath (2006) argues that focus in Hungarian is intonational, much like it is in English. The well-known overt movement of the focus-phrase to the preverbal position is not triggered by some [focus] feature, but by the particle *only* or its null counterpart, the Exhaustive Identification (*EI*) operator; i.e. it is a case of syntactic association with focus. Horvath assumes both *only* and *EI* to be heads of projections right above IP.[81]

The connection between Horvath's *EI* and Chierchia and colleagues' O is interesting, since the traditional claim about Hungarian, from Szabolcsi (1981) to Kiss (2009), has been that numeral indefinites receive an 'exactly n NP' interpretation when the numerals or the containing phrases are in focus, and an 'at least n NP' interpretation when out of focus. (Fretheim 1992 makes a similar claim about the correlation between focus stress and numeral interpretation in Norwegian.) To make this more precise, Hungarian bare numerals receive an irrevocably exhaustive interpretation in and only in Region 3. Spector's paradigm can be fully replicated in Hungarian by varying narrow vs. broad focus and the scope of the universal with respect to focus. In (17) 'every student' takes widest scope. On the reading corresponding to (16a), *EI* associates with narrow focus on *KÉT* 'two'; on the reading corresponding to (16b) focus projects from *KÉT* 'two' to the right (here, to the verb phrase).

(17)   Minden diáknak   KÉT problémát   kell   megoldania.
        every   student.dat two   problem.acc must perf.solve.inf

    a.   'every student must solve at least two problems, and the maximum permitted number is two'; cf. (16a)

    b.   'every student must solve at least two problems, and the maximum required number to solve is two'; cf. (16b)

On the reading corresponding to (16c) 'every student' takes narrower scope than focus; the most natural way to achieve this effect is to left dislocate (contrastively topicalize) the universal.

(18)   MINDEN diáknak   – KÉT problémát   kell   megoldania.
        every   student.dat – two   problem.acc must perf.solve.inf
        'the maximum requirement shared by every student is to solve at
        least two problems'; cf. (16c)

When however the numeral indefinite is not in Region 3, it receives an
obligatorily non-exhaustive interpretation in the presence of verum-focus
on the verb, and an 'at least' reading that can be strengthened according
to the neo-Gricean scenario elsewhere. (19) exemplifies the latter case:

(19)   Minden diáknak   meg kell   oldania   két problémát.
        every   student.dat perf must solve.inf two problem.acc
        'every student has to solve two problems (infer exactly two, if the
        number is relevant and the speaker is knowledgeable and cooper-
        ative)'

The interpretations outside Region 3 do not seem to be predicted by the
Chierchia–Fox–Spector hypothesis. Hungarian appears to have more than
one source for 'exactly n' interpretations.

9.3   Cardinal vs. individual readings of numeral indefinites

Sentences containing *how many*-expressions exhibit a cardinal vs. individual ambiguity, most clearly discernible in interaction with modals or
intensional predicates.

(20)   How many people should I talk to?
        a.   cardinal 'What number n is such that there should be n-
             many people that I talk to?'
        b.   individual 'What number n is such that there are n-many
             people that I should talk to?'

Following Higginbotham (1993), Cresti (1995) decomposes *how many NP*
into two component quantifiers, as is suggested by the paraphrases in
(20). The cardinal reading arises when *should* intervenes between the two
components. Modal and intensional operators are privileged in being allowed to intervene; quantifiers and negation cannot do so. The individual
reading arises when both components scope over *should*, or a quantifier,
or negation.[82] More formally, the two readings of (20) are as in (21)–
(22). Following Hamblin (1973), the question is interpreted as a set of
propositions: the alternatives it introduces into the discourse. They are its
possible (not necessarily true) literal answers. The same are the alternatives that focus on the numeral would generate in Rooth (1992); see Krifka
(2006) for association with focus phrases. The propositions defined in (21)
are of the shape *It should be the case that there are one/two/three/four*

... *people that you talk to*; those defined in (22) are of the shape *There are one/two/three/four ... people that you should talk to.*

(21)   Cardinal reading:
$$\lambda p \exists n[num(n) \wedge p = {}^{\wedge}should'({}^{\wedge}\exists_n x[person'(x) \wedge talk'(I, x)])]$$

(22)   Individual reading:
$$\lambda p \exists n[num(n) \wedge p = {}^{\wedge}\exists_n x[person'(x) \wedge should'({}^{\wedge}talk'(I, x))]]$$

The derivation involves extracting *wh-how*, leaving behind *t-many people*; the cardinal reading is obtained when *t-many people* reconstructs into an intermediate position below the modal. Cresti proposes so-called semantic reconstruction, which affects interpretation but not syntactic material, and the implementation was already discussed in some detail in **§2.3.5**; see (39)–(40). (Heycock 1995, Romero 1998, and Fox 1999 among others argue that syntactic reconstruction must be involved, because the existential scope of the nominal restriction interacts with Binding Theory. This debate is orthogonal to present concerns.) The encircled modal and trace t' in the tree below will remind the reader of how the ambiguity comes about; but we focus on the derivation of a simple unambiguous example, and the step-by-step interpretation does not take the encircled material into account. Steps (b) and (h) involve abstraction over y and m, respectively, not just plain functional application.

(23)   How many people [did] I talk to?

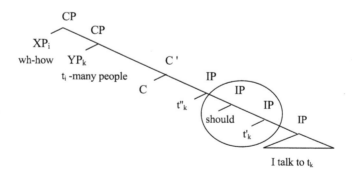

a. t'' $\mathcal{P}$ (of the generalized quantifier type)
b. $[t''\ IP]$ ${}^{\wedge\wedge}\mathcal{P}({}^{\wedge}\lambda y[talk'(I', y)])$
c.   C $\lambda q \lambda p[p = q]$
d.   C' $\lambda p[p = {}^{\wedge\wedge}\mathcal{P}({}^{\wedge}\lambda y[talk'(I', y)])]$

e. t-many people $\qquad \lambda Q \exists^m x[person'(x) \land Q(x)]$

f. $[_{CP} \; t$-many people $C']$ $\quad \lambda p[p = {}^{\wedge}\exists^m x[person'(x) \land talk'(I', x)]]$

g. wh-how $\qquad\qquad \lambda R \lambda p \exists n[num(n) \land R(n)(p)]$

h. $[_{CP} \; wh$-how CP] $\qquad \lambda p \exists n[num(n) \land$
$\qquad\qquad\qquad\qquad\qquad p = {}^{\wedge}\exists^n x[person'(x) \land talk'(I', x)]]$

Cresti settles on another derivation that adjoins wh-how to t-$many$ $people$ and not to CP, maintaining their constituency. But (23) is simpler to interpret; it also has the same structure as the scope-splitting analysis of comparatives quantifiers in Hackl (2000) that is going to be discussed in §10.3, so it is more useful to us.[83]

Cresti (1995) naturally does not consider the choice-functional treatment of indefinites (a later invention), but the above might be recast using existential closure over choice functions:

(24) Cardinal reading:
$\lambda p \exists n[num(n) \land p = {}^{\wedge}should'({}^{\wedge}\exists f[talk'(I', f(n(people')))])]$

(25) Individual reading:
$\lambda p \exists n[num(n) \land p = {}^{\wedge}\exists f[should'({}^{\wedge}talk'(I', f(n(people'))))]]$

If existential closure of choice functions is abandoned, then (24) can be distinguished from (25) by f having a world-parameter bound by the modal quantifier $should$.

The next section surveys morpho-syntactic correlates of the cardinal vs. individual readings as well as D-linking.

9.4 Numeral interpretation, agreement, and the split-DP hypothesis

Although sophisticated semantic analyses of numeral indefinites are available in the literature and all make rather concrete claims about the syntax/semantics interface, they are built on little morpho-syntactic evidence. It may thus be interesting to consider a domain of data that potentially offers such evidence. In many languages the presence or absence of number/gender agreement correlates with the interpretive options of numeral indefinites. These data lend syntactic reality to the locus of the existential closure of the nominal restriction (or whatever semantic equivalent performs the same job). Their consideration may inform the choice between semantic accounts.

A much-discussed feature of French is that the presence or absence of participle agreement interacts with the interpretation of 'how many'-phrases originating as internal arguments (Obenauer 1992; Déprez 1998; Rizzi 2000; Koopman and Sportiche 2008). Russian exhibits a somewhat similar phenomenon with respect to numeral indefinites as subjects (Pesetsky 1982). This section pulls these together. We hope to draw the attention of semanticists to the existence of morpho-syntactic correlates of scope and specificity; also to facilitate the communication between linguists working on Romance and Slavic.[84]

This section can be read in either of two ways: concentrating just on the examples and the description of their interpretations, or paying attention also to the syntactic proposal outlined. I trust that even the description-oriented reading has its benefits.

French examples such as (26) exhibit a cardinal vs. individual ambiguity that Koopman and Sportiche (2008) describe as a scope ambiguity between the existential quantifier of the nominal restriction (*de voitures* 'cars') and the modal auxiliary (*doit* 'must, epistemic or deontic'), just as we saw Cresti does for English.

(26)   Combien   de voitures doit-il   avoir conduit?
        how.many of cars   must-he have driven

    a.   'for what number n, it must be that there are n cars that he drove' (cardinal)
    b.   'for what number n, there are n cars that he must have driven' (individual)

In contrast, (27) only has a cardinal reading, indicating that the existential quantifier of *de voitures* is stuck, or obligatorily reconstructs, below *doit*.

(27)   Combien   doit-il   avoir conduit de voitures?
        how.many must-he have driven   of cars

    a.   'for what number n, it must be that there are n cars that he drove' (cardinal)
    b.   #(individual)

In (26)–(27) the past participle *conduit* does not agree with the direct object in gender and number. In the presence of participle agreement (*conduites*) (26) loses its cardinal (a) reading and (27), which only had a cardinal reading, becomes unacceptable:

(28)   Combien   de voitures doit-il   avoir conduites?
        how.many of cars   must-he have driven.fem.pl

    a.   #(cardinal)
    b.   'for what number n, there are n cars that he must have driven' (individual)

(29)   *Combien   doit-il   avoir conduites   de voitures?
        how.many must-he have driven.fem.pl of cars

It is not the case, though, that agreement is incompatible with cardinal readings. When the 'how many'-phrase originates as an internal argument but surfaces as an unaccusative subject or as a passive subject, participle agreement is obligatory but both readings are available. (30) illustrates this with a passive:

(30)   Combien   de femmes doivent avoir été   admises   cette fois?
        how.many of women must   have been admitted this   time

      a.   'for what number n, it must have been that there were n women admitted' (cardinal)

      b.   'for what number n, there were n women that must have been admitted' (individual)

There exists an additional kind of interaction between participle agreement and interpretation: when agreement is optional, the presence of agreement indicates Discourse-linking (i.e. talk about entities under explicit discussion – see Pesetsky 1987 and much subsequent literature). We have seen above that the only case where agreement is optional is when *combien* does not visibly split from its nominal restriction and moreover the phrase is a direct object; cf. (26) and (28).

(31)   Combien de voitures doit-il avoir conduit(es)?

But one must be careful not to read the generalization as a biconditional. As was noted in Obenauer (1992), Discourse-linking is possible even in (27), where *combien* is extracted alone and thus agreement is excluded. So (27) can be used in a situation where various numbers are under explicit discussion and the speaker is asking, roughly, which of those numbers is the correct one.

The interest of these facts is two-fold. The agreement data can be used to sharpen delicate judgments. They also raise a question:

(32)   What information do the different agreement options provide about the syntactic position of the nominal restriction in the various readings; how does that guide the compositional semantics?

Below we develop the outlines of an analysis drawing from Kayne (1989), Sportiche (2005), and Koopman and Sportiche (2008), and from extensive helpful discussions with H. Koopman and D. Sportiche (p.c.) that fleshed out their 2008 proposal. We also point out some connections with subject–verb agreement in Russian.

Participle agreement is thought to signal that the nominal restriction of the internal argument has passed through some designated agreement-position. The nominal restriction must be the part relevant for agreement, because whenever the *wh*-part (*combien*) is fronted on its own and the restriction is left in-situ, agreement is impossible. The main idea of our analysis will be to draw the demarcation line between A-movement and A-bar

movement cases. The A-movement cases are those that involve the subject
position (passives and unaccusatives in French, agreeing subjects in Russian). Here the nominal restriction passes through the agreement-position
as a by-product of movement to the subject position. But A-movement is
known to allow scope reconstruction. Therefore, the A-movement cases are
predicted to be ambiguous. In contrast, French direct objects do not move
for plain well-formedness; their movement must be A-bar movement motivated by interpretation. A-bar movement is known to show reconstruction effects with respect to Binding Theory but not with respect to scope.
Therefore A-bar-movement cases that exhibit agreement are predicted to
unambiguously carry the high existential scope, i.e. individual, reading.
Finally, when the nominal restriction stays in-situ (*combien*-extraction in
French, postverbal *skol'ko*-extraction in Russian) and has no chance to
trigger agreement, it also does not have a chance to acquire high existential scope – it will only carry the cardinal reading.

These ideas can be accommodated in various different theories, but
we sketch a particular execution based on Sportiche's (2005) Split-DP
structure, given its principled approach to syntactic reconstruction.

In almost all of the literature it is taken for granted that expressions
that end up in one DP constituent were generated that way. Sportiche
(2005) radically departs from this assumption. Motivated by selection and
reconstruction facts, he proposes that the arguments of the verb are NPs,
not DPs. Determiners (D) are generated in a different layer of syntactic
structure, outside the VP, and NPs move in order to join their determiners. The motivation from selection is that whereas verbs often select for
arguments whose noun components are [animate], [abstract], etc., verbs
do not select for arguments with particular determiners. The motivation
from reconstruction is that in the case of operator (A-bar) movement only
the NP is interpreted in a low position (as seen from binding effects) but
the determiner is not (as seen from scope effects). Sportiche concludes
that we have evidence that the NP originates in the VP-internal position,
but we do not have evidence that the D does. So,

(33)   "[T]he sentence in (a) has a structure like (b) as underlying struc-
        ture. To put it in equivalent terms, the sentence in (a) contains a
        substructure similar to (b) so that a full representation is (c):
        a. [the/every/some cat] ... will ... sleep
        b. ... the/every/some ... [cat sleep]
        c. [the/every/some cat]... will ... [cat sleep]
        in which the determiner *the/every/some* (as well as other deter-
        miners) are part of the functional structure of the clause ... Note
        that since lowest traces must always be interpreted, the interpre-
        tation for the (c) structure will be (say for *every* and ignoring the

future):

d.   every cat [cat sleep]: $\forall x$ cat (x), sleep$(x) \wedge$ cat(x)"

(Sportiche 2005: 43)

Using these assumptions, let us return to the ambiguous A-movement case (30), *Combien de femmes doivent avoir été admises cette fois?* According to Koopman and Sportiche (2008), the cardinal and the individual readings differ in that in the initial structures the existential D is inserted at the vP-level (below the modal) in the first case and at the CP-level (above the modal) in the second.[85] The existential D scopes in the position where it is initially inserted. In other words, if DP occurs higher in surface syntax, the locus of the initial of D-insertion indicates where it reconstructs.

The initial (pre-movement) structures are as follows:

(34)   A-movement case, cardinal reading, obligatory agreement:
       Combien > Subject of TP > Tense Agreement > Modal > **D$_\exists$** >
       vP > Participle Agreement > VP > NP

(35)   A-movement case, individual reading, obligatory agreement:
       Combien > **D$_\exists$** > Subject of TP > Tense Agreement > Modal >
       vP > Participle Agreement > VP > NP

NP raises just in order to join its D. The participle-agreement position is at the VP-level. NP triggers agreement when it inescapably passes through Participle Agreement. The full DP then lands a little above the subject position.

The French direct object data are more difficult. First, agreement is optional. As H. Koopman and D. Sportiche (p.c.) point out, the optionality of agreement with direct objects indicates that participle agreement is triggered in two different ways in French. The VP-level agreement-position that was invoked for the A-movement cases is either absent or deficient in (26) and (28); but apparently there exists another agreement-position higher than the vP-edge position of D; call it High Agreement. Second, the non-agreeing (26) (*Combien de voitures doit-il avoir conduit?*) is ambiguous, whereas the agreeing (28) (*Combien de voitures doit-il avoir conduites?*) only carries the individual reading, where the existential D of the nominal restriction scopes over the modal. Third, the agreeing version is additionally inherently Discourse-linked.

As above, NP raises only to join its D. One might stipulate that the VP-level agreement does not accept accusative NPs.[86] Then the cardinal reading will not have agreement: the existential D is inserted at the vP-level, NP stops at D, and High Agreement is located somewhere higher than D. See (26). The same non-agreeing version also has an individual reading. This indicates that NP may unite with a CP-level D without passing through High Agreement. On the other hand, the agreeing version (28) has only an individual reading, so NP passes through High Agreement only if it is headed for a CP-level D. It is not quite clear exactly where the high agreement-position is in the space above the vP-edge D. If its position with respect to the CP-level D were variable, i.e. if both *High Agreement* > D and D > *High Agreement* were available, that would account for the optionality of agreement on the individual reading.

(36)   A-bar movement case, cardinal reading, no agreement:
        Combien > High Agreement > Subject of TP > Tense Agreement
        > Modal > $D_\exists$ > vP > VP > NP

(37)   A-bar movement case, individual reading, no agreement:
        Combien > High Agreement > $D_\exists$ > Subject of TP > Tense
        Agreement > Modal > vP > VP > NP

(38)   A-bar movement case, Discourse-linked individual reading, with
        agreement:
        Combien > $D_\exists$ > High Agreement > Subject of TP > Tense
        Agreement > Modal > vP > VP > NP

It is still mysterious why the High Agreement position exists and why a direct object whose restriction passes through it is irrevocably Discourse-linked. The spirit of Sportiche's overall proposal is that agreement itself has no interpretive effect, its presence or absence merely indicates how high NP raised to join its D. We may then assume that D may be inserted at three, not just two points: at the vP-level, as in (34) and (36); right above TP, as in (35) and (37); and right above High Agreement, as in (38) – and this last position is dedicated to Discourse-linking. This implies that there are two kinds of Discourse-linking, namely, grammaticized Discourse-linking involving a dedicated position, perhaps topicalization, and pragmatic Discourse-linking. For example, the Discourse-linked cardinal readings of split *combien* are clearly pragmatic.

Finally, we have (27) and (29), where *combien* and *de voitures* are discontinuous. As the spell-out shows, NP never moves out of VP, it does not trigger any agreement, and its D only scopes below the modal.[87]

On this proposal the fact that agreement entails Discourse-linking in French if and only if agreement is optional is an epiphenomenon; optionality is not a determining factor. Rather, the relevant distinction is between cases where agreement occurs as a by-product of A-movement (which is for independent reasons obligatory) and cases where agreement occurs because the phrase moves to an A-bar position dedicated to Discourse-linking (optional in the sense that it is not necessary for plain well-formedness). It appears that this approach is supported by Russian. Subject agreement with numeral NPs is optional, but it is definitely not the case that agreeing forms are all irrevocably Discourse-linked. In other words, the optionality of agreement does not correlate with Discourse-linking.

In Russian the pertinent agreement is between the subject and the finite verb. The Russian data are clearly similar to the French data in that contiguous *skol'ko akterov* 'how.many actors' is compatible with both agreement and non-agreement (the latter is neuter singular).[88] In Russian the agreeing versions are ambiguous, whereas the non-agreeing version only has a cardinal reading.

(39) *skol'ko akterov* with 3pl agreement:
   Skol'ko   akterov   mogut ego uvazhat'?
   how.many actor.gen.pl may.3pl him respect.inf
   a. 'for what number n, it may be that there are n actors who respect him' (cardinal)
   b. 'for what number n, there are n actor who may respect him' (individual)

(40) *skol'ko akterov* without agreement:
   Skol'ko   akterov   mozhet ego uvazhat'?
   how.many actor.gen.pl may   him respect.inf
   a. 'for what number n, it may be that there are n actors who respect him' (cardinal)
   b. #(individual)

From our perspective (39) definitely falls into the A-movement category: it involves movement to the subject position, as does the ambiguous passive example (30) in French.

(41) A-movement case, cardinal reading, with agreement:
   Skol'ko > Agreement in TP > Tense Agreement > Modal > $\mathbf{D}_\exists$ > vP > VP > NP

(42) A-movement case, individual reading, with agreement:
   Skol'ko > $\mathbf{D}_\exists$ > Agreement in TP > Tense Agreement > Modal > vP > VP > NP

I leave open the analysis of (40), the non-agreeing cardinal reading.

Russian is of further interest in that the optionality of agreement with numerals is not restricted to interrogatives. It is also present in plain numeral indefinites. *Pjat' akterov* 'five actors' replicates the *skol'ko akterov* patterns seen above. In addition, *pjat' akterov* can take extra-clausal scope when it triggers subject agreement in the complement clause, but not in the absence of agreement. For some speakers these are just tendencies, for others hard and fast rules. This contrast is suggestive of classical choice-functional behavior in agreeing numeral DPs, and assimilates the non-agreeing counterparts to Winter's (2000) purely quantificational DPs.[89]

9.5 Summary

The present chapter started with Winter's flexible DP hypothesis that relates type multiplicity, cf. **§5.3**, to internal structure in the spirit of the choice-functional analysis. We then discussed two major topics in the interpretation of numeral indefinites: their 'at least' vs. 'exactly' interpretation, and their cardinal vs. individual interpretation. The currently most debated issue concerning the former pertains to how implicatures contribute to 'exactly' readings. Regarding cardinal vs. individual readings syntacticians and semanticists seem to agree that the ambiguity is due to the scope interaction of modals with two separate quantificational layers in numeral indefinites. The ingredients of this analysis will be particularly relevant in connection with comparative quantifiers: see the next chapter.

10

Modified numerals

The treatment of unmodified indefinites and universals has undergone major revisions in recent decades, but the original generalized-quantifier-theoretic analysis of modified numeral expressions took the brunt of the criticism, as seen in Chapter 5. The present chapter looks at some interesting properties of modified numerals in their own right. These are the absence of scalar ('exactly') implicatures; the question whether comparative (*more than*) and superlative (*at least*) modifiers yield interchangeable expressions; the interaction of comparative determiners with modals; and the compositional interpretation of amount-superlatives (*(the) most NP*). After this we attempt a preliminary characterization of a class of items that have been dubbed counting quantifiers. The next chapter will return to modified numerals with a discussion of their scope behavior.

10.1 The absence of scalar implicatures in modified numerals

The unmodified numeral expressions discussed in the previous chapter were associated with a scalar implicature that stronger alternatives on the Horn-scale are false. But modified numeral expressions do not carry such an implicature. The interpretations given below are incoherent or are unfaithful to the sentence, depending on what one thinks the numbers greater than at least three might be. Parallel observations hold for *at most four boys* and *fewer than four boys*.

(1)   At least three boys left.
       #'At least three boys left and it is false of all numbers n greater than at least three that n boys left'

(2)   More than three boys left.
       #'More than three boys left and it is false of all numbers n greater than at least three that n boys left'

Krifka (1999) is the first to address why this is so. He analyzes n *NP* phrases as predicates of pluralities, and builds *at least n NP* and *more than n NP* by combining those units with the modifiers. By itself, *three boys* denotes $\lambda x[3(x) \wedge boys'(x)]$, i.e. the set of pluralities whose elements are boys and whose cardinality is exactly three. This is consonant with (13) in the previous chapter. But, in contrast to the traditional GQ-theoretic treatment as well as Winter's, on Krifka's analysis the modifiers *at least/at most* and *more/less* modify this whole phrase and do not form a constituent with the numeral *three* (a feature to which we return below). A further crucial observation is that the modifiers are focus-sensitive operators. Consequently in the presence of these modifiers either *three* or the whole of *three boys* must have focus. The gist of Krifka's analysis is that focus-sensitive operators use, and use up, the alternatives introduced by focus on the numeral and no alternatives are left for scalar implicatures to negate. This is an application of Rooth's (1992) proposal regarding the competition among focus-sensitive operators. The diagram in (3) specifies the constituent structure, (4a) the truth-conditional contribution of *THREE boys*, and (4b) the ordered alternatives due to focus on *three*.

(3)   Krifka (1999)

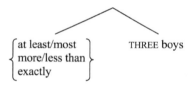

(4)   a.   *THREE boys'* $= \lambda x[3(x) \wedge boys'(x)]$
        b.   *THREE boys'*$_A = \{\langle \lambda x[n(x) \wedge boys'(x)],$
               $\lambda x[m(x) \wedge boys'(x)]\rangle : n \leq_N m\}$

Krifka's main goal is to attend to the needs of *at most*-modified phrases in sentences such as (5):

(5)   a.   At most THREE boys left.
        b.   At most THREE boys ate at most SEVEN apples.
               (cumulation)
        c.   Mary is at most an ASSOCIATE professor.
               (no entailment among alternatives)

Krifka argues that "*at most*-sentences do not have any meaning proper, but rather come with alternatives that are marked as being excluded by the speaker." Specifically, their illocutionary force is the assertion that the speaker claims that the higher ranked alternatives are false. This carries over very nicely to the otherwise difficult (5b)–(5c). The difficulty with the cumulative reading is, as was mentioned in §4.1.4, that its most intuitive analysis involves existential quantification over witness sets of the quantifiers involved, but this has to be accompanied by a maximality condition when the quantifiers are not increasing. The difficulty with (5c) is that the titles assistant, associate, and full professor do not form an entailment scale, so standard neo-Gricean treatments do not apply to them.

The analysis has less of a dramatic effect for *at least*. *At least*-sentences assert that at least one of the alternatives is true and thus introduce a discourse referent, predicting the contrast in (6):

(6)   a.   At most three boys left. ?They found the play boring.
      b.   At least three boys left. They found the play boring.

Sentences involving *more/less than*, *exactly*, etc. are analyzed in an analogous manner.

The fact that these modifiers can occur in complement clauses is not compatible with the view that the clauses that contain them have no meanings proper:

(7)   Mary was aware that at most three boys were present.

Therefore Krifka specifies a way to translate appropriate alternatives to meanings. This also applies to root sentences, correctly interpreting *At most three boys left* as 'it is not the case that more than three boys left', to which the assertion operator applies and from which no scalar implicatures arise.

See Fox and Hackl (2006) for a different proposal pertaining to the absence of scalar implicatures in modified numeral NPs.

Krifka's constituent structure for modified numerals, cf. (3), contrasts with the traditional GQ-theoretic one in that it does not group the modifier together with the numeral (hence the title of his paper, "At least some determiners aren't determiners"). Is there independent motivation for this syntactic analysis?

On independent grounds Ionin and Matushansky (2006: Appendix) are led to the same structure as Krifka. Their paper concerns the cross-linguistic syntax and semantics of complex cardinals involving multiplication (e.g. *two hundred*) and addition (e.g. *twenty-four*) in Russian, Inari Sami, Finnish, and a number of other languages in addition to English. They derive complex cardinals from simplex ones of type $\langle\langle e, t\rangle, \langle e, t\rangle\rangle$ compositionally. For example (the *xNP* notation in the place of NP or DP is used to indicate that it is irrelevant which functional layers are projected and which are not):

(8)

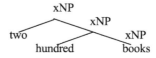

(9)   a.   *hundred books′* = the set of entities y such that y is a plural individual divisible into 100 non-overlapping individuals π such that their sum is y and each π is a book

        b.   *two hundred books′* = the set of entities y such that y is a plural individual divisible into 2 non-overlapping individuals π such that their sum is y and each π is divisible into 100 non-overlapping individuals p_k such their sum is π and each p_k is a book

As Ionin and Matushansky note, the analysis requires the cardinal to combine with the lexical xNP before combining with comparative or superlative modifiers, forcing them to adopt the same constituency for modified numerals as Krifka's.[90]

    Ionin and Matushansky also conclude that numerals are nouns. Kayne (2005c) offers a detailed argument to the effect that *few* and *many* are adjectives, but instead of modifying "head nouns" directly, they modify an unpronounced noun that he dubs NUMBER (capitals indicate nonpronunciation):

(10)

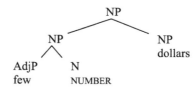

Zweig (2005a) extends Kayne's argument to simplex and complex numerals in a manner compatible with Ionin and Matushansky's conclusion:

(11)   a.   [NP [AdjP three] NUMBER]

        b.   [NP [AdjP three] thousand]

In sum, Ionin and Matushansky's analysis converges with Krifka's analysis.

    In support of the *[more than][three dogs]* constituency both Krifka and Ionin and Matushansky note that *more than* can modify categories other than numerals. One of Krifka's examples:

(12)   The aggressors wanted more than the southern province.

Let us examine whether this kind of data is evidence that *more than n NP* has *more than* as a constituent. Based both on English and Hungarian, I argue that it is not. Observe that the following sentence is ambiguous:

(13)   Peter drank more than one glass of wine.
    a.   'Peter drank two, or three, or four … glasses of wine'
    b.   'Peter drank something more intoxicating than a glass of wine'

The ambiguity might be attributed to differences in focus (although Krifka does not recognize this option with *more than*, only with *at least*). On that view, the first reading would have focus just on *one*, so the alternatives are amounts of wine, whereas the second would have focus on the whole of *one glass of wine*, so the alternatives are drinks. Whether this would be correct, it could not be the whole story. The insertion of *last night* into (13) disambiguates it:

(14)   Peter drank more last night than one glass of wine.
    'Peter drank something more intoxicating than a glass of wine'

Hungarian morphology makes it plain that the two readings of (13) are syntactically distinct. In (15), which carries the amounts of wine interpretation, the word *több* 'more' has no case-marker, whereas in (16), which carries the kinds of drinks interpretation, *több* is in the accusative.

(15)   Péter több, mint egy pohár bort   ivott.
    Peter more than one glass   wine.acc drank
    'Peter drank two, or three, or four … glasses of wine'

(16)   Péter többet   ivott, mint egy pohár bort.
    Peter more.acc drank than one glass   wine.acc
    'Peter drank something more intoxicating than a glass of wine'

Case-marking on an adjective or a quantifier word is a fairly sure sign of a phonetically empty noun, so that (16) amounts to (17a) or, along the lines of Kayne (2005c), (17b):

(17)   a.   [more STUFF accusative] [than one glass wine accusative]
    b.   [more AMOUNT STUFF accusative] [than one glass wine accusative]

Another difference is that while the complement of case-marked *több* is often extraposed, cf. (16) and also English (14), unmarked *több* cannot be separated from its complement:

(18)   *Péter több ivott, mint egy pohár bort.
    Peter more drank than one glass   wine.acc

Finally, when *több* applies to expressions other than amount-denoters (i.e. when its exhibits cross-categorial behavior), it invariably has a case-marker:

(19)   a.   A   következő utamon   ...
              the next   trip.my.on
              'On my next trip ...'
        b.   Többet   akarok látni,   mint Párizst.
              more.acc want.I   see.inf than Paris.acc
              'I want to see more [places] than Paris'
        c.   *Több, mint Párizst   akarok látni.
              more than Paris.acc want.I   see.inf
        d.   *Több akarok látni,   mint Párizst.
              more want.I see.inf than Paris.acc

The conclusion seems to be that we are dealing with two different comparative constructions. The fact that English *more than* can co-occur with various XPs is not an argument for analyzing the strictly amount-focused comparatives with a [*more than*][*two dogs*]-style bracketing. Possibly, the data just reviewed actually rule out Krifka's and Ionin and Matushansky's structures for comparative (though not for superlative) modifiers.

10.2 The non-synonymy of comparative and superlative modifiers

As was mentioned in §5.5, Geurts and Nouwen (2007) set out to demonstrate that *at least n* is not equivalent to *more than n-1*, nor *at most n* to *fewer/less than n+1*, pace the standard assumption within generalized quantifier theory as well as Krifka (1999). They point out three main differences between the superlative and comparative members of the pairs. (i) The superlative is more specific, as shown by the continuations in (20):

(20)   a.   I will invite at most/least two friends, namely Jack and Jill.
        b.   ?I will invite fewer than two/more than one friend(s), namely Jack and Jill.

(ii) Inferences with comparatives can be drawn from sentences with plain numerals; inferences with superlatives are questionable.

(21)   Beryl had three sherries
        a.   ✓ ⇒ Beryl had more than two sherries
        b.   ✓ ⇒ Beryl had fewer than five sherries
        c.   ?⇒ Beryl had at least three sherries
        d.   ?⇒ Beryl had at most four sherries

(iii) Occasionally comparatives are ambiguous in a way their superlative counterparts are not:

(22)   The waitress can carry fewer than twenty glasses.
          (i) ✓¬◇ more   (ii) ✓◇¬ more

(23)   The waitress can carry at most twenty glasses.
          (i) ✓¬◇ more   (ii) *◇¬ more

The main ingredient of Geurts and Nouwen's account is that superlative modifiers have epistemic modal meanings, consisting of what the sentence says and a conventionalized conversational implicature.

(24)   At most four girls danced.
          Says: It is possible (for all we know) that there is a plurality of four girls who danced.
          Implies: It is certain that no more than four girls danced.

(25)   At least three girls danced.
          Says: It is certain that there is a plurality of three girls who danced.
          Implies: It is possible (for all we know) that more than three girls danced.

These richer interpretations account for the questionability of the last two inferences in (21), for example. If *Beryl had three sherries* has the (neo-Gricean or grammaticized) implicature that she did not have more than three sherries, then it cannot automatically imply also that it is possible that she did have more than three. The argument runs similarly for the *at most*-inference. In contrast, the comparative modifiers do not carry modal meanings and the *more than two*-inferences go through as the tradition in semantics would have it.

10.3 The split-scope analysis of comparative quantifiers

As was discussed at some length in §5.6, Hackl (2000, 2002) accepts the surface constituency that generalized quantifier theory assigns to *more than n NP*, but not as a syntactic primitive. His central claim is that only a compositional analysis of comparative quantifiers has the ability to explain their distinctive behavior. We do not repeat those aspects of the analysis that have already been reviewed; instead, the present section complements the informal discussion in §5.6.

Hackl follows Heim (2001) in interpreting the comparative morpheme *-er* as a relation between two sets of degrees (i.e. as a degree-determiner). This is one of many current analyses of comparatives; see von Stechow (1984), Kennedy (1999), Schwarzschild and Wilkinson (2002), and Heim

(2006a), among others. The analyses differ as to what component of the
construction is a quantifier and what is not. Hackl analyzes *more/fewer
than three people* in a way that shares crucial aspects with the Higginboth-
am/Cresti-analysis of *how many people*; see **§9.3**. First, the whole phrase
undergoes Quantifier Raising; second, *more/fewer than three* extracts
(just like *how* does), leaving behind *d-many people* at the extraction site.
(A third step is copying an intensionalized version of *d-many people smile*
into the restriction of *more/fewer than three*, but this does not play a
role in the explication of counting quantification, so we stick with the
simplification.)

(26)   More than three people smile.

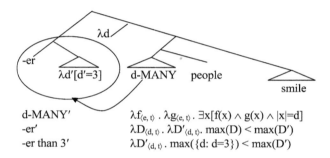

d-MANY′	$\lambda f_{\langle e, t\rangle} . \lambda g_{\langle e, t\rangle} . \exists x[f(x) \wedge g(x) \wedge |x|=d]$
-er′	$\lambda D_{\langle d, t\rangle} . \lambda D'_{\langle d, t\rangle}. \max(D) < \max(D')$
-er than 3′	$\lambda D'_{\langle d, t\rangle} . \max(\{d: d=3\}) < \max(D')$

In words, *More than three people smile* says that the maximal degree in
the interval that coincides with 3 is smaller than the degree equal to the
cardinality of the set/plural individual consisting of people who smile. In
simpler terms that suffice here, the number n such that n-many people
smile is greater than 3.

The reasons for scope-splitting in comparatives are essentially the
same as with *how many*-questions. Heim (2001) observes that various
intensional operators interact with the *-er than 3* and the *d-many* parts
as separate semantic units. For example, (27) allows two interpretations;
the critical one is (b) and it is in fact the easier reading.

(27)   This paper is 10 pages long. It is required to be exactly 5 pages
        longer than that.
        a. 'in every permitted world w exactly 5 pages longer than 10
            pages is the maximal degree d such that the paper is d-long
            in w'   (the maximum permitted length is 15 pages)
        b. 'exactly 5 pages longer than 10 pages is the maximal degree
            d such that in every permitted world w the paper is d-long
            in w'   (the required minimum length is 15 pages)

On the latter reading 'in every permitted world' intervenes between the degree-determiner and its trace *d-MANY*. The intervention of a nominal quantifier, as opposed to a modal/intensional operator, between the degree-determiner and its trace would be disallowed (see (28b)), as observed by Kennedy (1999) and Heim (2001), a fact seen as evidence for the decomposition.

(28)   Some/Every girl is exactly 1 in. taller/less tall than 5 ft.

   a.   'for some/every girl, her maximal height d is exactly 1 in. more/ less than 5 ft'

   b.   #'the maximal height d such that some/every girl has height d is exactly 1 in. more/less than 5 ft'

In **§6.1** we observed that comparative quantifiers are poor inverse scope takers even clause-internally. Hackl (2000) hints that this could follow from their split structure and intervention, and Takahashi (2006) works out a detailed proposal; see **§11.4**. In fact, the same scope behavior is characteristic of other quantifiers in English, e.g. *at least/most six NP*, *as many/few as six NP*, and *SIX NP*. One possibility, not yet investigated, is to assume similar scope splits for all of them and derive their general scope behavior from that. Monotonicity issues arise, but they need not be qualitatively different from what has already been considered for *less than*-comparatives; see Heim (2006b) and the literature cited therein.

10.4   *More than half, most of the,* and *the most*

Hackl (2009) observes that the fact that *most* is the superlative of *many* is not reflected in the standard semantic definitions; see (38) in **§4.2.2**. The superlative character of this determiner is not a peculiarity of English, although many languages do not have a literal counterpart and use a construction like 'the majority of' instead. His paper is the first to undertake the task of building a compositional semantics that takes the superlative character of the determiner seriously. The discussion below picks up the thread from **§5.6**.

Hackl's point of departure is an ambiguity of adjectival superlatives. On its absolute reading *the highest mountain* compares all mountains, possibly within a contextually relevant domain, say, in Wales. But the truth of the comparative/relative reading of (29) is only concerned with how the height of the mountain John climbed compares with the heights of the mountains other people climbed.

(29)   John climbed the highest mountain.

   a.   absolute reading: 'John climbed the highest among the mountains'

     b.   comparative/relative reading: 'John climbed a mountain that was higher than how high a mountain anyone else climbed'

There are two types of analyses of this ambiguity, carefully compared in Heim (2004). Heim (1985) and Szabolcsi (1986) localize the source in Logical Form: the *-est* component of the superlative takes DP-internal scope in the absolute reading and sentential scope in the relative reading. In contrast, Farkas and Kiss (2000) and Sharvit and Stateva (2002) argue that the two readings have the same LFs and the difference should be captured in terms of what is contextually relevant. Hackl implements the *-est*-extraction view with Heim's semantics:

(30)   a.   Absolute reading: $[\![$ [-est C]$_i$[d_i-high mountain] $]\!]$
         $= \lambda x \forall y [(y \in C \land y \neq x) \to max\{d : x \text{ is a } d\text{-high mountain}\} > max\{d : y \text{ is a } d\text{-high mountain}\}]$
   b.   Relative reading: $[\![$ [-est C]$_i$ climbed [d_i-high mountain] $]\!]$
         $= \lambda x \forall y [(y \in C \land y \neq x) \to max\{d : x \text{ climbed a } d\text{-high mountain}\} > max\{d : y \text{ climbed a } d\text{-high mountain}\}]$

A parallel ambiguity is exhibited by amount-superlative *most*: *most of the NP*. English favors two different forms of the DP for the two readings, whereas German and Hungarian employ the same form (*die meisten NP* and *a legtöbb NP*). Hackl does not address the English-internal difference and uses German examples.

(31)   John climbed most of the mountains (die meisten Berge).
       absolute: 'John climbed the majority of the mountains'

(32)   John climbed the most mountains (die meisten Berge).
       relative: 'John climbed more mountains than anybody else did'

So, how does the well-known proportional reading of *die meisten NP / most of the NP* come about? Hackl's key observation is that the proportional reading is identical to the absolute one, both with respect to truth conditions and with respect to the environments where they occur. This observation allows him to subsume the proportional reading of *die meisten / most of the* under the standard semantics for superlatives.

(33) $[\![$ MANY $]\!](d)(A) = \lambda x[A(x) \land |x| \geq d]$
      $[\![$ -EST $]\!]$ (C)(D)(x) is defined iff x has an alternative in C. If defined, $[\![$ -EST $]\!](C)(D)(x)$ is true iff
      $\forall y[(y \in C \land y \neq x) \to max\{d : D(d)(x)\} > max\{d : D(d)(y)\}]$

We focus on the absolute, i.e. proportional reading:

(34)   *most of the mountains*
      $[\![$ [-est C]$_i$ [d_i-many mountains] $]\!] =$

$$\lambda x \forall y [(y \in C \land y \neq x) \rightarrow$$
$$max\{d : mountains(x) \land |x| \geq d\} >$$
$$max\{d : mountains(y) \land |y| \geq d\}]$$

(34) requires that when the set of mountains is partitioned (exhaustively and disjointly divided) into pluralities, the cardinality of x be greater than the cardinality of any other plurality in the partition. This holds if and only if x contains at least 51% of the mountains, and the presupposition in (33) guarantees that x does not contain all the mountains. For good measure below is Hackl's interpretation of the relative reading, with the predicate *climbed* filled in for transparency:

(35) *the most mountains*
   [[[-est C]$_i$ [climbed [the$_\exists$ d_i-many mountains]]] =
   $\lambda x \forall y [(y \in C \land y \neq x) \rightarrow max\{d : \exists z[mountains(z) \land |z| \geq d \land$
   $x \; climb \; z]\} > max\{d : \exists z[mountains(z) \land |z| \geq d \; \land y \; climb \; z]\}]$

Notice now that *fewest of the NP / die wenigsten NP* does not have a proportional reading at all; for example, it cannot mean 'less than 50% of the NP'. As Hackl points out, that reading would require for $|x|$ to be smaller than the cardinality of any other plurality in the partition. If $|x|$ is at least 1 and as per presupposition there is another plurality in C, then $|x|$ is not the smallest. The largest plurality could vacuously satisfy the asserted condition but it would run afoul of the presupposition. The 'less than 50% of the NP' reading is perfectly coherent and capable of being true, so the fact that *fewest of the NP / die wenigsten NP* does not mean that can only be due to the fact that it is not produced by the grammatical algorithm that computes the meanings of superlatives. In contrast, the relative reading of *the fewest NP / die wenigsten NP*, which compares individuals with respect to numbers of mountains climbed, is safely in place.

Various aspects of the compositional analysis of *(the) most (of the)*-phrases remain to be explored. But significant progress has been made with making these phrases look like ordinary good citizens.

10.5 Counting quantifiers

Szabolcsi (1986) notices that superlatives on the relative reading are non-specific indefinites. This can be seen from their occurrence in existential *there* and relational *have* contexts.[91]

(36) a. #In whose plans were there the errors?
   b. In whose plans were there the most/fewest/costliest errors?
       'In whose plans were there more/fewer/costlier errors than in anyone else's plans?'

(37)   a. #Who has the nephews?
          b.   Who has the most/fewest/youngest nephews?
             'Who has more/fewer/younger nephews than anyone else?'

We may now add that relative superlative *the most* readily combines with binominal *each*. Imagine a situation with grown-ups and children, where the grown-ups give the individual children various numbers of books.

(38)   Who gave the children the most/fewest books each?
           'Who gave more/fewer books per child than how many books anyone else did?'

Contrast this with an absolute superlative:

(39)   #Who showed the children most of the books each?
           ought to mean 'Who showed each child a possibly different absolute majority of the books?'

Sutton (1993) characterized those quantifiers that host binominal *each* as counters; see **§8.4**. It appears that relative superlative *the most NP*, in contrast to the absolute superlative, is one of them.

What are counting quantifiers? Table 10.1 draws up a partial inventory. Notice that *two NP* and *many NP* occur in both columns. The suspicion is that when just the numeral part bears focus accent, the phrase definitely shares properties with modified numerals; in contrast, when the phrase bears no focus or the whole phrase is focused, it may or may not behave as a counting quantifier. Focus on the numeral in modified phrases will only be indicated by small capitals when its presence is specifically under discussion (cf. Krifka's work above). *No NP, not every NP, any NP, sm NP, more NP$_1$ than NP$_2$, each NP*, and bare plural *NP* are not included in either column. Some of them may fit, but we do not wish to make claims about them here. An exhaustive typology is not necessary for present purposes.

The significance of the two classes into which the binominal *each* data split quantifiers is further supported by observations about inverse scope in English (Liu 1997; Beghelli and Stowell 1997), and by constituent order in Hungarian (Szabolcsi 1995, 1997a). English modified numerals fall among the counting quantifiers, and they are poor inverse scope takers. The Hungarian counterparts of the English counting quantifiers all occur in Region 3 of the preverbal field, whereas the counterparts of the non-counters all occur in Region 1 or 2; cf. Table 8.1 in **§8.3**.[92]

One of Sutton's important observations, also made in Hackl (2009), is that the class of counting quantifiers cannot be delimited in truth-conditional terms. For example, notice that *more than 50% of the NP* and *most of the NP* receive the same interpretation in Barwise and Cooper

Table 10.1 *Counting vs. not counting quantifiers*

Counting q's in English	Not counting q's in English
more than two NP	the NP
less than two NP	a (certain) NP
exactly two NP	some NP
TWO/two NP	two NP
MANY/many NP	many NP
few NP	all of the NP
as many/few as six NP	these NP
at most/least two NP	every NP
two or more NP	both of the NP
more than 50% of the NP	most of the NP
the most NP	
and their partitive versions	and their partitive versions

(1981). However, as Sutton observes, the former but not the latter combines with binominal *each*:

(40)   The boys have seen more than 50% of the films each.

(41)   #The boys have seen most of the films each.

How come 'more than 50% of the NP' may serve as a counter? My guess is that from a grammatical perspective the noun *percent* (Hungarian *százalék*) is much like nouns denoting inalienable possessions; grammar does not recognize its specific mathematical content. 'More than 50% of the boys' is not unlike 'more than thirty-five legs of the centipede'.

Szabolcsi (1995, 1997a) proposes that the difference between Regions 1–2 versus Region 3 concerns the mode in which the quantifier operates; i.e. it is a procedural distinction. The inhabitants of Regions 1 and 2 are monotonically increasing quantifiers whose witness sets serve as logical subjects of predication. The combination of a Region 1–2-quantifier with a predicate asserts that the predicate holds, or does not hold, of that witness set or its elements. In contrast, the counting quantifiers that inhabit Region 3 specify the size of a participant of the atomic or plural event described by the verbal predicate in conjunction with the counting quantifier's restriction. For illustration recall examples (47) and (48) of **§8.3**, repeated below, that contain a quantifier that occurs in more than one region. There it was observed that *több, mint n NP* is unambiguously distributive in Region 2, but not in Region 3. The paraphrases below are slightly reworded to highlight the additional difference that is relevant to the present discussion.[93]

(42)   In Region 2: logical subject of predication
        Több, mint hat gyerek felemelte az asztalt.
        more than six child   up.lifted the table.acc
        'There is a set of more than six children such that each
        element of this set lifted up the table'

(43)   In Region 3: counter
        Több, mint hat gyerek emelte fel az asztalt.
        more than six child   lifted   up the table.acc
        'Greater than six is the number n such that there was an
        event of table-lifting by children whose collective agent,
        or the individual agents of its subevents, numbered n'

Positing a procedural distinction is not unique to this approach. The two interpretations above recall Brentano's categorical and thetic judgments; see Ladusaw (1995) for recent discussion. Likewise, Kamp and Reyle (1993) and other versions of dynamic semantics make a procedural distinction between truth-conditionally equivalent DPs. Unsurprisingly, logical subjects of predication correspond to discourse referents that support singular or plural anaphora.

Let us attempt to characterize logical subjects of predication and counting quantifiers exploiting the notions introduced earlier in this book.

(44)   An expression operates as a logical subject of predication if the
        output of its compositional interpretation is a witness set of the
        generalized quantifier it can be said to denote.

Recall from Chapter 7 that the values of our choice functions are witnesses of the pertinent generalized quantifiers. Therefore all expressions analyzed in terms of choice functions will qualify. But (44) covers a potentially wider range. Suppose that the choice-functional treatment is reserved for expressions that are capable of taking extra-wide existential scope. (44) allows for expressions that clause-internally operate as subjects of predication but do not take extra-wide scope, in case their non-choice-functional compositional interpretation delivers a witness set. If however it turns out that such cases do not exist, then (44) should be replaced by (45):

(45)   To be a logical subject of predication is to be the value of a
        (grammatically motivated) choice function.

It is more of an open question whether counting quantifiers can be given a uniform formal characterization. We will not try to decide; as a preliminary hypothesis, we may contemplate (46) or (47):

(46)   Counting quantifiers are "scope-splitters": they involve a distinct
        layer of degree (number, amount) quantification. Syntactically

or semantically significant sentence-level material may intervene between the two layers.

(47) In counting quantifiers degree (number, amount) alternatives are introduced by focus or by a *wh*-expression.

The scope-splitting approach is inspired by the Higginbotham–Cresti–Heim–Hackl line of work; the focusing approach is inspired by Krifka's work. The relevance of focus is corroborated by the fact that the inhabitants of Region 3 of the Hungarian preverbal field all have focus, or a focussed constituent. See §9.2 for some discussion of focus in Hungarian. Wedgwood (2005) explores the procedural distinctions in a Relevance Theory cum Dynamic Syntax framework.

10.6 Summary and experimental evidence

This chapter has discussed research that is very much in progress, aiming to devise compositional analyses for expressions that were left unanalyzed in classical work in generalized quantifier theory. Along the way systematic distinctions have been found in the distribution and in the interpretation of quantifier phrases that are truth-conditionally indistinguishable; some of these have been successfully attributed to differences in internal structure.

An interesting question is whether these finer distinctions have psycholinguistic correlates. Hackl (2009) and Koster-Moeller, Varvoutis, and Hackl (2008) have conducted experiments using a new paradigm, self-paced counting, making progress towards uncovering the specific ways in which speakers verify sentences involving one subclass of counting quantifiers, comparative quantifiers (*more than n NP, more than half of the NP*) as opposed to non-comparative *at least n NP* and *most of the NP.*

In incremental verification tasks involving self-paced counting participants are presented with dot-arrays and judge whether statements involving the quantifiers are true. The standard design of a self-paced counting array is to evenly distribute the targets and non-targets. (E.g. if the participant hears *Most/More than half of the dots are blue*, they will see a red dot and two blue dots, and then a blue dot and a red dot, then two blue dots, then a red and a blue, and so on.) This environment seems amenable to both "vote counting" (comparing the number of red to the number of blue dots) and "criterion counting" (counting up the number of blues), although "vote counting" is a bit easier. To test what verification strategies participants use the experimenter creates an environment that makes one kind of counting easy and the other difficult. One environment that has this effect is a "weighted" array, where either most of the blue dots come first, or most of the blue dots come in the second half of the array.

Seemingly denotationally equivalent quantifiers (e.g. *most* versus *more than half* and *more than six* versus *at least seven*) show different verification profiles: participants apparently use different counting strategies to verify the statements containing them. The difference in verification profiles can be related to a difference in the form of the quantifiers contrasted. In the standard design verifying sentences with *most* is overall easier than verifying those with *more than half*, but in a weighted environment *most* suddenly gets harder. Furthermore, there is no difference between the two weighted conditions for *more than half*, but there is for *most*, indicating that the ease of comparing targets and non-targets is a significant determinant for verifying *most*-statements, but not for *more than half*-statements. *Most* seems to trigger "vote counting"; *more than half* on the other hand seems to trigger "criterion counting". If these two quantifiers were equivalent, this would be unexpected. For modified numeral quantifiers (*more than six* versus *at least seven*) the particular numeral occurring in the quantifier plays a crucial role in defining the verification profile. Again, the authors conclude that this would be unexpected if the form of the quantifier were not a crucial determinant of the meaning.[94]

11

Clause-internal scopal diversity

The Montague/May/Hendriks-style approach has a single scope-assignment strategy and therefore predicts that all DPs have the same scope behavior. Starting with Chapter 6 we have seen that this prediction is incorrect; the recognition of this fact has played a key role in rethinking the treatment of quantifier phrases. Three main classes have emerged from the foregoing discussion. The first two classes, plural (in)definites and singular universals, both have unbounded existential scope, but the distributive vs. collective readings of (in)definites depend on the predicate, whereas *every NP* associates with a special functional head, Dist. The third class is that of counting quantifiers, which do not take extra-clausal scope. The three main classes also differ clause-internally. In languages like English, where quantifier scope is rarely disambiguated by word order and intonation, this manifests itself in differences in the ability to take inverse distributive scope.

This chapter supplements §**2.3.4** with a survey of the current generative syntactic approaches to clause-internal scope, with an emphasis on how they account for scopal diversity, and comments on how the treatment of scope relates to certain general assumptions of syntactic theory. We start with a quick recapitulation of the basic data in §**11.1** and a characterization of the feature-checking and the economy approaches in §**11.2**. They are discussed in some detail in §**11.3** and §**11.4**. §**11.5** concludes with cross-linguistic variation.

11.1 The basic facts

Most of the data in (1) through (6) have been introduced in previous sections.

Every NP and *each NP* are excellent inverse scope takers; see (1): they are poster children for Montague/May/Hendriks-style theories.

(1)   a.   More than one soprano sings in every show.
             OK 'every NP > more than one NP'
       b.   More than one soprano sings in each show.
             OK 'each NP > more than one NP'

Counters as direct objects or prepositional objects on the other hand do
not take inverse scope over subject *every NP*, e.g. (2a), although they may
scope over an *a(n)*-indefinite or another counter in subject position; see
(2b)–(2c). Much less known is the fact that a VP-internal direct-object–
indirect-object pair is properly ambiguous; see (3a)–(3b), after Takahashi
(2006):[95]

(2)   a.   Every soprano sings in more than one show.
             #'more than one NP > every NP'
       b.   A soprano sings in more than one show.
             OK 'more than one NP > a(n) NP'
       c.   At least two sopranos sing in more than one show.
             ? 'more than one NP > at least two NP'

(3)   a.   John submitted every paper to more than one journal.
             OK 'every NP > more than one NP'
             OK 'more than one NP > every NP'
       b.   John submitted more than one paper to every journal.
             OK 'more than one NP > every NP'
             OK 'every NP > more than one NP'

Downward monotonic DPs are especially reluctant to take inverse scope
(see Stabler 1997). Why this is so is not well-understood, but the observation explains a well-known but mysterious constraint on negative polarity
item licensing, namely, that the licensor must have the NPI in its scope in
virtue of its overt syntactic position (inverse scope due to LF-movement
does not suffice). If *no meal* cannot take inverse scope, it naturally cannot
license *ever* in (5a); the "overt syntax" qualification is not necessary.

(4)   A boy has missed no meal.
       #'No meal was missed by any boy'

(5)   a.   *He has ever missed no meal.
       b.   No meal/few meals has he ever missed.

Definite and indefinite plurals may take inverse distributive scope, but
not nearly as readily as *every NP*. The reasons are debated. They may lie
in the semantics of predicates, or in the burden such sentences place on
working memory; see the discussion in **§8.2**.

(6)   More than one soprano sings in those (six) shows.
       ? 'six NP > more than one NP'

Japanese, German, and Mandarin are sometimes called scope-freezing or scope-rigid languages because (at least on the canonical "Subject precedes Object" order) they do not allow inverse scope. See Hoji (1985); Aoun and Li (1993); Liu (1997); Pafel (2006); Richards (2008); and Wurmbrand (2008); also Bruening (2008) on Passamaquoddy. Likewise the double object construction exhibits scope freezing in English; see Larson (1990) and Bruening (2001). Unfortunately, not all descriptions of freezing comment on the behavior of quantifier phrases other than 'some NP' and 'every NP'. Hungarian is also a scope-freezing language in the sense that it rarely exhibits scope ambiguity, but it differs from the above type in that its surface constituent order specifically correlates with scope relations and not with grammatical functions. See the discussion below. How languages like Japanese, German, Passamaquoddy, Hungarian, etc. visibly classify their quantifiers and express particular readings in overt syntax should be an important source of information to those who approach the big universal questions by working on English, a language that rather more modestly covers up its methods of scope assignment.

11.2   The basic approaches

Two robustly different approaches to the observed clause-internal scopal diversity have been proposed. Both are discussed in some detail below.

One of the approaches belongs to the "cartographic" paradigm best known for Rizzi's (1997) analysis of the fine structure of the left periphery and Cinque's (1999) cross-linguistic study of adverbs and functional heads. On this view there exist a variety of functional projections that are dedicated to the checking of specific "morpho-semantic" features. Scope relations and sometimes surface order follow from the movement of operators to the specifiers of such functional projections in order to check features. Proponents of this approach typically also assume that different DPs take scope using different semantic mechanisms, discussed in Chapter 7 and in §10.5. See Beghelli and Stowell (1997) and Kayne (1998) for English, and Brody (1990), Kiss (1991, 1994), Szabolcsi (1997a), and Brody and Szabolcsi (2003) for Hungarian.

The other approach essentially maintains the assumption of a single uniform QR (see FOX 2002a for an overview). Whether proponents subscribe even to the basic "extra-wide-scoping indefinites vs. the rest" distinction is not clear. QR is regimented by Scope Economy (Fox 2000). The QR-plus-economy approach is not designed to capture differential scope behavior. When however quantifier phrases are assumed to have an articulated internal structure that is visible to external syntax, the peculiarities of their behavior become amenable to treatment in such terms, as demonstrated in Takahashi (2006) for comparative quantifiers.

Orthogonal to the above is the commonality that many if not most instances of inverse scope are now attributed to reconstruction, as opposed
to moving the inversely-scoping quantifier into a higher position than
the one scoped over. In terms of the copy-theory of movement, reconstruction amounts to the interpretation of a lower copy of a superficially
higher-positioned operator. This entails that representations carrying inverse readings are often ambiguous to a point (the ambiguity is resolved
if the uninterpreted copy is deleted):

(7)   Inverse scope via reconstruction/copy-interpretation:
        $[\ldots A_i \ldots [\ldots B \ldots [\ldots A_i \ldots]]]$
        'A > B' when the higher A_i is interpreted
        'B > A' when the lower A_i is interpreted

This is in marked contrast with the Montagovian strategy, where structures are at no time ambiguous. The copy-interpretation approach appears to originate with Aoun and Li (1993) and Hornstein (1995), and
characterizes theories as different as Beghelli and Stowell (1997), Johnson
and Tomioka (1997), Fox (2002a,b), and Takahashi (2006). I am not sure
whether the battle between the disambiguators and the reconstruction-
ists has ever been fought, or researchers have peacefully converged on the
realization that many movements motivated purely by scope assignment
can be dispensed with, but this position is now widely shared.[96]

Recent work has begun to employ shared structure (i.e. multi-domin-
ance) in syntax. Bachrach and Katzir (2006) use it for the explanation
of the scopal properties of right-node-raised quantifiers, which obey a
generalization that they state as follows:

(8)   Height Generalization: The scope of a shared quantifier in Right
        Node Raising is not clause-bound within each conjunct but is
        clause-bound above the conjunction.

Johnson (2007) addresses the fact that Trace Conversion (Fox 2002a)
makes determiners ambiguous. He invokes shared structure in proposing
that copies of α are one and the same α in different syntactic positions, and
combines this with a treatment of quantifiers along the lines of Elbourne
(2005) and the approach detailed in §8.3.

11.3   Scope as a by-product of feature checking

Beghelli and Stowell's (1997) analysis of distributive universals and plurals
has been reviewed in §8.2 and §8.3; this section focuses on their theory
in general. The view is that (in)definites, *wh*-phrases, distributive universals, and negative quantifiers check features in the specifiers of dedicated
functional projections (Referential Phrase, Complementizer Phrase, Dis-

tributive Phrase, Share Phrase, and Negative Phrase), whereas counting quantifiers do not move beyond their Case positions (Agreement Phrases), at least in English. Moreover, the two kinds of positions are interleaved in the syntax of English in a particular hierarchy, as follows:

(9)   English LF
$[_{RefP}\cdots[_{CP}\cdots[_{AgrSP}\cdots[_{DistP}\cdots[_{ShareP}\cdots[_{NegP}\cdots$
$[_{AgrIOP}\cdots[_{AgrOP}\cdots[_{VP}\cdots]]]]]]]]]$

Unmodified indefinites check features in RefP or ShareP, both of which are headed by existential quantifiers. In the former case they scope above, and in the latter case below, *every NP* and *each NP*, which check features in DistP, headed by a universal quantifier. RefP, DistP, and ShareP are operator positions. Once a phrase lands there it does not reconstruct for scope (as is generally the case with A-bar movement). It follows that such a phrase may only be outscoped by operators that land in higher positions. In contrast, counting quantifiers just check Case features, which means that they may reconstruct into lower positions of their chains for scope (as is generally the case with A-movement). The fact that the Case-position of the subject, AgrSP, is very high entails that even a counting-quantifier subject can always take widest scope; but counting quantifiers may also reconstruct into the scope of any other operator. The low positions of indirect and direct objects entail that counting-quantifier objects may only scope inversely over something that reconstructs into their scope.

The idea that some operators move into high operator positions and do not reconstruct while others remain in case-agreement positions and do reconstruct offers a plausible handle on the difference between scopally capable vs. scopally deficient quantifiers. The specific execution derives many of the complicated English scope data, but the strategic positioning of AgrSP is stipulative, and the system does not work quite as well for the interaction of two non-subject quantifiers; it definitely falls short of accounting for Takahashi's data in (3). Also, *a(n) NP* is not a counter but it readily reconstructs (unless it has a modifier like *certain*); it is not explained why.

The syntax of scope in Hungarian can be seen to directly support many of Beghelli and Stowell's ideas, although not the role of AgrP positions in the syntax of scope. It was recognized as early as in Kiss (1981) and Szabolcsi (1981) that topics, foci, and quantifiers occupy distinct positions in the preverbal field in Hungarian. Subsequent research uncovered the finer distribution of quantifier phrases. It turns out that there is a remarkably good match between the positions Beghelli and Stowell (1997) postulate for English LF and those that had been identified for Hungarian surface structure, both in terms of what operators are grouped together and in terms of the ordering of the positions. In Table 11.1 the first row specifies

Table 11.1 *Positions in the preverbal field in Hungarian*

RefP	DistP	ShareP/AgrP		
Topic	Quantifier	Focus	Verb	Postverbal field
Region 1	Region 2	Region 3	Verb	Postverbal field
Hat fiút	minden tanár	egynél többször	akart	megbuktatni.
six boy.acc	every teacher.nom	one.loc more.times	wanted	flunk.inf

the labels of the Beghelli-Stowell-projections, the second row the widely used labels of the distinguished positions in Hungarian linguistics, and the third row the pre-theoretical "regions" in terms of which this book has referred to the data. The fourth row gives one example sentence. For additional information regarding the membership of the three regions, see Tables 8.1, 10.1, and the discussion of counting quantifiers in §10.5. Regions 1 and 2 can be multiply filled; Region 3 may host only one phrase at a time.[97] Grammatical functions (subject, object, etc.) do not play a role in the ordering. Contrastive topics are omitted from the left edge and are ignored in the discussion.

In the preverbal field left-to-right order translates into potential distributive scopal order: A can make B referentially dependent iff A precedes B. (In other words, an appropriate B can be independent of an A to its left, but cannot make an A to its left dependent.) The sentence in Table 11.1 is unambiguously interpreted as (10):

(10)   'there are six boys such that every teacher wanted to flunk them more than once'

Alternative preverbal orderings of the same material are unacceptable:

(11)   a.   *Minden tanár egynél többször hat fiút akart megbuktatni.
            b.   *Egynél többször hat fiút minden tanár akart megbuktatni.

The unacceptability of (11a)–(11b) does not have to do with scope relations or grammatical functions. The problem is that individual quantifiers occur in the wrong preverbal regions. The fact that *hat fiút* in (11a) occurs immediately preceding a verb whose infinitival complement is postverbal entails that it is in Region 3 (bears focus). This prevents *egynél többször* from occurring in Region 3, which is its only possible position in the preverbal field. This problem is avoided in (12) by relegating *hat fiút* 'six boys' to the postverbal field (more on the postverbal field below). The distributive scopal order matching the left-to-right order in (11a) can be expressed by (12):

(12) Minden tanár   egynél többször   akart   hat fiút
every   teacher.nom one.loc more.times wanted six   boy.acc
megbuktatni.
flunk.inf
'for every teacher there was more than one occasion where he/she
wanted to flunk six boys'

The second example, (11b), suffers from several positional problems.
One is that *minden tanár* occurs in Region 3, instead of Region 2. This
is unacceptable independently of whether or not the quantifier is in interaction with another; see below. (Region 3 is not the only possible source
of problems, but these are the easiest to illustrate.)

(13)   a.   *Minden tanár   akar   aludni.
           every   teacher wants sleep.inf
   b.   Minden tanár aludni akar.
   c.   Aludni akar minden tanár.

The distributive scopal order matching the left-to-right order in (11b)
could be expressed as follows:

(14)   Egynél többször   akart   megbuktatni hat fiút   minden
one.loc more.times wanted flunk.inf   six   boy.acc every
tanár.
teacher.nom
'there was more than one occasion where there were six potentially different boys whom every teacher wanted to flunk'

In sum, the correct placement of quantifiers is part and parcel to the
basic syntax of Hungarian, just as the fronting of at least one *wh*-phrase
in constituent questions is part and parcel to the basic syntax of English.

The fact that the potential scopal dependency order in the preverbal
field is isomorphic to left-to-right order calls for a way to assign scope
that is sensitive to syntax, but not necessarily to grammatical functions.
Because quantifiers do not simply line up in an arbitrary desired scopal
order, and occurrence in particular positions is not contingent on making
a truth-conditional difference, feature-checking movement resembling *wh*-
movement seems a fitting analysis. Consonant with this is the fact that
when a quantifier occurs in the specifier of a larger DP, the containing DP
inherits its positional requirements. *Minden tanár kalapja* 'every teacher's
hat' occurs in the same position as *minden tanár* (Region 2), and *egynél
több tanár kalapja* 'more than one teacher's hat' occurs in the same position as *egynél több tanár* (Region 3). Brody and Szabolcsi (2003) define
scope in terms of featural dominance, not in terms of c-command, and
subsume such data under feature inheritance and pied piping.

We briefly mention that the structure of the postverbal field is debated. Szabolcsi (1997a), Kiss (1998), and Brody and Szabolcsi (2003) propose that the sequence of operator positions reiterates itself above each of the inflectional projections (although each of the three papers offers a different execution of the reiteration idea). On this view postverbal quantifiers are in operator positions, but not necessarily all within the same sequence. Preverbal operators typically scope over the postverbal field, but Brody and Szabolcsi also point out two distinct ways in which a postverbal quantifier may take inverse distributive scope over a preverbal one. One involves alternative phrase-internal orders of the specifier and its sister, the other involves reconstruction. Reconstruction produces some readings that cannot be expressed otherwise, but it also gives rise to some ambiguities. (Naturally, postverbal indefinites may also take wide existential scope over the preverbal field, without inducing referential dependencies there.) Surányi (2003a,b) and Kiss (2008) reject postverbal operator positions.

The feature-checking approach to quantifiers shares two important problems with Cinque's (1999) approach to adverbs. Based on the data of over 100 languages Cinque postulates a universal hierarchy of ca. 40 different semantically significant functional heads in whose specifiers the various adverbs occur. One evident question is what the order in the hierarchy follows from. Ernst (2002) proposes that the order derives from semantics, which sounds plausible, although Nilsen (2003) argues that Ernst's particular analysis is only partially viable; see Butler (2007) for an alternative.

On the other hand, Nilsen (2003) points out that Cinque's method of establishing the hierarchy crucially assumes that the order is linear (transitive, antisymmetric, and total), whereas adverb order in Norwegian is not linear. Specifically, Nilsen observes that some adverbs are polarity sensitive and thus must scope either above or below negation. Therefore they are ordered with respect to negation and, in the presence of negation, with respect to each other. In the absence of negation however their order is free.

Similarly, the feature-checking approach to quantifiers stipulates that topical plurals precede distributive singulars and those precede focalized counters. Here too it is natural to expect a semantic explanation, although none is known yet. On the other hand, Bernardi and Szabolcsi (2008: Part II) show that a larger set of Hungarian quantifiers cannot be totally ordered. They argue, like Nilsen does for adverbs, that quantifier positions form a partially ordered set (reflexive, transitive, antisymmetric). This means that category requirements are checked for subsumption, not for identity. This raises larger questions because, unlike many other theories, Chomskyan generative syntax does not recognize partial orderings.

11.4   Scope restrictions, internal structure, economy

One prominent line of recent research involves Scope Economy, or Interface Economy (Fox 2000; Reinhart 2006). The view is that covert scope shifts, such as QR in English are allowed only if they make a truth-conditional difference, i.e. if they are motivated by needs of the syntax/semantics interface. At first blush it may seem that this principle does not affect interpretive possibilities. But it does, because it may block a necessary intermediate step in the derivation of some structure that would carry a distinctive interpretation (if it could be derived). Fox (2000) uses this principle to explain the lack of ambiguity in (17).

(15)   An aide admires every politician.
        (ambiguous)

(16)   An aide admires every politician, and a journalist does too.
        (ambiguous)

(17)   An aide admires every politician, and every journalist does too.
        (not ambiguous, the same aide admires all the politicians)

(17) is not ambiguous, because (i) VP-ellipsis requires a parallelism between the two conjuncts, and (ii) QR in the second clause would not make a truth-conditional difference and is therefore disallowed.[98]

See §11.5 on Bobaljik and Wurmbrand (2008), a recent approach to economy that pertains to both covert and overt scope shifts and focuses on mismatches between Phonetic Form and Logical Form.

Apart from why the distributive scope of *every NP* is clause-bounded (§2.3.4 and §8.3.5), the central descriptive question that calls for an answer is why decreasing and counting quantifiers are so much poorer inverse scope takers than *every NP*.

Takahashi (2006) argues that the reluctance of comparative quantifiers to take inverse scope over the subject follows from their decomposition, in view of Scope Economy and the Intervention Constraint that was illustrated in (28b) of §10.3. In contrast, derivations involving *every NP* do not involve the separation of a DegreeP from its restriction and thus they are not subject to Intervention; moreover the semantic vacuity patterns are naturally different. This will explain the greater clause-internal scopal freedom of *every NP*.

We are considering Takahashi's proposal here, as opposed to the chapter on modified numerals, because it seems like an excellent methodological model of how the internal structure of a phrase can be used to predict its detailed external behavior.

The main ingredients of the specific account are as follows:

(18)   a.   The decomposition of *more than n NP* into *-er than n* and
               t-many NP (Heim 2001; Hackl 2000).
        b.   Quantifier Raising forced by type mismatches, subject to
               Shortest Move.
        c.   Optional Quantifier Lowering, subject to Shortest Move.
        d.   Shortest Move: QR/QL targets the closest node of type t
               (Fox 2000).
        e.   Intervention constraint: A quantificational DP cannot inter-
               vene between DegreeP and its trace (Kennedy 1999, Heim
               2001, and much literature on weak islands).
        f.   Scope Economy: Covert QR/QL cannot be semantically vac-
               uous (Fox 2000).
        g.   Results regarding when scope commutativity obtains with
               comparative quantifiers (Heim 2001).

As Takahashi points out, while direct-object comparative quantifiers
do not take inverse scope over a universally quantified subject, they do
take inverse scope over a vP-internal universal quantifier.

(19)   a.   Every student read more than one paper.
               #'more than one NP > every NP'
        b.   John submitted more than one paper to every journal.
               OK 'more than one NP > every NP'
        c.   John submitted every paper to more than one journal.
               OK 'more than one NP > every NP'

The reason will be that the two internal arguments are equidistant from
the closest node of type t, i.e. vP (see Bruening 2001) and so Shortest
Move does not affect their interaction. So Takahashi's immediate goal is
to explain (19a).

Takahashi follows Hackl's analysis of comparative quantifiers. When
decomposed, the two parts of *more than three books* might in principle
enter into three configurations with a subject quantifier, notated as QP
below. The fourth option (not shown) is certainly unavailable, because
t-many books contains a trace of *-er than three* and therefore cannot
outscope it.

(20)

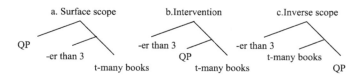

The plain inverse reading is out, because it would require the subject (notated as QP) to lower into the scope of the object crossing two quantifiers (the parts of *more than 3 books*). This violates Shortest Move, since both involve a node of type t. Also, the subject cannot lower before the object decomposes into two parts, because obligatory movements (here: decomposition) must precede optional ones. If they did not, the type clash that makes decomposition obligatory would prevent the movement from making a truth-conditional difference (Fox 2000: 26). So the lowering of the subject could at best proceed in two steps. The task is to show that the step involving QP between *-er than three* and *t-many books* is impossible. If it is impossible, it cannot be part of a legitimate derivation. It is indeed ruled out by Intervention.

Takahashi's more general goal is to show that the stipulative Intervention Constraint follows from Scope Economy, in conjunction with results as to when the scopal order between *-er than n* and particular intervening operators makes a truth-conditional difference, also including *less than n NP* as well as interaction with negation. The overall finding is that the predictions of the Intervention Constraint account and the Scope Economy account largely overlap but are not identical, each having an edge in relation to some data.

Because comparative quantifiers are not alone in being poor inverse scope takers, it would be important to see how Takahashi's approach fares for those data.

Going back to Hungarian, Takahashi's approach would account for some of the contrasts. If the fact that counting quantifiers bear focus accent ensures that they immediately precede the verb, Takahashi's reasoning regarding scope-split will explain why they do not take inverse scope over operators that precede them. On the other hand, the fact that the other operators line up in the order they do and that they do not freely take inverse scope among them does not seem to follow. So it remains to be seen whether applying Takahashi's approach to the counter vs. others contrast is a good partial solution, or perhaps it does not pick out a natural class.

11.5   Cross-linguistic hypotheses

In the early 1990s many researchers became aware that different quantifiers exhibit different scopal behavior. This observation served as a stepping stone for the differentiated analyses of quantifier phrases that many of these chapters have surveyed, but the results are fragmentary as regards scope itself.

Likewise much has been learned about the cross-linguistic differences in quantifier scope behavior, but no theory to my knowledge spans the full spectrum. Kayne (1998) proposes, somewhat programmatically, that quantifier scope in English is assigned in overt syntax, much like it is in Hungarian, but further leftward movements mask the results.

Williams (2003) offers a theory of Shape Conservation to account for the cross-linguistic variation in how languages use overt syntax to represent either case or scope relations.[99] Bobaljik and Wurmbrand (2008) address a question similar to Williams's in asking why some languages (like English) abound in scope ambiguities whereas others (like German and Japanese) severely restrict them. Their main conclusions are as follows:

(21)   There exist 'soft' constraints (economy conditions) that value a particular type of correspondence between LF and PF representations. For example, Scope Transparency requires that scope at LF be matched by precedence at PF.

(22)   These constraints are unidirectional: LF (broadly construed) is calculated first, and determines PF (surface word order).

(23)   Scope rigidity (the apparent absence of QR) is not a property of languages, but of specific configurations, and the distribution of rigidity effects is (largely) predictable from independent variation in the syntactic resources of various languages (e.g. possibilities for scrambling). There is no ±QR parameter.

The existence of both German/Japanese-style and Hungarian-style scope rigidity seems compatible with this proposal, but the proposal as it stands does not yet shed light on the nature of the difference between them.

12

Towards a compositional semantics of quantifier words

In the past decade different lines of research have been converging on the claim that there is no sharp demarcation line in grammar corresponding to word boundaries. One such line is Distributed Morphology, which argues for "syntactic hierarchical structure all the way down" (see Halle and Marantz 1994, and a more recent overview in HARLEY AND NOYER 2003). Another line leading to similar results was initiated in Kayne (2000, 2005a). This expansive view of syntax also converges with recent work at the syntax/semantics interface that has been busy dissecting items that traditional generalized quantifier theory took to be unanalyzed primitives; much of the second half of this book has surveyed such work. The closely related literature on polarity items and free-choice items, not reviewed here, is another rich source of decompositional analyses. Higginbotham (1991) is one of the early examples, with an analysis of *whether* as the *wh*-counterpart of *either*.

It seems useful to formulate the general thrust of this work, even though it is very programmatic at the moment:

(1)   Compositional analysis cannot stop at the word level.

This contrasts with the more traditional strategy, which does not shy away from postulating fairly complex semantics for lexical items, but does not systematically strive to link their ingredients to morpho-syntactic components of the lexical items or to account for all the morphemes in evidence. A striking example is the determiner *most*, because its being the superlative of *many* and *more* is uncontroversial. Yet, the first attempt to derive the well-known truth-conditional content in a compositional fashion is Hackl (2009); see §**5.6** and §**10.4**.

The present chapter will survey some further very recent research in this spirit, directed specifically at universal quantifiers. Some of the work is primarily syntactic, but of course compositional semantics must interpret what is there in the syntax, and the proposals to be discussed will prove to be directly relevant. Beyond specific details two larger semantic questions emerge. One pertains to where quantifier domain restriction is anchored in syntax and whether its locus is cross-linguistically invariant. Another is how the composition of quantifier words meaning 'every' and 'some' reflects their relationship to other fundamental operators, such as those meaning 'and' and 'or'. The discussion will be based on work directed at Lillooet, Mandarin, Modern Greek, Hungarian, German, Swedish, Japanese, Korean, and Malayalam, with occasional glimpses at English.

12.1   Is there interesting syntax in and around universal quantifiers?

Chapters 7 and 8 argued that sentences involving quantifier phrases such as *every dragon* are built in the following semi-formal steps:

(2)   *dragon'* $f(Pow(dragon'))$
          every   sends *every dragon* to Spec, DistP
          Dist' $\lambda P \lambda Q \forall x[x \in P][Q(x)]$
          Every dragon coughed' $\forall x[x \in f(Pow(dragon'))][cough'(x)]$

The NP *dragon* denotes one element of the powerset of dragons that a contextually given choice function f selects. The fact that the set of dragons quantified over is selected by a choice function (which could be Skolemized in other examples) captures the domain restriction. What the particular choice function is must be clearly contextually given: it is not enough for the existence of some choice function to be asserted or presupposed. According to §7.2.3 this is what distinguishes *Every dragon coughed* from *Some dragons coughed*, although both sentences can be true when every element of a proper subset of all the world's dragons coughed. The word *every* is not a universal quantifier; it merely signals that the set of dragons picked by f is going to be quantified over by a phrase-external universal quantifier; in the jargon of one kind of syntax, *every* sends the phrase *every dragon* to the Specifier of Distributive Phrase (DistP) to check a [dist] feature. On this proposal, the universal quantifier is the head of DistP.

Providing that this is by and large correct, can we say more about the compositional derivation of the phrase *every dragon* and its relatives, in English and cross-linguistically? Unlike modified numeral phrases such as *more than five dragons*, whose syntactic complexity is visible to the naked eye, the internal syntax of phrases such as *every dragon* initially seems quite banal. It turns out that there is more interesting syntax in them than meets the eye.

12.2 The view from Lillooet: quantifier words operate on DP

Matthewson (1999: 109) puts forth the following proposal, by now familiar from Chapter 7:

(3) a. All non-polarity determiners are obligatorily interpreted as variables which range over choice functions.
     b. The polarity determiner is not interpreted as a variable that ranges over choice functions.
     c. The choice-function variables are always existentially closed at the highest level.

She specifically argues that St'át'imcets (Lillooet Salish) encodes the distinction between the two kinds of determiner, discontinuous *(t)i ... a* being a marker of the choice-functional interpretation, while *ku* is a polarity determiner. Matthewson (2001) uses *i ... a* to make a novel proposal regarding the composition of quantifier phrases. She observes that all argumental phrases in Lillooet require the presence of *i ... a*, and conversely, this element only occurs with arguments. Matthewson dubs *i ... a* a determiner, D, but emphasizes that the label has no particular significance.

(4) i   smúlhats-a   smúlhats
     det woman-det   woman
     'the/a woman, argument' vs. 'the/a woman, predicate'

The claim directly relevant to present concerns is that quantifier words must combine with an argumental DP: a nominal flanked by *i ... a*:

(5)

Matthewson translates *tákem* and *zí7zeg* variably as 'all', 'every', and 'each'; *cw7it* is 'many'. In the data of Matthewson (1999) *i ... a* may actually flank *zí7zeg* itself, e.g. *i zí7zeg'-a pukw* 'each book' in her (48), or the noun: *zí7zeg' i smelhmúlhats-a* 'each woman' in her (47), or *i ... a* can be entirely absent: *zí7zeg' smelhmúlhats* 'each woman' in her (46), in addition to other constructions in which *zí7zeg* participates. In unmodified numeral indefinites where *i . . . a* is present it appears to consistently flank the numeral, not the noun, e.g. *i án' was-a sqaycw* 'two men' in her (39). This variation in the attachment site of *i . . . a* may be relevant to the compositional semantics (see §**12.3**); I restrict attention to *tákem* 'every, all'. All the 1999 *tákem*-data conform to the 2001 claim.

Regarding the compositional semantics, Matthewson (2001) proposes that the noun is first pluralized by Link's (1983) *-operator. Because plural morphology is not obligatory on the surface, * is the denotation of an abstract plural feature. D combines with *N and returns one plural individual from the join semi-lattice. *Tákem* universally quantifies over the atoms of this plural individual. The head of DP, *i . . . a*, which delivers the plural individual argument of *tákem* ensures that the complement of Q is an argument, not a predicate, makes the denotation of this argument specific or contextually unique, and restricts the domain of quantification. (We return to the argument-maker property of *i . . . a* below. Specificity or contextual givenness follows from the widest scoping choice-functional interpretation. The assimilation of quantifier-domain restriction to choice-functional interpretation was discussed in Chapter §**7.2.3**.)

Matthewson (2001: 153–154) points out that her analysis would be fully compatible with the choice function being contextually given as opposed to existentially closed, or with using an iota-operator instead of a choice function (i.e. an epsilon-operator). What matters to her is that specificity and domain restriction are achieved in a way that makes the complement of the quantifier word denote an entity (type e), not a set (type $\langle e, t \rangle$). On her analysis quantifier words are of type $\langle e, \langle \langle e, t \rangle, t \rangle \rangle$, not $\langle \langle e, t \rangle, \langle \langle e, t \rangle, t \rangle \rangle$, as in generalized quantifier theory.

On this basis Matthewson puts forth the interesting proposal that by taking the cue from Lillooet in analyzing quantifier words in English (French, Italian, etc.) one can make better sense of their distribution and interpretation. She first considers the fact that the majority of quantifier words enter into overt partitive constructions. The contrasts below reflect what is known as the Partitive Constraint:

(6)   most/many/some/three/few/all/both **of the (ten) chiefs**

(7)   *most/many/some/three/few/all/both of **chiefs/ten chiefs/every chief**

The complement of partitive *of* must be a definite plural; see Ladusaw (1982) and PETERS AND WESTERSTÅHL (2006: Sections 4.6 and 7.11). Ladusaw proposes that the complement denotes a group of individuals, and the role of *of* is to convert this group into a set that the quantifier word (semantic determiner) can operate on. On Matthewson's analysis *of* can be meaningless; as seen from Lillooet, the complements of quantifier words are always definite/specific plural individuals. This of course entails that the same holds even when no overt partitive construction is present. In what is probably the first illuminating discussion of these data she proposes that *all* and *most* modify bare plurals. Pulling together well-known and novel observations she points out that the distribution and interpretation of *all NP* and *most NP* matches that of bare plurals on the generic reading (Partee 1995; Brisson 1998; Gil 1995) or on Condoravdi's (1994) so-called functional reading, known for her haunted campus example. They contrast with *all (of) the NP* and *most of the NP*. Below are some examples with *all*; Matthewson suggests that the *most*-data are more complicated but the basic pattern is the same.

(8)   a.   Desks are brown.
      b.   All desks are brown.
      c.   #All pages in this book were torn.
      d.   All the pages in this book were torn.

(9)   a.   I admire linguists.
      b.   I admire all linguists.
      c.   #I talked to all linguists.
      d.   I talked to all the linguists.

(10)   In 1985 there was a ghost haunting the campus. . .
      a.   Students were aware of the danger.
           'the students on campus', not 'there were students who'
      b.   All students were aware of the danger.

Matthewson adopts Chierchia's (1998) version of Carlson's (1977) theory that bare plurals in English denote kinds and, therefore, individuals. (Focus-sensitive *all*, as in *There were all* WOMEN *at the bar* in §4.2.2, is likewise compatible with Carlson's kind-based analysis of the existential reading of bare plurals.)

The quantifier word *every* is problematic for this analysis, because it always takes a singular complement and never a definite DP. If *every* is a determiner and selects the individual corresponding to the maximal contextually salient subset of the set denoted by NP, it is similar to *the*. But then what accounts for the distributive interpretation of *every linguist*? Here Matthewson proposes to follow Beghelli and Stowell (1997) and Szabolcsi (1997a) in assuming that *every* merely associates its DP with a distributive operator; it is not a distributive operator itself. In sum, the contrasting structures she proposes are as follows. The indices on syntactic categories indicate semantic types.

(11)

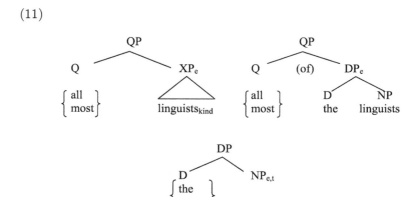

12.3　A closer look at determiners: Mandarin, Modern Greek, and Hungarian

Matthewson (2001) attributes a rather complex role to the determiner *i* ... *a*: its output is (i) argumental, (ii) of type *e*, (iii) maximal, and (iv) context-dependent. She moreover glosses over some variation in the attachment of *i* ... *a* in her earlier data. Giannakidou (2004) and Cheng (2008) single out particular aspects of the analysis of Lillooet for adoption in generalizing the proposal to other languages, Modern Greek and Mandarin among them.

Cheng's (2008) starting point is Lin, Jo-Wang's (1998) analysis of Mandarin *dōu*, as in (12):

(12)　Měi-ge　　　xuéshēng *(dōu) mǎi-le　shū.
　　　every-classifier student　**dou**　buy-perf book
　　　'Every student bought a book'

Měi is typically glossed as 'every'. It requires the presence of *dōu*, normally glossed as 'all'. Following Beghelli and Stowell (1997) Lin, Jo-Wang proposed that *měi* is like English *every* in that it is not a distributive operator; it merely carries a [dist] feature. The real distributive operator is *dōu*.

Cheng notes, drawing from Lin, Tzong-Hong (1998) and Huang, Shi-Zhe (1996) that *dōu* is possible in non-distributive contexts, and that *měi* can sometimes do without *dōu*, but in its absence requires an element like *zhèr* 'here':

(13)　Tāmén dōu yīqǐ　　lái.
　　　they　**dou** together come
　　　'All of them came together'

(14) ⟨Zhèr⟩ Měi yī-ge   chúshī ⟨dōu⟩ zuò-le   yī-daò
      here every one-classifier chef **dou** make-perf one-classifier
      cài.
      dish
      'Every chef here made a dish'

Cheng concludes that *dōu* is not a distributive operator; instead, it is
a definite determiner, contributing familiarity, maximality, and domain
restriction. In line with this, the optional presence of *dōu* with weak determiners makes the interpretation specific or definite. *Měi* on the other
hand is indeed a universal, and it demands domain restriction, which may
be accomplished by *dōu* or *zhèr* 'here'. In this respect *měi* is like other
strong determiners, such as *dàbùfèn* 'most' and *suǒyǒu* 'all'.

Dōu is in VP-adjoined position. As long as it was considered a distributive operator, this did not raise a problem. But, Cheng observes, the
definite determiner analysis makes this fact surprising – unless Sportiche's
Split-DP hypothesis is adopted. According to this hypothesis verbs take
NPs as arguments, and determiners are always generated in a separate
layer, somewhere outside VP; see §9.4. In languages like French and English NP typically raises in overt syntax to join its D; in Mandarin it
apparently does not. In Cheng's view the Split-DP hypothesis may offer
a new way to look at languages that are traditionally thought not to have
determiners, like Mandarin.

Giannakidou (2004) argues that familiarity and the restriction of the
domain of quantification are not necessarily expressed on the complement of the quantifier, as Stanley and Szabó (2000) and, following them,
Matthewson would have it; it may be expressed on the determiner, as is
proposed in Westerståhl (1985). According to Giannakidou, the sole function of *i . . . a* is to embody familiarity by contributing a context-variable.
When it attaches to NP *i . . . a* effectively produces a definite generalized quantifier, which is then shifted to a predicate by a "silent *of*". In
other words, *i . . . a* is not a predicate-to-individual shifter. Giannakidou
observes that *i . . . a* can alternatively attach to the universal quantifier
word *zíʔzeg* (see above), and in many languages the attachment of the definite article to the quantifier word is the norm. Such a language is Modern
Greek, where for example 'each' is composed of the definite article (with
gender agreement) plus *kathe* 'every':

(15) o   kathe fititis
      the.masc.sg every student
      'each student'

Thus, Giannakidou argues, Modern Greek expresses domain restriction
on the quantifier word (semantic determiner), and Lillooet has both ty-

pological options available. Etxeberria (2008) supports the possibility of domain restriction on the semantic determiner based on Basque.

There may be alternative ways to look at the fact that the definite determiner is sometimes higher and sometimes lower than quantifier words. Definite articles in Hungarian initially seem to be in complementary distribution with quantifier words. But both obligatorily surface when something linearly intervenes between them, and so it becomes clear that QPs are dominated by a DP layer, headed by *a(z)* 'the' (Szabolcsi 1994). One eligible intervener that reveals the co-occurrence is a nominative pronominal possessor. Because personal pronouns never take articles, the definite article unambiguously belongs to the larger construction:

(16)   az én   minden / legtöbb / ezen szavam
        the I-nom every / most   / this word.poss.1sg
        'every/most/this word(s) of mine'

Szabolcsi (1994) draws a syntactic parallelism between DP and CP, assimilating D to C in its subordinator (argument-maker) function.[100] She contrasts argumental DPs not with predicates but with vocatives, the analogues of main clauses. She observes that definite articles are cross-linguistically absent from vocatives, just as subordinating complementizers are absent from main clauses. A simple illustration comes from languages or dialects in which proper names have definite articles (German, Modern Greek, Portuguese, Hungarian, etc.):

(17)   a.   Der Hans kommt.
              'Hans is coming'

        b.   (*Der) Hans, komm her!
              'Hans, come here'

She likens quantifier words to clause-type indicators (interrogative, declarative, etc.). Many languages, Korean, Japanese, Kashmiri, and Hungarian among them, systematically lexicalize subordinators and clause-type indicators separately. A Korean example:

(18)   Bill-un [John-i   wa-ss-**nya-ko**]   mwule-ss-**ta**.
        Bill-top John-nom come-past-**interrog-subord** ask-past-**decl**
        'Bill asked if John came'

In the same spirit, Hungarian lexicalizes D and Q separately. *A(z)*, the item glossed as 'the', is not a definite article in the traditional semantic sense, just a subordinator. Definiteness is encoded by a phonetically null feature [def]; Szabolcsi (1994) places [def] in the same position as Q-words. The relation between *a(z)* and 'every', 'most', 'this', and [def] is analogous to the matching relation between *that* and finiteness vs. *for* and non-finiteness in English. The subordinator D that co-occurs with indefinites in Hungarian is phonetically null.

Focusing on the determiner–quantifier issue and setting aside the rest of the DP–CP analogy, putting Hungarian together with Lillooet one might obtain (19). The high D2 is what Szabolcsi (1994) and the related syntax literature call D. The low D1 is what Matthewson (2001) calls D, but it is now stripped of its argument-maker function:

(19)

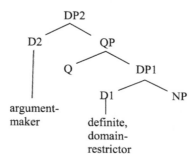

When a language does not have three separate overt elements corresponding to D1, Q, and D2, one may think of what overt elements it does have either as mono-functional heads that are accompanied by null heads in the other positions, or as portmanteau words that spell out multiple heads, possibly glummed together by head movement. The predictions of the two analyses could be distinguished if parts of the structure undergo movement, but this does not concern us here. Relevant to us is the fact that the argument-maker and the maximalizer/domain-restrictor functions are performed by different heads. It is then possible for one language (Hungarian) to possess an overt argument-maker D2, and another (Lillooet, as in the examples Matthewson 2001 discusses) an overt maximalizer/domain-restrictor D1. This would reconcile the high D vs. low D data. But even with argument-making factored out, Matthewson, Giannakidou, and Cheng attribute rather complex activities to D. Definiteness (maximalization) and context-dependency (domain-restriction) are not logically inseparable and thus need not be ensured by the same operator. It may be necessary to add a new player.

Which D does the Modern Greek definite article represent? Its surface position recalls the Hungarian argument-maker. But Greek also differs from Hungarian in that the article bears agreement morphemes. In §12.4 a proposal will be reviewed that pays special attention to languages whose definite articles carry agreement morphology, such as German and Modern Greek.

12.4   And finally, the deep end: diving into quantifier words in German

The line of research reviewed above makes it natural to look for syntactic structure, and thus compositionality, inside quantifier words as well. Sometimes etymology makes it clear that the word is composed of several relevant morphemes. Take German *jeder, jede, jedes* 'every'. It consists of the independently known distributive particle *je*, the *d-* of the definite article plus, somewhat surprisingly, adjectival inflection. Notice that its agreement morphemes are not identical to the ones that articles followed by nouns take:

(20)   je - d - er Mann   cf.   gut-er Mann   vs.   der Mann
          je - d - e Frau   cf.   gut-e Frau   vs.   die Frau
          je - d - es Kind   cf.   gut-es Kind   vs.   das Kind

The question is whether such facts have synchronic syntactic significance. Leu (2008, 2009) argues that they provide the key to the internal syntax of determiners, broadly speaking. His starting point is the syntax of the determiner/adjective interaction.[101]

German has two different adjectival declensions: the so-called strong one in indefinites (with agreement, to be glossed as AgrA) and the so-called weak one in definites. In definite DPs the strong adjectival declension appears on the article instead. Updating an analysis by Milner and Milner (1972), Leu proposes to relate these in the following way. Definites reflect the original "article > agreement > adjective" hierarchy. Agreement attaches to the article. The notation xAP, as earlier, stands for an unspecified adjectival projection.[102]

(21)   d-er   gute Wein
          the-AgrA good wine
          [$_{xAP}$ d- ... AgrA ... Adj ...]

Indefinites have no article in xAP. The adjective moves into initial position. Agreement attaches to the moved adjective.

(22)   gut-er   Wein
          good-AgrA wine
          [$_{xAP}$ Adj$_i$ ... AgrA ... ~~Adj$_i$~~ ...]

Leu observes that not only run-of-the-mill adjectives may occupy these two different positions: certain quantifier words do too. Swiss German *bäid-* 'both' (German *beid-*) is an example. Observe that (23) replicates the (21) pattern in the plural: strong declension appears on the initial article *di*, followed by the quantifier in its weak form *bäidä*; (24) replicates the (22) pattern: the quantifier is in initial position and carries strong declension: *bäidi.*[103] (As was mentioned in §8.2, in Swiss German the first pattern is optionally distributive, whereas the second one is obligatorily so. Colloquial Dutch lacks the same interpretive correlates.)

(23) **D-i**   **bäidä** mäitli hend es piär trunkä.
the-AgrA both   girls   have a beer drunk
[$_{xAP}$ d- ... AgrA ... both ...]

(24) **Bäid-i**   mäitli hend es piär trunkä.
both-AgrA girls   have a beer drunk
[$_{xAP}$ both$_i$ ... AgrA ~~both~~$_i$ ...]

Leu argues that constituent order and morphology indicate that such quantifier words are, syntactically speaking, adjectives.

Before moving on to the analysis of quantifier words it will be useful to spell out the derivation of (21) in some detail. The derivation involves remnant movement, whereby a smaller constituent A is moved out of a larger B, followed by the movement of the remnant of B. The semanticist reader will immediately want to know how remnant movement affects interpretation. It doesn't. One may think of the movement of remnants as one that will undergo "semantic reconstruction", i.e. one that leaves a higher-order variable as its trace. One reason why it must reconstruct is that the remnant contains the trace of a moved element that needs to be bound. This means that the initial structures obtained by Merge must get the interpretation right; remnant movement will not change the interpretation; it just delivers the order and constituency observed on the surface.

Leu's analysis is designed to unify the structures for *der gute Wein*, Scandinavian double definiteness (exemplified below with Swedish), and Greek determiner spreading. The latter constructions contain a definite article that is directly dependent on the presence of the modifier, in addition to the regular definiteness marking.[104]

(25) den   stora bil-en
the.agr big   car-definite
'the big car'

(26) to   megalo (to) vivlio
the.agr big   (the) book
'the big book'

The unification explains the presence of the second D, which I notate as D*, and the resulting unorthodox constituent structure highlighted in (27).

(27)

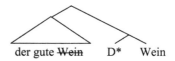

The derivation goes as follows. NP first moves to the Specifier of AgrA to trigger gender/number agreement, and then out of xAP. The structure of xAP is analogous to a relative clause (Kayne 1994; Koopman 2001, 2005); its initial D is the relative complementizer. After NP leaves xAP, AgrA cliticizes to D. D* is merged and the remnant xAP that dominates *der gute* and traces of *Wein* moves to its Specifier.

(28)   der gute Wein

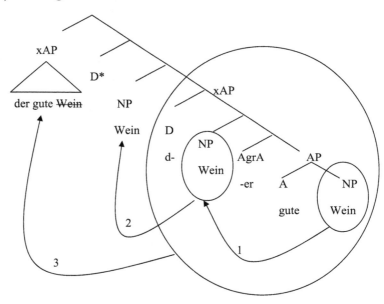

Elaborating on these ideas Leu (2008) works out analyses for the *ein–kein–mein* 'one–not even one–my' series and the *welch–solch* 'which–such' series, which we do not detail here. Instead, we consider Leu's (2009) extension to *jed-* 'every'. As was mentioned at the outset, *jed-* incorporates a quantificational morpheme and a definite article, and takes adjectival agreement. The derivation differs from (28) in one step. In contrast to the derivation with AP, the one with (what I label as) je-P involves preposing the remnant je-P to the Specifier of xAP, forming *jeder*:

(29)   jeder Junge

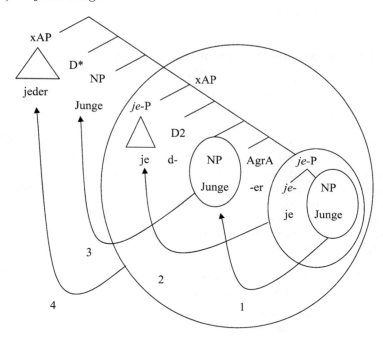

This proposal revises the analysis of *jeder* in Kallulli and Rothmayr (2008). The latter is more like Matthewson's (2001) for Lillooet *tákem i smelhmúlhats-a* 'every woman, all the women':

(30)

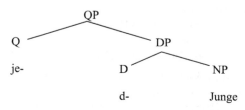

Leu (2009) points out that (30) predicts the wrong kind of morphology on *jed-* (article agreement, not the strong adjectival declension that actually occurs). He also believes that the complement of *je-* is NP, not DP. Recall that Matthewson (2001) proposes that the complement of English *every*, in contrast to *all*, is NP, not DP.[105] In Leu's view D* is the definite article that also appears in the absence of adjectival modification (argument-maker and/or definiteness marker).

12.5 Word-internal compositionality? Cross-linguistic isomorphy?

The very new line of research reviewed in this chapter is significant from multiple perspectives. Although the analysis of the "logical words" of natural languages is one of the classical tasks of a formal semanticist, we often play fast and loose with the precise differences between similar quantifiers within one language (say, *every*, *each*, *all*, *all the*, etc.) and across languages (assuming that whatever holds true of a quantifier in one language works for its dictionary equivalents in other languages). Such practices do not only result in inaccurate descriptions – they may well affect general theoretical conclusions regarding quantification.

In addition to such specific issues, two fundamental questions in this domain are as follows:

(31)   To what extent does compositionality systematically extend below the word level, at least in "logical words"?

(32)   If word-internal compositionality turns out to be the norm, how uniform is the composition of "logical words" across languages (give or take some well-motivated null elements)?

There is a set of data that raises such questions particularly sharply. It is well known that in many languages morphemes that may be said to signify disjunction and conjunction build connectives, discourse particles, quantifier words, and clause-type indicators. Japanese is one example (Nishigauchi 1990, Yatsushiro 2002, Shimoyama 2006, among others).

(33)   a.   Taro-ka Akira-ka   'Taro or Akira'
        b.   dare-ka 'someone'
        c.   dono NP-ka   'some NP'
        d.   Dare-ga odorimasu ka   'Who dances?'
        e.   Taro-ga odorimasu ka   'Does Taro dance?'

(34)   a.   Taro-mo Akira-mo   'Taro and Akira'
        b.   dare-mo   'everyone/anyone (depending on stress)'
        c.   dono NP-mo   'every/any NP (depending on stress)'
        d.   Taro-mo   'also/even Taro (depending on stress)'

Similar data are discussed by Hunyadi (1989) for Hungarian; Ramchand (1997) for Bengali; Jayaseelan (2001) for Malayalam; Amritavalli (2003) for Kannada; Borzdyko (2004) for Belorussian; Paul (2005) for Malagasy; Zimmermann (2009) for Korean and Hausa; and by HASPELMATH (1997) and GIL (2008) from a wider typological perspective. Much of the literature focuses on the fact that some of the relevant morphemes can also attach to a larger phrase containing an indeterminate ("*wh*") pronoun. An example is (35) from Shimoyama (2006). The analysis has been either in terms of movement or in terms of the expansion of alternatives introduced by the indeterminate pronouns in a Hamblin/Rooth-style semantics:

(35)   [[Dono gakusei-ga   syootaisita] sensei]-mo   odotta.
        which student.nom invited   teacher-**mo** danced
        'For every student x, the teacher(s) that x invited danced'

In contrast, my interest here is in the "multi-functionality" of the conjunction and disjunction morphemes, which typically remains unaddressed in the literature. I propose that *ka* and *mo* signify the general lattice-theoretic operations:

(36)   a.   *ka*   least upper bound (join, union, disjunction)
        b.   *mo*   greatest lower bound (meet, intersection, conjunction)

This assumption makes the range of uses associated with each morpheme coherent. First, recall (4) of **§4.1.1**, repeated here:

(37)   a.   The generalized quantifier *everyone'* is the intersection (greatest lower bound) of the Montagovian individuals.
        b.   The generalized quantifier *someone'* is the union (least upper bound) of the Montagovian individuals.

(36) explains why *mo* builds a universal and *ka* an existential quantifier. Second, 'also, too' and 'even' have conjunctive semantics in that part of the interpretation of *I saw X too/even X* is that I saw *X* and another entity *Y*; it is not surprising that the morphemes carrying these meanings come from the greatest lower bound family. Third, *Who dances?* is understood as denoting the set of propositions such that, for some individual or other, the proposition is that this individual dances (mutatis mutandis, similarly for yes/no questions); it is not surprising that question-markers are morphemes that belong to the least upper bound family. Or, the range of uses of *ka* and its cross-linguistic counterparts may follow from the Hamblin-style alternative semantics for disjunction. What this latter view would imply for *mo* and its counterparts is an open question.[106]

Recognizing the operations least upper bound and greatest lower bound as dramatis personae in quantification does not throw us back to the traditional position according to which natural language quantifiers are one-step primitives. Jayaseelan (2005) observes that the distributive universal quantification exemplified in Malayalam (38) involves the numeral 'one' and the disjunction morpheme in addition to the conjunction morpheme:

(38)   oor-**oo**   kuTTi-(y)uDe-(y)**um** paraati
        one-disjunction child-gen-conjunction complaint
        'each child's complaint'

His analysis is that the numeral 'one' plus the disjunction morpheme
serve to form a partition of the class of 'child', such that each cell of the
partition has just one element. The conjunction morpheme ensures that
the elements of the cells, taken together, exhaust the class of 'child'. The
added complexity in *oor-oo kuTTi-. . . -um* is due to the fact that it has a
nominal restriction, unlike *dare-mo*.

How far can such analyses be pushed cross-linguistically? Jayaseelan
(2005) draws attention to the fact that according to the Oxford English
Dictionary *every* is composed of *ever* and *each*; the *each* part is preserved
in the -*y* of *every*:[107]

(39)   [OE. ǽfre ǽlc, *ǽfre ylc: see EVER adv. and EACH.
        The OE. *ǽlc, ylc*, was a compound of *á*, synonymous with *ǽfre*;
        but, owing to umlaut and contraction, the etymological force of
        the word had become obscured, and *ǽfre* was prefixed in order to
        express more distinctly the original sense. Although the phrase
        was always written in OE. (as sometimes in ME.) as two words, it
        had in 10th c. already come to be felt as a compound, and when
        it is governed by a prep. this is placed before the first of the two
        words. . . .
        1558 Q. KENNEDY *Compend. Tract. in Wodr. Soc. Misc.* (1844)
        117 Bot everilk faithfull minister to bestowe the grace quhilk God
        hes gevin hym.   OED: *every*

Jayaseelan goes on to note that *each* was often followed by the number
word *one* or its weakened form *a(n)* before the noun, and that *each* was
at least sometimes used to carry the meaning of 'any'.

(40)   a1300 Cursor M. 510 (Gött.) Iornays . . . fourti mile euerilk a day.
        c1325 Pol. Songs (1839) 157 Everuch a parosshe heo polketh in
        pyne. 1352 MINOT Poems x. 51 God save sir Edward his right In
        everilka nede. c1440 HYLTON Scala Perf. (W. de W. 1494) II. xli,
        Eueryche a soule resonable owyth for to coueyte . . . nyghynge to
        Jhesu.   OED: *every*

(41)   † 2. After *without*: = ANY. Cf. ALL A. 4.
        c1300 Beket 480 Withoute ech delay.   OED: *each*

Thus Jayaseelan suggests that *every child* is underlyingly *ever each one
child*. Because *ever* occurs in *whoever, whatever*, etc. and contributes universal quantification, Jayaseelan takes *ever* to be the conjunction operator
and conjectures that *each* is the disjunction operator. If this is correct,

then Old and Middle English, perhaps even Modern English, compose the meaning of the operator the same way as Malayalam does.

Are these semantically reasonable and cross-linguistically prevalent patterns the stuff of compositional semantics? Some of the questions that we have to answer are the following.

One, it is sometimes proposed that not all uses of the same superficial morpheme represent the same lexical item; e.g. Shimoyama (2006) argues, based on the absence of intervention effects, that *mo* 'every' and *mo* 'also' are distinct. Do these *mo*'s then share a semantic core and differ in what some phonetically null material contributes, or are they truly independent and their identical shapes a historical accident?

Two, not all languages possess as elaborate an inventory as Japanese. Is there a principled explanation for the gaps (or, can they at least be thought of as normal products of language change)?

Three, there is significant cross-linguistic variation in what stretches of the sentence such morphemes operate on, cf. (35), addressed in Ramchand (1997), Kratzer and Shimoyama (2002), and Zimmermann (2009). Is this variation compatible with a unified semantics?

Four, if Jayaseelan's conjecture about English is correct, then the morphological matches sometimes break down: *ever* may be a conjunction (greatest lower bound) operator, but its shape does not bring *and* to mind. How fine-grained should the compositional analyses be, then?

Five, recognizing *ever* as a component of *every* is not too controversial, but is it legitimate to treat *-y* as a representative of *each*? Where should the line be drawn between diachronic and synchronic analysis in this domain? How suggestive is the Malayalam data of the analysis of English? How strong is the English-internal motivation?

Six, the Malayalam construction in (38) works only with the numeral 'one'; with higher cardinalities Malayalam uses reduplication, and neither disjunction nor conjunction is present. It is an interesting question whether sorting-key reduplication in Malayalam creates a blocking effect, or the divergence is semantically significant. If the former is correct, how should compositional semantics deal with blocking effects?

These questions go beyond the ones we are familiar with from sentence-level compositional analysis. Answering them calls for novel theorizing, in addition to commonsensical case-by-case argumentation. Since the questions arise at the intersection of productive lines of research in morphology, syntax, and semantics, the theories and the best practices of all these fields can and should inform the development of the requisite methodology and analytical standards.

Despite the fact that so many important questions are currently open, the issues arising from the work reviewed in this chapter seem to be among the most intriguing ones that research on quantification has recently begun to tackle, and they promise genuinely new insights.

Notes

1. Many of the ideas in PTQ were apparently in the air at UCLA at the time; Lewis (1970) outlines a proposal that is extremely similar to Montague's.
2. For the historical record, PTQ (Montague 1974a) treated *every* and its brothers syncategorematically, but this practice was abandoned soon afterwards.
3. Well, almost all DPs. Reflexives and reciprocals for example do not denote generalized quantifiers, nor do the noun phrases in *Different people like different books* (Keenan 1992; Ben-Shalom 1996) or denotationless expressions like idiom chunks and expletives.
4. For semantic type theory, see ALLWOOD ET AL. (1977), Section 8.5, and GAMUT (1991), Vol. 2., Section 4.2.
5. Thus in Heim and Kratzer's syntactic representations the λ-operator that helps form the property that the QP combines with is notated as a numeral, corresponding to the index of the trace of the quantifier.
6. To see weak crossover in action, consider singular *a different NP*. Because it is not a pronominal, it helps exhibit the full range of scope effects (see Beghelli and Stowell 1997). (i) shows that the prepositional object *every girl* can scope over both the subject and the direct object.

    (i) a.   A different person sent a gift to every girl.
        b.   Vlad sent a different gift to every girl.

    But none of the pronouns in (ii) can be interpreted as linked to *every girl*:

    (ii) a.   She sent a gift to every girl.
         b.   Her aunt sent a gift to every girl.
         c.   Vlad sent her gift to every girl.

    Bach and Partee's (1984) explanation is that there is simply no syntactic binding in (ii), regardless of scope, because the argument position of the quantifier does not c-command the pronoun.
7. It is important to have a solid intuitive grasp of how the generalized-quantifier-type (higher-order) variables A and B versus the entity-type (first-order) variables x and y make a difference for scope. Consider two

possible ways of putting together *every book'* and *some student borrowed'*. In the first case *some student borrowed'* has an entity-type variable x in the direct-object position; this is abstracted over by the λ-operator. *Every book'* is the function that applies to this as an argument. Because *some student borrowed'* replaces the variable P in the course of λ-conversion, the universal quantifier of *every book'* remains outside the scope of the existential quantifier of *some student'*. That is how this derivation assigns wide scope to *every book'*.

(i) a. *every book'* : $\lambda P \forall y[book'(y) \rightarrow P(y)]$
   b. *some student borrowed'* : $\lambda x \exists z[student'(z) \wedge borrowed'(x)(z)]$
   c. $\lambda P \forall y[book'(y) \rightarrow P(y)](\lambda x \exists z[student'(z) \wedge borrowed'(x)(z)]) =$
        $\forall y[book'(y) \rightarrow \lambda x \exists z[student'(z) \wedge borrowed'(x)(z)](y)] =$
        $\forall y[book'(y) \rightarrow \exists z[student'(z) \wedge borrowed'(y)(z)]]$

The second version differs from the first in that *some student borrowed'* now has a generalized-quantifier-type variable C in the direct object position, abstracted over by the λ-operator. (There is also an entity-type variable x in there, which is important, but it doesn't play a role in the present argument, so ignore it and focus on C.) Now this is the function that applies to *every book'* as an argument. C is exactly the same size as *every book'*, so lambda-conversion in (ii) inescapably stuffs all of *every book'* into the C slot within the scope of the existential quantifier. Therefore the universal quantifier falls within the scope of the existential, and *some student'* takes wider scope.

(ii) *every book'* : $\lambda P \forall y[book'(y) \rightarrow P(y)]$
    some student borrowed' : $\lambda C \exists z[student'(z) \wedge C(\lambda x[borrowed'(x)(z)])]$
    $\lambda C \exists z[student'(z) \wedge C(\lambda x[borrowed'(x)(z)])](\lambda P \forall y[book'(y) \rightarrow P(y)])$
    $= \exists z[student'(z) \wedge \lambda P \forall y[book'(y) \rightarrow P(y)](\lambda x[borrowed'(x)(z)])]$
    $= \exists z[student'(z) \wedge \forall y[book'(y) \rightarrow \lambda x[borrowed'(x)(z)](y)]]$
    $= \exists z[student'(z) \wedge \forall y[book'(y) \rightarrow borrowed'(y)(z)]]$

8. Hendriks presents the rules type-theoretically. Bernardi (2010) shows that Argument Raising is not derivable in the non-associative Lambek calculus (NL). Value Raising and Argument Lowering are derivable.

9. I thank S. Charlow for discussion.

10. Steedman's pied-piping combinator, discussed in Szabolcsi (1992), performs the same job. It turns *everyone*, $\lambda f \forall x[f(x)]$, into $\lambda g \lambda h \forall x[h(g(x))]$, where g may be a preposition or whatever else *everyone* combines with; quantificational properties are passed on to the result.

11. These complications become unnecessary in a variable-free semantics that follows Jacobson (1999) in interpreting pronouns as maps $\lambda x[x]$, as opposed to free variables. A reformulation of the dynamic treatment of cross-sentential anaphora along these lines is given in Szabolcsi (2003).

12. *Every dragon lumbers'* will be $\lambda p[\forall x[(dragon'(x) \rightarrow lumber'(x))] \wedge p]$, where p falls outside the scope of $\forall$.

13. The composition of the functions f and g, notated as $f \circ g$, is defined as $\lambda x[f(g(x))]$.

14. Lift applied "below the line", Scope involving three levels, and Lower involving three levels all require slight generalizations of the basic operations given above, both in terms of towers and in terms of λ's.

15. A variable-free semantics is, more precisely, free of variable binding. It has no operation that takes an expression with a free (assignment-dependent) variable and returns one where the variable is bound (no longer dependent on assignments). Variable-ful and variable-free systems have the same expressive power, but they build their expressions differently. The reader may be interested to know that the interpretations of the propositional connectives and of the existential and universal quantifiers can also be defined in this way, as is shown in Henkin (1963), extended to modal operators in Gallin (1975: 15–17). A basic idea can be seen from the following definitions. The variable x is of type t:

(i) $\mathbf{T} = [\lambda x.x \equiv \lambda x.x]$

(ii) $\mathbf{F} = [\lambda x.x \equiv \lambda x.\mathbf{T}]$

(iii) $\sim\, = \lambda x[\mathbf{F} \equiv x]$

(iv) $\forall y_\alpha.A = [\lambda y_\alpha.A \equiv \lambda y_\alpha.\mathbf{T}]$

Informally, (i) defines Truth, because everything is identical to itself; (ii) defines Falsehood, because it says that every proposition is True; (iii) defines negation as a function that equates its argument with Falsehood. The definition of universal quantification in (iv) is based on the fact that two functions are identical iff they assign the same value to every argument. (iv) says that the function that maps any y to A is the same as the one that maps any y to Truth. Notice that the definitions only use closed typed λ-terms (viz. combinators) and equality.

16. As Z. Szabó (p.c.) observes, one of the reasons most philosophers treat modality as an operator, not a quantifier is that we do not seem to have pronouns picking out possible worlds in English, and presumably in other natural languages either. Since philosophers commonly assume that variables are the formal equivalents of pronouns, they are disinclined to postulate possible world variables. But Iatridou (1994) and Percus (2000) argue that the word *then* refers to worlds, in addition to times.

17. Gutiérrez-Rexach (1997) subsumes the interpretation of questions directly under generalized quantifier theory, with *wh*-phrases playing the role of determiners. In a world where just John and Mary walk, *Who walks?* assigns True to a set iff it is identical to {j, m}. Thus *who* relates two sets of individuals, the *walk*-set and the answer-set {j, m}, the former being the restriction. This replicates Groenendijk and Stokhof's (1984) partition semantics in an extensional setting, and makes the standard results of generalized quantifier theory straightforwardly applicable.

18. The paraphrase for *begin* should really be stated with respect to Kaplanian characters, not propositions.

19. Montague (1974a) attributes this example to J. Moravcsik. PTQ does not offer a treatment.

20. I thank Andrea Cattaneo, Jeroen Groenendijk, and Laziz Nchare for data and discussion on Italian, Dutch, and Shupamem. The fact that English (9) carries the same two readings was pointed out to me by Ed Garrett.

21. The LO reading could not be accommodated by saying that there was an event in which only Mary got good roles. Quantification, such as the explication of *only*, does not "fit" into an event.

22. In the Dutch (a) example verb movement to second position is followed by subject movement to first position. The wide scope of such subjects is a general phenomenon in Dutch and German, giving rise to their well-known "scope rigidity". I thank W. Lechner for discussion.

23. The prevalence of the passive in the examples is due to how a simple and efficient Google-search could be designed, and it is not necessarily a statistical feature of LO readings.

24. The assumption, necessary here, that English *don't* comprises both negation and the existential quantifier over events is stronger than what is forced by the plain event semantics and what may hold cross-linguistically. Zimmermann (2007) argues that in Bura (Central Chadic) an overt existential closure operator appears between negation and an eventive verb:

(i) kubili **adi** [tsi mtika-ni] **wa.**
Kubili **exist** slaughter chicken.def **neg**
'Kubili did not slaughter the chicken'

Here *adi* and *wa* do not appear to form a unit.

25. PETERS AND WESTERSTÅHL (2006) systematically distinguish the local and the global perspectives on quantifiers. The local perspective is confined to a particular finite universe, the global one is not. The claims in the present book are typically local; for the global perspective the reader is referred to Peters and Westerståhl and §**5.7**.

26. *Every* is not felicitous when its restrictor set has less than three elements, but we want to avoid drawing Hasse-diagrams for larger sets.

27. Consider the partially ordered set of rational numbers that are greater than or equal to 2 but smaller than or equal to 3. This set is infinite, but it has a least upper bound (top), namely 3, and a greatest lower bound (bottom), namely 2. It forms a so-called bounded lattice.

28. On other aspects of *more than n NP*, see Chapters 9, 10, and 11.

29. Notice that the set of witnesses of an increasing quantifier do not form an increasing quantifier; on the other hand, the fact that the witness sets in Figure 4.8 are disconnected is to some extent an artifact of how the Hasse-diagram was drawn.

30. (19a) does not hold for decreasing quantifiers and conversely, (19b) does not hold for increasing ones. But, as M. Solomon (p.c.) observes, the following does hold for all three monotonicity types:

(i) For any X, $X \in GQ$ iff $\exists W[(X \cap L) = W]$.

31. More on cumulative readings in §**8.2.1**. Both cumulation and branching were originally assumed to require polyadic quantification (going beyond the Frege boundary, in the words of Keenan 1992); see Hintikka (1974) and Scha (1981). The polyadic assumption has been successfully questioned, among others, by van der Does (1992); Schein (1993); Beghelli,

Ben-Shalom, and Szabolcsi (1997); and Schlenker (2006a). The issue of polyadicity is orthogonal to the monotonicity problem discussed in the text and will not be discussed here. See Scha (1981); May (1989); Landman (2000); KEENAN AND WESTERSTÅHL (1997); Beck and Sauerland (2000); Sternefeld (1993); and PETERS AND WESTERSTÅHL (2006).

32.   Elegant but limited approaches to the monotonicity issues in branching are to be found in Barwise (1979) and Westerståhl (1987). Exactly what the truth conditions of the non-increasing cases are is debated in the literature; see Beghelli, Ben-Shalom, and Szabolcsi (1997) for discussion.

33.   More on the cardinality-adjective view in Chapter 9. Maybe "cardinality marker/modifier" would be a more prudent name than "cardinality adjective", since nothing in the analysis hinges on them being adjectives. Ionin and Matushansky (2006) argue that cardinals are nouns, though modifiers indeed.

34.   "Currying" (or "Schönfinkelization") turns a two-place function into a function that has one argument and its value is another one-place function. In doing so it is forced to rank one of the two arguments of the original function as the first argument of the result and the other as its second argument.

35.   There are 2^{4^n} semantic determiners in a universe with n elements; conservativity cuts the number down to 2^{3^n}. Thijsse (1985) outlines an elegant proof suggested by Johan van Benthem, rephrased here in the terms of (35). For any permutation-invariant semantic determiner DET, whether or not its second argument Pred$'$ is an element of DET(NP$'$) only depends on the way NP$'$ and Pred$'$ are situated in the universe (call it E). But instead of listing the members of NP$'$ and Pred$'$, we could specify for any element of E whether it belongs to area (i), (ii), (iii), or (iv). Call this set 4. In this way any mapping in $f : E \to 4$ determines a pair $\langle$NP$'$,Pred$'\rangle$. Now we identify any DET with the set of $\langle$NP$'$,Pred$'\rangle$ pairs such that Pred$'$ is an element of DET(NP$'$). Without conservativity, there are 2^{4^n} DETs (where 2 is the set {true, false}). Conservativity says that area (iii) need not be considered, so there are only 2^{3^n} conservative DETs.

36.   This is essentially Keenan's (2000) sortal reducibility. Keenan warns that "whether a quantifier is sortally reducible and whether it is first order definable are independent properties, though it happens that the properly proportional quantifiers fail both conditions: they are neither sortally reducible nor are they first order definable, not even over finite universes. But the quantifiers *just finitely many* and *all but finitely many* are sortally reducible but not first order definable. And the quantifiers *both, neither,* and *the ten* are first order definable but not sortally reducible."

37.   Szabó (2008), in a workshop presentation, raises the possibility that bare quantifiers are at work in sentences like (i).

(i)   This election could have two winners.

On the most natural interpretation (i) does not mean that there are two winners such that this election could have them, nor that it is possible for this election to wind up with two winners; rather, it means that there are two people/things such that they could be winners of this election. A quantifier occurs bare if it is not restricted either by the context or by a predicate in the sentence. Szabó notices that counting quantifiers support such readings. In his comments on the paper J. Stanley notes that these interpretations are similar to cases of number or degree quantification that some languages, e.g. French, express overtly:

(ii) Combien   as-tu   conduit de camions?
    how.many have-you driven   of trucks
    'for what number, you have driven trucks of that number'

See also Herburger (2000) re: (47). Herburger also claims that her focus-affected readings are possible only with intersective determiners; see de Hoop and Solà (1995) for a different opinion.

38. Shu (2008) proposes that sentential adverbs like *evidently*, *certainly*, *unfortunately*, and their counterparts in Chinese, Icelandic, and other languages are focus-sensitive operators.

39. Note the grammaticality of (i) in the jargon of philosophers and logicians.

(i) All and only triangles have three angles.

Assuming that like categories are conjoinable, if *only* is not a determiner, *all* is not one, either, and indeed alongside *only the triangles* we have *all the triangles*.

40. But see Beaver and Clark (2003), who argue that adverbs of quantification differ from *only* in that they are not focus-sensitive; instead, they are sensitive to more pragmatic factors.

41. The distributive readings could not be obtained by meaning postulates pertaining to predicates. A meaning postulate merely adds a new interpretation to the basic one, which in this case would be the collective interpretation. We cannot start out with the ontological assumption that collectives sneeze, give live birth, and so on.

42. Linguists typically treat presuppositions semantically and thus in terms of truth-values; philosophers overwhelmingly see them as a pragmatic phenomenon.

43. Z. Szabó (p.c.) observes that the majority of philosophers agree with Kripke's view in *Naming and Necessity* that there are no unicorns in any possible world; he also finds it difficult to detect a modal flavor in (12a).

44. The discussion of *all* and *most* in the literature is tainted by the tacit or explicit assumption that *all unicorns* is synonymous with *all the unicorns* and *all of the unicorns*, and *most unicorns* with *most of the unicorns*, and so they can be used interchangeably to obtain judgments. They are far from synonymous. As Matthewson (2001) observes, the distribution of *all NP* is similar to that of bare plurals on the kind reading; similarly for *most NP*. More on this in §12.2.

45. Hackl's own paraphrase of *More than three students were at my party* is his (145c), *More students were at my party than how many students there are such that 3 students would be at my party*. My hope is that (16) preserves the spirit, although it sacrifices the ungrammaticality.

46. The algebra of syntax consists of the set of all expressions of the language (lexical and complex) plus the set of its syntactic operations (by which the complex expressions are obtained from the lexical ones). The algebra of semantics consists of the set of all meanings of the language (lexical

and complex) plus the set of its semantic operations (by which the complex meanings are obtained from the lexical ones). The view is entirely neutral as to what meanings are. The two algebras have to be similar in the sense that they contain the same number of operations and the paired operations have the same arity. Compositionality is ensured by the requirement that the function that associates complex expressions with meanings extend the interpretation of lexical items to a homomorphism. Let E be an expression, M a meaning, Syn a one-place syntactic rule, and Sem a matching one-place semantic rule. Then, the meaning assignment function h is a homomorphism iff $h(Syn(E)) = Sem(h(E))$. In our diagram: $Syn(E)$ is E^* and $h(E)$ is M. Because h is a homomorphism, $h(E^*)$ coincides with $Sem(M)$, i.e. the value of both is M^*.

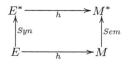

47.   The worry may arise that *every blue* as a constituent is still a source of trouble. It need not be if the grammar allows for a certain amount of optional rebracketing, like categorial grammars that include functional composition. See also **§12.4** for syntactic arguments for precisely such a constituent in German.

48.   I thank S. Charlow and Z. Szabó for discussion.

49.   Unfortunately, current theories of quantification do not produce underspecified representations, or at least no non-disjunctive ones.

50.   On various aspects of specificity, see Cormack and Kempson (1991), Liu (1997), Farkas (2002), and the references towards the end of **§7.2.2**. In the present context it is useful to recall Cormack and Kempson's argument against defining specificity for indefinites as "what the speaker has in mind". Suppose I am looking at two women and, having the taller one in mind, I say, *One of these women/A woman here is French*. Now the taller woman is in fact Italian, but the other, unbeknownst to me, is French. If my sentence meant 'The woman I have in mind is French', it would have to be false. But what I said is true, plain and simple.

51.   Starting with Hamblin (1973) and Karttunen (1977) *wh*-words have been assimilated to indefinites. Reinhart (1998) argues that *wh*-in-situ exemplifies choice-functional indefinites. Garrett (1996) and Dayal (2002) observe that sentences with *wh*-in-situ only allow a list of pairs as an answer if the in-situ *wh*-phrase is clausemate to the moved wh-phrase:

(i)   Q: Which linguist likes which philosopher?
      A: ok B likes C, and D likes E.

(ii) Q: Which linguist thinks that we invited which philosopher?
      A: B thinks that we invited C, #(and D thinks that we invited E).

This follows naturally from the clause-boundedness of distributivity. One exception to the generalization is *Who remembers where we bought which book?*, where Dayal proposes to exploit the pair-list interpretation of the complement question.

52. Winter's (1997) choice functions yield generalized quantifiers (Montagovian individuals), not first-order individuals, as values. When the restriction is empty, they pick the empty quantifier: the one that does not include any set of individuals.

53. Geurts (2000) makes various objections to choice functions. One of them is that a sentence like (i) on the given interpretation appears to claim that Bill believes in choice functions:

    (i) Bill believes that you buy every book that is illustrated by a certain artist.
    'Bill believes that there is a choice function such that you buy every book that is illustrated by the individual that this function picks from the set of artists'

    But a similar problem arises with sets, and indeed with all the formal apparatus of semantics, and so one should not view this as an argument against the use of choice functions in particular. Also, if one thinks of choice functions as ways of selecting (just as possible worlds are ways things could be), it is not implausible that we do believe in them. Cf. 'Bill believes that there is a way to select an artist such that you buy every book that is illustrated by her.' I thank Z. Szabó for discussion.

54. NumP, or Number Phrase, was introduced in Ritter (1991) to account for the plural (or, in some languages, singular) morphology on nouns in the presence of numerals: the N-head is assumed to move to the Num-head, whose specifier hosts the numeral. The label NumP is also used informally in the literature to designate a category that contains a numeral; but especially semanticists use plain NP for the same purpose.

55. There is an unsettled terminological and conceptual issue here. Both the parameters and the arguments of a function can take on different values, but if a careful distinction is made, parameters are part of the function's definition, whereas the function's action is to apply to its arguments. So these correspond to two different compositional manners in which to achieve the result that the ultimate function value depends on a particular thing. The linguistic literature talks variably and largely interchangeably of "Skolem arguments" or "Skolem parameters" when referring to the dependence of the function value on some individual. The set that the choice function chooses from is invariably called an argument, but maybe contextually salient choice functions ought to be said to have set parameters instead – see the remark at the end of this section.

56. Z. Szabó points out that in the spirit of free enrichment (Recanati 2002) one might think that the relevant reading of (18) is elliptical for *If each student makes progress in an area (of his weakness), nobody will flunk the exam.*

57. The observation that non-monotonic quantifiers create the same logical problem as decreasing ones is due to P. Schlenker (Chierchia 2001: fn.10; Schlenker 2006a):

    (i) Exactly two linguists studied every solution that some problem might have.

Chierchia proposes to take care of this based on the fact that non-monotonic quantifiers are intersections of increasing and decreasing quantifiers. But is this intersection visible enough in the grammar for existential closure to appear in the immediate scope of the decreasing component?

We add that intuitions regarding the truth conditions of examples with non-monotonic numerals like *exactly two* or with decreasing numerals such as *fewer than five* are not as clear as those involving *not every*. The same holds for the truth conditions of quantified possessive constructions, which are quite similar in that they involve a context-dependent element: the possessive relation that may involve ownership, authorship, and a multitude of other relations between possessor and possessee.

(ii) Exactly two men's books are valuable.

(iii) Fewer than five men's books are valuable.

Is (ii) true, for example, if one of the men is the owner and the other the author of his books? Is (ii) true if there are exactly two authors, but also one owner, whose books are valuable? The answers are not clear and different people may judge the sentences differently. The difficulties are reminiscent of the disagreement in the literature regarding the truth-conditions of branching readings with non-increasing quantifiers. Sher (1990) proposed that these require the existence of an appropriate cross-product that is maximal in the relevant relation; but Schein (1993) and Spaan (1992) disagreed with Sher and with each other about what cross-products count as maximal; see Beghelli, Ben-Shalom, and Szabolcsi (1997: 53–55). The similarities with our choice function examples are not surprising; Chierchia's problem is also a maximalization problem due to existential quantification over a component of (what can be seen as) a complex non-increasing quantifier.

58.   Just like the negated examples most often discussed, (i) has two readings, as originally observed in Schwarz (2004):

(i)   If every student reads every paper that a professor who gave a lecture in class wrote, I'll be happy.
'if every student reads every paper that *the professor assigned to them by the presupposed choice function* wrote, then I'll be happy'
'if for every student *there is some way of choosing professors* (not necessarily the presupposed way) such that the student reads every paper which the professor wrote, I'll be happy'

The second reading is truth-conditionally weaker than the first. It corresponds to the case where there is an existential quantifier binding $f(x)(professor)$, within the antecedent of the conditional, while in the first reading the choice function is left free and therefore read anaphorically. Mascarenhas's proposal accounts for (i) in just the same way it accounts for negated cases, while the denial proposal does not.

59.   It may be interesting to note that in naturally-occurring texts the typical use of *every* is not with nouns like *child*, *bottle*, or *idea*, but with "indeterminate pronouns" such as *one, body, thing, where*, or with nouns denoting time periods such as *minute, hour, morning, evening, day, night, month*,

year, etc. A quick Google search turns up 1,320 million hits for the word *every*. If one excludes the above-listed items from the search, the number drops to 425,000. In other words, only ca. 1 in 3,000 uses involves a noun other than an indeterminate pronoun or a temporal noun.

60. If Mascarenhas's (2009) proposal is adopted, then this may be recast as follows: specific indefinites presuppose the existence of a contextually relevant choice function, whereas universals require the actual choice function to be part of the common ground. How the contextual requirements of *every NP* differ from those of *the NP[plural]*, *all (of) the NP*, and *each NP* remains to be investigated.

61. I am grateful to B. Schein for many discussions of plurals and events over the years and for comments on this chapter.

62. More precisely, a free i-join semi-lattice. To link this to the parlance of the previous sections, the set $\{\{a, f\}, \{a\}, \{f\}\}$ in (2) is the powerset of $\{a, f\}$ minus the bottom element, the empty set. The removal of the bottom element prevents the partially ordered set from being a lattice or a complete atomic Boolean algebra. See LANDMAN 1991: 254–267.

63. There are proposals in the literature that seek to handle cumulativity without reference to events. These proposals however are often based on examples that feature only two semantically interacting noun phrases. (An exception, as E. Zweig points out to me, is McKay 2006: 247–250.) As noted above, Schein's (1993) argument to the effect that events are indispensable crucially involves examples with three relevant noun phrases enabling the co-occurrence of cumulation with a distributive dependency. The proposals for the simpler examples do not necessarily scale up. Pietroski (2005) builds the whole semantics on the idea of Conjunctivism.

64. It is thought to be a trivial fact that English *and* may scope under negation and receive the 'not both' interpretation predicted by the de Morgan laws. Szabolcsi and Haddican (2004) observe that this obtains only when the connective is stressed, as in (i).

(i)　He didn't visit Budapest AND Tokyo.

If the connective is unstressed, speakers judge the negated conjunction to be degraded or, in the presence of additional circumstances detailed in the paper, they interpret it as homogeneously negated ('neither').

65. In §4.1.4 we pointed out that Chierchia's analysis does not carry over to non-increasing quantifiers supporting pair-list readings. This is not a problem here, since Beghelli and Stowell only analyze increasing quantifiers in this way.

66. The concord-marker proposal is not an innocuous one, because its interpretation probably involves unselective binding (Lewis 1975 and much literature following him). Unselective binding could only be traded for a simple variety of polyadic quantification, resumptive quantification (May 1989) if each of the participating DPs contained a semantically significant instance of negation, existential, or universal quantification – which is precisely what the view denies.

67. *Kati is felemelte az asztalt* 'Kate too lifted up the table' is distributive in that it cannot mean that Kate formed a collective with some other person(s) to lift up the table; it can only mean that Kate performed her

own table-lifting and in addition some other individual or collective did so.

68.   The reader will have noticed that numeral expressions in Hungarian do not trigger plural morphology on the sister noun, although the language has nominal plural morphology. Cheung (2003) addresses a similar situation in connection with Mandarin and Jingpo, following Li (1999). The gist of the proposal is that even seemingly count nouns in such languages are mass nouns, and NumP contains an overt or (more typically) silent classifier. Hungarian, traditionally not thought of as a classifier language, exhibits the same properties that Cheung describes for Jingpo.

69.   The interpretation of a non-distributive *every NP* can be likened to that of *three relatives* in (6) of **§7.1.1**, where it takes extra-wide scope. It is not capable of inducing referential dependency, although no "collective action" is implied. Beghelli and Stowell regard the licensing of the bound reading of singular *a different NP* as the hallmark of the universal being in the Specifier of DistP. Indeed, when *every NP* is within the scope of negation, it does not license *a different NP*.

(i)   I showed every boy a different book.
      OK 'a book that was different from what I showed to the other boys'

(ii) I showed the boys/all the boys a different book.
      # 'a book that was different from what I showed to the other boys'

(iii) below is acceptable only as a response to an accusation, i.e. as denial or metalinguistic negation:

(iii) I didn't show every boy a different book.
      only as denial of 'a book that was different from what I showed to the other boys'

Brody and Szabolcsi (2003: 32) discuss DP-internal occurrences of *every NP*. They define scope in terms of featural dominance:

(iv) *A* scopes over *B* if *A*'s features dominate *B* in view of standard agreement and percolation conventions.

When *every girl* occurs in the Specifier of DP, its features are inherited by the container DP, and so the latter moves to the sentence-level Spec, DistP. When *every girl* occurs in a complement position inside DP, it finds a DP-internal Dist to check features with. This assumption is supported by the fact that many speakers find that the scope of such a universal is trapped inside the DP. These speakers judge that while (vb) can mean the same thing as (va), (vib) cannot mean what (via) can.

(v) a.   Every girl's oldest relative attended the potluck.
    b.   The oldest relative of every girl attended the potluck.

(vi) a. Every girl's oldest relative brought a different dish.
         OK 'a dish that was different from what the other girls' oldest relatives brought'

b. The oldest relative of every girl brought a different dish.
'a dish that was different from what the other girls' oldest relatives brought'
OK 'a dish different from one previously mentioned'

This is explained if the occurrence of *every girl* in the Specifier of some DP-internal Dist prevents the percolation of its [dist] feature to *the oldest relative of every girl*, and so the latter does not occur in the Specifier of Dist at the sentence level.

70. On the other hand it may be interesting to note that the 'none' reading is completely impossible in Norwegian (Nilsen 2003), Modern Greek (Giannakidou 2000), Hausa (M. Zimmermann 2008), and Hungarian; Norwegian is not a negative concord language, so this cannot generally be the effect of competition from negative concord.

71. At least in American English *every NP* often binds the plural pronouns *they, their*, but that is thought to achieve gender-neutrality, not the semantic effect of plurality.

72. Safir and Stowell (1988) also find such examples acceptable. The only speakers who systematically rejected them were semanticists. I generally have no qualms about using experts as informants, but my suspicion is that rejection here is a normative judgment.

73. Pereltsvaig (2008b) observes that when *po* attaches to a numeral phrase in Russian, it has the interpretation cross-linguistically characteristic of distributive numeral reduplication and binominal *each*; see the discussion of the "more than one overall" requirement proposed in Balusu (2005), following Zweig (2005b), below. When however *po* attaches to a bare singular, it requires a one-to-one map. (i) is true in a situation with three boys where two of them drew the same girl, but (ii) is only true if each of the three drew a different girl:

(i) Kazhdyj mal'chik narisoval po odnoj devochke.
every boy drew po one girl

(ii) Kazhdyj mal'chik narisoval po devochke.
every boy drew po girl

74. Farkas (1997b and other papers) discusses Hungarian numeral reduplication and concludes that, with the exception of one set expression, it does not have event-key readings. Thus the present discussion revises the standard analyses of both English and Hungarian, based on the insight that Telugu offers.

75. I thank Asja Pereltsvaig for sharing her ongoing cross-linguistic work with me, and Bill Haddican and Arantzazu Elordieta for the Basque data, judgments, and discussion.

76. Scha uses a polyadic cumulative schema that stipulates the 'exactly' reading. Krifka's (1999) initial motivation for treating numeral phrases as predicates $\lambda x[n(x) \land NP(x)]$ as opposed to generalized quantifiers comes from cumulative quantification. I am assuming that his $n(x)$ has an 'exactly' interpretation.

77. Partee (1986) assumes that *two dogs* of type $\langle e, t \rangle$ undergoes an existential shift to type $\langle \langle e, t \rangle, t \rangle$. Winter (2000) assumes that the NP in (11) becomes the complement of a functional head D, interpreted as a choice function, which is then existentially closed. These differences are immaterial from the present perspective. The informal discussion is intended to facilitate neutrality.

78. We assume thematic unicity for atomic events: "If there is a proposed event with, say, two themes, then there are (at least) two events and not one" (Carlson 1984: 274). That is, such a proposed event is non-atomic, so we have (at least) e_1, e_2, and $e_1 \oplus e_2$.

79. This is remarkable: modified numerals do not produce this so-called non-maximal-anaphora effect; recall also (10) in **§6.1**.

    (i) At least/more than two dogs were hungry. They barked.

    In (i) *they* refers to all the dogs that were hungry. Suppose five dogs were hungry, but only three of them barked – now (i) is false. Kamp and Reyle capture this by treating modified numeral expressions as quantifiers: their discourse referents are introduced into subordinate DRSs. They do not introduce plural referents for them into the current DRS or into a superordinate one.

80. Stressed numerals in English are not always interpreted as 'exactly n'. Krifka (1999) observes that the following question-answer pair is fine:

    (i) How many children does Nigel have?
        Nigel has fourteen$_F$ children, perhaps even fifteen$_F$.

    Recall that the main text does not suggest that cross-linguistically focus prosody associates with an exhaustivity operator. Rather, the suggestion is that exhaustivity operators associate with focus.

81. Earlier analyses that assumed that exhaustivization is a by-product of focusing (e.g. Szabolcsi 1981) ran into a "double exhaustivization" problem with *csak* 'only', given that *csak* clearly latches onto a focused phrase. On Horvath's analysis the problem disappears, because the phonetically null exhaustive operator *EI* and the particle *csak* are in complementary distribution. See Wedgwood (2005) and Balogh (2009) for alternative views on the interpretation of focus in Hungarian.

82. See also Dobrovie-Sorin (1994); Rullmann (1995); Honcoop (1998); SZABOLCSI (2006); Fox and Hackl (2006); Abrusán (2007); Lassiter (2009). Szabolcsi and Zwarts (1993/1997) recognize a three-way interpretive distinction. *How many laps* supports a "counting-conscious" reading; see (ii):

    (i) How many people talked to every girl / no girls?
        OK 'what is the number of people who talked to all the girls?'
        OK 'what is the number of people who talked to no girls?'

    (ii) How many laps bring every swimmer / no swimmers into shape?
        OK 'what is the number of laps that bring all the swimmers into shape?'
        #'what is the number of laps that bring no swimmers into shape?'

(iii) How much pain tormented every patient / no patients?
#'what is the amount of pain that tormented all the patients?'
#'what is the amount of pain that tormented no patients?'

Szabolcsi and Zwarts attribute the differences to the algebraic structures of the denotations of certain segments of the sentences that crucially enter into the computation of the *wh* > quantifier scope relation.

83. Lahiri (2002) shows that a combination of Cresti's analysis of *how many* and Dayal's (1994) analysis of *wh*-scope marking correctly predicts that Hindi, Hungarian, German, etc. sentences that literally translate as, 'What does Mary think how many people came?' only have an embedded-clausal reading for 'how many people', in contrast to the ambiguity of *How many people does Mary think came?*, where *how many people* moves.

84. I thank Andrea Cattaneo for help with the French data.

85. As was discussed in connection with (24)–(25), I assume that existential quantification over individuals can be converted into existential quantification over choice functions or into Skolemized choice functions; but Koopman and Sportiche's existential D will be retained in the discussion below.

86. As O. Savescu Ciucivara (p.c.) points out, the morphological reflex of agreement invariably occurs on the participle, i.e. inside VP. To ensure this one might say that VP-level agreement can accept accusative NPs, but when it does it must be bound by High Agreement; so VP-level agreement with an accusative NP is grammatical only if the accusative NP moves to a D above High Agreement, as described below.

87. R. Kayne (p.c.) points out that the *combien ... de voitures* construction probably involves remnant movement, rather than just extraction of *combien*; cf. Kayne (2005b). The same probably applies to *skol'ko*, discussed below. I do not attempt to figure *combien/skol'ko*-extraction into the discussion, but in the interest of further research I note that in the preverbal (as opposed to postverbal) position Russian allows agreement in the split construction, and both versions are ambiguous between the cardinal and the individual readings:

(i) Skol'ko   mogut/mozhet   akterov ego uvazhat'?
    how.many may.3pl/may.3sg actors   him respect.inf
    'How many actors may respect him?'

I thank I. Livitz and I. Yanovich for help with judgments; they suggest that there may be speaker variation.

88. Although Pesetsky (1982) claims that non-agreeing QPs must be underlyingly VP-internal direct objects, Franks (1994: 614–615) observes that "speakers fairly readily accept 'non-agreeing' (i.e. neuter singular) verbs with quantified subjects of both unergative and transitive verbs". This is consonant with the judgments of Rapoport (2000), I. Yanovich (p.c.), and I. Livitz (p.c.), who kindly helped me with the data discussed in the main text.

89. Russian has no overt definite articles, so one must carefully check (i) and (ii) in contexts that ensure that 'five actors' is not a definite.

(i) Kazhdyj rezhissjor dumajet, chto pjat'   akterov   ego
    every   director thinks   that five.nom actor.pl.gen him
    uvazhajut.
    respect.3pl
    OK 'There are five actors such that every director thinks that they
    respect him'

(ii) Kazhdyj rezhissjor dumajet, chto pjat'   akterov   ego
     every   director thinks   that five.nom actor.pl.gen him
     uvazhajet.
     respect.3sg
     # 'There are five actors such that every director thinks that they
     respect him'

Rapoport (1999) extends the flexible DP analysis to Russian comparative DPs, which by and large follow the same pattern as the unmodified
numeral indefinites illustrated in the main text. Cattaneo (2007) makes
a congenial proposal about Italian clefts, extending an observation by F.
Beghelli reported in Szabolcsi and Zwarts (1993/1997):

(iii) Sono cinque donne   che (non) ho   invitato.
      are five   women that not   have invited.I
      'There are five women who I did (not) invite'

(iv) È cinque donne   che (*non) ho   invitato.
     is five   women who not   have invited.I
     'The number such that I did (*not) invite that many women is five'

90. I thank T. Ionin and O. Matushansky for discussion.

91. Hackl (2009) assumes that the definite article in relative superlatives is an
    existential in disguise; see (35). In Szabolcsi (1986) *the -est* is a unit that
    occurs at the N''' level in absolute superlatives and at the N'' level in rela-
    tive superlatives. In then-current terms N''' is the position of definiteness
    markers and quantifiers, and N'' of numerals.

92. The regions of Table 8.1 give a rather coarse-grained classification, sim-
    ilarly to the fact that Table 10.1 does not list all the important DP-
    types of English. For a finer-grained classification see Bernardi and Sza-
    bolcsi (2008). Bare singulars and plurals, polarity items, negative (con-
    cord) quantifiers and *nem minden NP* 'not every NP' are not counters,
    but they do not occur in Regions 1 or 2. Contrastive foci and *only*-phrases
    also have a separate rubric in the finer-grained classification and are not
    lumped with counters. The identification of the counter vs. non-counter
    division with regions has to be taken with these qualifications.

93. In other words, *több, mint n NP* in Region 3 is a counting quantifier, but
    in Region 2 it is not. See also note 89 for Russian. It is an open question
    whether English *more than n NP* has a similar dual behavior. See Szabolcsi
    (1997a: 134–137) for some discussion.

94. I thank J. Koster-Moeller for generous help with the explanation of the
    self-paced counting tasks and their interpretation.

95. The indirect object linearly follows the direct object but is structurally higher. Whichever factor is relevant for scope, inverse scope is available.

96. It is not quite clear how this approach interacts with the widely-held view that the subject is introduced by a functional head outside VP, i.e. by vP or VoiceP (Kratzer 1996 and others).

97. See a detailed discussion of counting quantifiers and contrastive/exhaustive foci in Wedgwood (2005). In Szabolcsi (1997a) the position of counting quantifiers is labeled PredOp for Predicate Operator; in Brody and Szabolcsi (2003) it is labeled CountP. These two works are not concerned with the focusing of other expressions.

98. The standardly quoted example uses a proper name in the subject position of the second conjunct, but because QR of names may be dubious anyway, it is important to see that Scope Economy does more than exclude just that.

99. Williams (2003: 45–50) reanalyzes Brody and Szabolcsi's data, but neglects the examples that necessitate reconstruction, and surprisingly refers to a reordering operation in Brody and Szabolcsi (2003) that is strictly equivalent to his own Flip operation as "hyper-Kaynean remnant movement".

100. Szabolcsi (1994: 272) writes, "[in earlier work] I propose[d] the following semantic interpretations for the subordinator. In Montague Grammar, C and D may be regarded as lambda operators that bind variables over possible worlds and properties, respectively, thus yielding propositions and generalized quantifiers as canonical arguments. In Discourse Representation Theory, the subordinator may be claimed to serve as, or mark the existence of, a discourse referent (individual or group)."

101. I thank T. Leu for discussion of the contents of this section.

102. Leu (2008: Chapter 7) proposes a new analysis of the genitive/dative morphology in the noun phrase.

103. Leu (2008) is undecided as to whether the historical definite determiner at the end of *beid-*, *bäid-*, and *both* should be synchronically factored out. We will not pursue the decomposition here.

104. Leu (p.c.) suggests that the second (optionally pronounced) *to* has article agreement, as opposed to adjectival agreement. The adjectival article and the ordinary article (in D*) happen to be homonymous in Modern Greek, just as they are in most cases in German.

105. Strong adjectival agreement occurs on *jed-* even when it is followed by (another) adjective. Compare: *der kleine Baum* 'the little tree', *der schöne kleine Baum* 'the pretty little tree', *jeder kleine Baum* 'every little tree'.

106. I thank Z. Szabó, S. Mascarenhas, P. Schlenker, I. Yanovich, and D. Ben-Shalom for discussion on these matters.

107. I thank K.A. Jayaseelan for sharing and discussing this manuscript with me. See also Haspelmath (1995); Zerbian and Krifka (2008).

Bibliography

Abrusán, Márta 2007. *Contradiction and Grammar: The Case of Weak Islands.* PhD dissertation, MIT.

Abusch, Dorit 1994. The scope of indefinites. *Natural Language Semantics* 2: 83–135.

Allwood, Jens, Lars-Gunnar Andersson, and Östen Dahl 1977. *Logic in Linguistics.* Cambridge: Cambridge University Press.

Alonso-Ovalle, Luís and Paola Menéndez-Benito 2002. Two types of weak quantifiers: evidence from Spanish. In: *Proceedings of the 1st North American Summer School in Logic, Language and Information,* pp. 11–19. Stanford, CA.

Amritavalli, R. 2003. Question and negative polarity in the disjunction phrase. *Syntax* 6: 1–18.

Aoun, Joseph and Audrey Li 1993. *The Syntax of Scope.* Cambridge, MA: The MIT Press.

Bach, Emmon and Barbara Partee 1984. Quantification, pronouns, and VP-anaphora. In: Jeroen Groenendijk, Theo Janssen and Martin Stokhof (eds.), *Truth, Interpretation, and Information,* pp. 99–130. Dordrecht: Foris.

Bach, Emmon, Eloise Jelinek, Angelika Kratzer and Barbara Partee (eds.) 1995. *Quantification in Natural Languages.* Dordrecht: Kluwer.

Bach, Kent 2000. Quantification, qualification and context: a reply to Stanley and Szabó. *Mind and Language* 15: 262–283.

Bachrach, Asaf and Roni Katzir 2006. Spelling out QR. In: Estela Puig-Waldmüller (ed.), *Proceedings of Sinn und Bedeutung* 11, pp. 63–75. Barcelona: Universitat Pompeu Fabra.

Balogh, Kata 2009. *Theme With Variations: A Context-based Analysis of Focus.* PhD dissertation, University of Amsterdam.

Balusu, Rahul 2005. Distributive reduplication in Telugu. In: Christopher Davis, Amy Rose Deal, and Youri Zabbal (eds.), *Proceedings of NELS* 36, pp. 39–53. Amherst: GLSA.

Barker, Chris 2007. Direct compositionality on demand. In: Chris Barker and Pauline Jacobson (eds.), *Direct Compositionality*, pp. 102–131. Oxford: Oxford University Press.

Barker, Chris and Chung-chieh Shan 2006. Explaining crossover and superiority as left-to-right evaluation. *Linguistics and Philosophy* 29: 91–134.

Barker, Chris and Chung-chieh Shan 2008. Donkey anaphora is in-scope binding. *Semantics and Pragmatics* 1:1–42. doi: 10.3765/sp.

Barker, Chris and Chung-chieh Shan 2009. *Book on Continuations and Scope*, in progress.

Barwise, Jon 1979. On branching quantifiers in English. *Journal of Philosophical Logic* 81/1: 47–80.

Barwise, Jon and Robin Cooper 1981. Generalized quantifiers and natural language. *Linguistics and Philosophy* 4: 159–219.

Beaver, David and Brady Clark 2003. *Always* and *only*: Why not all focus sensitive operators are alike. *Natural Language Semantics* 11: 323–362.

Beck, Sigrid 1996. Quantified structures as barriers for LF-movement. *Natural Language Semantics* 4: 1–56.

Beck, Sigrid 2001. Reciprocals are definites. *Natural Language Semantics* 9: 69–138.

Beck, Sigrid and Uli Sauerland 2000. Cumulation is needed: a reply to Winter (2000). *Natural Language Semantics* 8: 349–371.

Becker, Misha 1999. The *some* indefinites. In: Gianluca Storto (ed.), *Syntax at Sunset 2*, UCLA Working Papers in Linguistics 3: 1–13.

Beghelli, Filipppo 1997. The syntax of distributivity and pair-list readings. In: Szabolcsi (1997b), pp. 349–409.

Beghelli, Filippo, Dorit Ben-Shalom, and Anna Szabolcsi 1997. Variation, distributivity, and the illusion of branching. In: Szabolcsi (1997b), pp. 29–70.

Beghelli, Filippo and Timothy Stowell 1997. Distributivity and negation: The syntax of *each* and *every*. In: Szabolcsi (1997b), pp. 71–108.

Bennett, Michael and Barbara H. Partee 1972/2002. Toward the logic of tense and aspect in English. In: *Compositionality in Formal Semantics*, pp. 59–110. Oxford: Blackwell.

Ben-Shalom, Dorit 1996. *Semantic Trees*. PhD dissertation, UCLA.

Bernardi, Raffaella 2010. Scope ambiguities through the mirror. In: H. de Mulder, M. Everaert, T. Lentz, Ø. Nilsen, and A. Zondervan (eds.), *The Linguistics Enterprise: Cognition, Methodology, Modelling*, pp. 11–54. Amsterdam: John Benjamins.

Bernardi, Raffaella and Michael Moortgat 2007. Continuation semantics for Symmetric Categorial Grammar. In: Daniel Leivant and Ruy de Queiroz (eds.), *Proceedings of the 14th Workshop on Logic, Language, Information and Computation*, pp. 53–71. Dordrecht: Springer.

Bernardi, Raffaella and Anna Szabolcsi 2008. Optionality, scope, and licensing: an application of partially ordered categories. *Journal of Logic, Language and Information* 17: 237–283.

Bittner, Maria 1993. *Case, Scope, and Binding*. Dordrecht: Reidel.

Bittner, Maria and Naja Trondhjem 2008. Quantification as reference: evidence from Q-verbs. In: Matthewson (2008), pp. 7–67.

Bobaljik, Jonathan D. 2001. Floating quantifiers: handle with care. In: Lisa Cheng and Rynt Sybesma (eds.), *The Second State-of-the-Article Book*, pp. 45–68. Berlin: Mouton de Gruyter.

Bobaljik Jonathan D. and Susi Wurmbrand 2008. Word order and scope: transparent interfaces and the 3/4 signature. To appear in *Linguistic Inquiry*.

Borer, Hagit 2005a. *In Name Only: Structuring Sense*, Vol I. Oxford: Oxford University Press.

Borer, Hagit 2005b. *The Normal Course of Events: Structuring Sense*, Vol II. Oxford: Oxford University Press.

Borzdyko, Oxana 2004. *La disjonction, l'indéfinition et l'interrogation: la particule ci du biélorusse*. PhD thesis, University of Western Ontario, London, CA.

Bosveld-de Smet, Leonie 1998. *On Mass and Plural Quantification: The Case of French des/du NPs*. PhD dissertation, University of Groningen.

Bott, Lewis and Ira Noveck 2004. Some utterances are underinformative: the onset and time course of scalar inference. *Journal of Memory and Language* 51: 437–457.

Braine, Michael and D. O'Brien (eds.) 1998. *Mental Logic*. Mahwah, NJ: Erlbaum.

Breheny, Richard 2003. Exceptional-scope indefinites and domain restriction. In: Matthias Weisgerber (ed.), *Proceedings of Sinn und Bedeutung 7*, pp. 310–323. Konstanz: Universitt Konstanz.

Breheny, Richard 2008. A new look at the semantics and pragmatics of numerically quantified noun phrases. *Journal of Semantics* 25: 93–139.

Brennan, Jonathan 2008. Indefinites, choice functions, and discourse anaphora. To appear in: S. Lima, K. Mullin, and B. Smith (eds.), *Proceedings of NELS 39*. Amherst, MA: GLSA.

Brisson, Christine 1998. *Distributivity, Maximality, and Floating Quantifiers*. PhD dissertation, Rutgers University.

Brisson, Christine 2003. Plurals, *all*, and the nonuniformity of collective predication. *Linguistics and Philosophy* 26: 129–184.

Brody, Michael 1990. Remarks on the order of elements in the Hungarian focus field. In: István Kenesei (ed.), *Approaches to Hungarian*, Vol. 3, pp. 95–123. Szeged: JATE.

Brody, Michael and Anna Szabolcsi 2003. Overt scope in Hungarian. *Syntax* 6: 19–51.

Bruening, Benjamin 2001. QR obeys superiority: ACD and frozen scope. *Linguistic Inquiry* 32/2: 233–273.

Bruening, Benjamin 2008. Quantification in Passamaquoddy. In: Matthewson (2008), pp. 7–67.

Butler, Alastair and Mark Donohue 2009. *A Semantic Grammar of Tukang Besi*. Submitted book ms.

Butler, Johnny 2007. The structure of temporality and modality: or, towards deriving something like a Cinque hierarchy. In: Pierre Pica (ed.), *Linguistic Variation Yearbook 2006*, pp. 161–201. Amsterdam: John Benjamins.

Büring, Daniel 1996. A weak theory of strong readings. In: *Proceedings of Semantics and Linguistic Theory VI*, pp. 17–35. Ithaca: Cornell.

Büring, Daniel 1997. The great scope inversion conspiracy. *Linguistics and Philosophy* 20: 175– 194.

Büring, Daniel 2005. *Binding Theory*. Cambridge: Cambridge University Press.

Cable, Seth 2008. Q-particles and the nature of wh-fronting. In: Matthewson (2008), pp. 67–105.

Cappelen, Herman and Ernest Lepore 2001. Insensitive quantifiers. In: Joseph Keim Campbell, Michael O'Rourke, and David Shier (eds.), *Meaning and Truth. Investigations in Philosophical Semantics*. New York: Seven Bridges Press.

Cardinaletti, Anna and Giuliana Giusti 2006. The syntax of quantified phrases and quantitative clitics. In: Martin Everaert and Henk van Riemsdijk (eds.), *The Blackwell Companion to Syntax*, Vol. V, pp. 23–93. Oxford: Blackwell.

Carlson, Gregory 1977. A unified analysis of the English bare plural. *Linguistics and Philosophy* 1: 413–457.

Carlson, Gregory 1984. Thematic roles and their role in semantic interpretation. *Linguistics* 22/3: 259–279.

Carstens, Vicki M. 1991. *The Morphology and Syntax of Determiner Phrases in Kiswahili*. PhD dissertation, UCLA.

Carston, Robyn 1998. Informativeness, relevance and scalar implicature. In: Carston, Robyn and Seiji Uchida (eds.), *Relevance Theory*, pp. 179–236. Amsterdam: John Benjamins.

Cattaneo, Andrea 2007. What verb agreement and specificity tell us about DPs and their structure: the case of Italian cleft constructions. Ms., New York University.

Cecchetto, Carlo 2004. Explaining the locality conditions of QR: consequences for the theory of phases. *Natural Language Semantics* 12: 345–397.

Chemla, Emmanuel 2008. Presuppositions in quantified sentences. To appear in *Natural Language Semantics*.

Cheng, L.-S. Lisa 2008. On *every* type of quantificational expression in Chinese. In: Monika Rathert and Anastasia Giannakiou (eds.), *Quantification, Definiteness, and Nominalization*, pp. 53–75. Oxford: Oxford University Press.

Cheung, Chi-hang (Candice) 2003. *An Investigation of the Jingpo Nominal Structure*. M.Phil. thesis, University of Hong Kong.

Chierchia, Gennaro 1984. *Topics in the Syntax and Semantics of Infinitives and Gerunds*. PhD dissertation, UMass.

Chierchia, Gennaro 1993. Questions with quantifiers. *Natural Language Semantics* 1/2: 181–234.

Chierchia, Gennaro 1995. *Dynamics of Meaning*. Chicago: The University of Chicago Press.

Chierchia, Gennaro 1998. Reference to kinds across languages. *Natural Language Semantics* 6: 339–405.

Chierchia, Gennaro 2001. A puzzle about indefinites. In: Carlo Cecchetto, Gennaro Chierchia, and Maria Teresa Guasti (eds.), *Semantic Interfaces*, pp. 51–90. Stanford: CSLI Publications.

Chierchia, Gennaro 2006. Broaden your views: implicatures of domain widening and the "logicality" of language. *Linguistic Inquiry* 37: 535–591.

Chierchia, Gennaro, Danny Fox, and Benjamin Spector 2008. The grammatical view of scalar implicatures and the relationship between semantics and pragmatics. To appear in Claudia Maienborn et al. (eds.), *Semantics: An International Handbook of Natural Language Meaning*. Berlin: Mouton de Gruyter.

Choe, Jae-Woong 1987. *Anti-Quantifiers and a Theory of Distributivity*. PhD dissertation, UMass, Amherst.

Chomsky, Noam 1977. *Essays on Form and Interpretation*. New York: North Holland.

Chomsky, Noam 1995. *The Minimalist Program*. Cambridge, MA: The MIT Press.

Chomsky, Noam 2001. Derivation by phase. In: Michael Kenstowicz (ed.), *Ken Hale: A Life in Language*, pp. 1–52. Cambridge, MA: The MIT Press.

Condoravdi, Cleo 1992. Strong and weak novelty and familiarity. In: *Proceedings of Semantics and Linguistic Theory II*, pp. 17–37. Columbus, OH: OSU.

Cooper, Robin 1983. *Quantification and Syntactic Structure*. Dordrecht: Reidel.

Cormack, Annabel and Ruth Kempson 1991. On specificity. In: Jay Garfield and Murray Kitely (eds.), *Meaning and Truth: Essential Readings in Modern Semantics*, pp. 546–581. New York: Paragon.

Cresswell, Max 1976. The semantics of degree. In: Barbara H. Partee (ed.), *Montague Grammar*, pp. 261–292. New York: Academic Press.

Cresswell, Max 1990. *Entities and Indices*. Dordrecht: Kluwer.

Cresti, Diana 1995. Extraction and reconstruction. *Natural Language Semantics* 3: 79–122.

Davidson, Donald 1967. The logical form of action sequences. In: Nicholas Rescher (ed.), *The Logic of Decision and Action*, pp. 81–120. Pittsburgh: U. of Pittsburgh Press.

Dayal, Veneeta 1993. Scope marking as indirect wh-dependency. *Natural Language Semantics* 2/2: 137–170.

Dayal, Veneeta 1998. *Any* as inherently modal. *Linguistics and Philosophy* 21/5: 433–476.

Dayal, Veneeta 2002. Single-pair and multiple-pair answers: Wh in-situ and scope. *Linguistic Inquiry* 33/3: 512–20.

de Hoop, Helen 1992. *Case Configuration and Noun Phrase Interpretation*. London: Routledge.

de Hoop, Helen and Jaume Solà 1995. Determiners, context sets, and focus. In: José Camacho, Lina Choueiri, and Maki Watanabe (eds.), *Proceedings of WCCFL 14*. Stanford: CSLI Publications.

de Jong, Franciska and Henk Verkuyl 1985. Generalized quantifiers: the properness of their strength. In: Johan van Benthem and Alice ter Meulen (eds.), *Generalized Quantifiers in Natural Language*, pp. 21–45. Dordrecht: Foris.

de Mey, Sjaak 1981. The dependant plural and the analysis of tense. In: Victoria A. Burke and James Pustejovsky (eds.), *Proceedings of NELS* 11, pp. 58–78. Amherst: GLSA, UMass.

de Swart, Henriëtte 1993. *Adverbs of Quantification: A Generalized Quantifier Approach*. New York: Garland.

de Swart, Henriëtte 2006. Aspectual implications of the semantics of plural indefinites. In: Svetlana Vogeleer and Liliane Tasmowski (eds.), *Non-definiteness and Plurality*, pp. 161–189. Amsterdam: John Benjamins.

Déprez, Vivien 1998. Semantic effects of agreement: the case of French past participle agreement. *Probus*, 10: 1–65.

Diesing, Molly 1992. *Indefinites*. Cambridge, MA: MIT Press.

Dobrovie-Sorin, Carmen 1994. *The Syntax of Romanian*. Berlin: Mouton de Gruyter.

Doetjes, Jenny 1992. Rightward floating quantifiers float to the left. *The Linguistic Review* 9: 313–332.

Doetjes, Jenny 1996. Mass and count: syntax or semantics? In: *Proceedings of Meaning on the HIL*, pp. 34–52. HIL/Leiden University.

Doetjes, Jenny 1997. *Quantifiers and Selection: On the Distribution of Quantifying Expressions in French, Dutch and English*. PhD dissertation, Leiden University.

Doetjes, Jenny and Martin Honcoop 1997. The semantics of event-related readings: a case for pair-quantification. In: Szabolcsi (1997b), pp. 263–311.

Dowty, David R. 1987. Collective predicates, distributive predicates, and *all*. In: Fred Marshall (ed.), *Proceedings of the 3rd ESCOL*. Columbus, OH: OSU.

Dowty, David R. 2007. Compositionality as an empirical problem. In: Chris Barker and Pauline Jacobson (eds.), *Direct Compositionality*, pp. 23–102. Oxford: Oxford University Press.

Dowty, David R. and Belinda Brodie 1984. The semantics of "floated" quantifiers in a transformationless grammar. In: Mark Cobler, Susannah MacKaye, and Michael T. Westcoat (eds.), *Proceedings of WCCFL 3*, pp. 75–90. Stanford, CA: Stanford Linguistics Association.

Eckardt, Regine 2006. To be or not to be a determiner. In: *Meaning Change in Grammaticalization*, pp. 202–235. Oxford: Oxford University Press.

Elbourne, Paul 2005. *Situations and Individuals*. Cambridge, MA: The MIT Press.

Ernst, Thomas 2002. *The Syntax of Adjuncts*. Cambridge: Cambridge University Press.

Etxeberria, Urtzi 2008. On Basque quantification and on how some languages restrict their quantificational domain overtly. In: Matthewson (2008), pp. 225–277.

Evans, Gareth 1980. Pronouns. *Linguistic Inquiry* 11: 337–362.

Faller, Martina and Rachel Hastings 2008. Cuzco Quechua quantifiers. In: Matthewson (2008), pp. 277–319.

Farkas, Donka 1981. Quantifier scope and syntactic islands. In: R. Hendrik et al. (eds.), *Papers from the Seventh Regional Meeting, Chicago Linguistic Society*, pp. 59–66.

Farkas, Donka 1997a. Evaluation indices and scope. In: Szabolcsi (1997b), pp. 183–217.

Farkas, Donka 1997b. Dependent indefinites. In: Francis Corblin et al. (eds.), *Empirical Issues in Formal Syntax and Semantics*, pp. 243–268. Frankfurt-am-Main: Peter Lang.

Farkas, Donka 2002. Specificity distinctions. *Journal of Semantics* 19/3: 213–243.

Farkas, Donka and Anastasia Giannakidou 1996. How clause-bounded is the scope of universals? In: *Proceedings of Semantics and Linguistic Theory VI*, pp. 137–155. Ithaca: Cornell.

Farkas, Donka and Katalin É. Kiss 2000. On the comparative and absolute readings of superlatives. *Natural Language and Linguistic Theory* 18: 417–455.

Fauconnier, Gilles 1978. Implication reversal in a natural language. In: Franz Günthner and S. J. Schmidt (eds.), *Formal Semantics and Pragmatics for Natural Languages*, pp. 289–303. Dordrecht: Reidel.

Feferman, Solomon 1997. Logic, logics, logicism. In memory of George Boolos. *Notre Dame Journal of Formal Logic* 40/1: 31–54.

Ferreira, Fernanda and Naomi Patson 2007. The "good enough" approach to language comprehension. *Language and Linguistics Compass* 1: 71–83.

von Fintel, Kai 1993. Exceptive constructions. *Natural Language Semantics* 1: 23–148.

von Fintel, Kai 1994. *Restrictions on Quantifier Domains*. PhD dissertation. UMass, Amherst.

von Fintel, Kai 1999a. NPI licensing, Strawson-entailment, and context dependency. *Journal of Semantics* 16: 97–148.

von Fintel, Kai 1999b. Quantifier domain selection and pseudo-scope. *Cornell Context-dependence Conference*, March 28, 1999.

von Fintel, Kai and Sabine Iatridou 2002. If and when *if*-clauses can restrict quantifiers. Paper for the *Workshop in Philosophy and Linguistics at the University of Michigan*, November 8–10, 2002.

Fodor, Janet 1970. *The Linguistic Description of Opaque Contexts*. PhD dissertation, MIT.

Fodor, Janet and Ivan Sag 1982. Referential and quantificational indefinites. *Linguistics and Philosophy* 5: 355–398.

Fox, Danny 1999. Reconstruction, binding theory, and the interpretation of chains. *Linguistic Inquiry* 30: 157–196.

Fox, Danny 2000. *Economy and Semantic Interpretation*. Cambridge, MA: The MIT Press.

Fox, Danny 2002a. On Logical Form. In: Randall Hendrick (ed.), *Minimalist Syntax*, pp. 82–124. Oxford: Blackwell.

Fox, Danny 2002b. Antecedent-contained deletion and the copy theory of movement. *Linguistic Inquiry* 33: 63–96.

Fox, Danny and Jon Nissenbaum 1999. Extraposition and scope: a case for overt QR. In: S. Bird, A, Carnie, J. D. Haugen, and P. Norquest (eds.), *Proceedings of WCCFL* 18. Somerville, MA: Cascadilla Press.

Fox, Danny and Martin Hackl 2006. The universal density of measurement. *Linguistics and Philosophy* 29: 537–586.

Fretheim, Thornstein 1992. Themehood, rhemehood and Norwegian focus structure. *Folia Linguistica* 26/1–2: 111–150.

Fromkin, Victoria (ed.) 2000. *Linguistics. An Introduction To Linguistic Theory*. Oxford: Blackwell.

Gallin, Daniel 1975. *Intensional and Higher-Order Modal Logic*. Amsterdam: North-Holland.

Gamut, L.T.F. 1991. *Logic, Language, and Meaning*. Chicago, London: The University of Chicago Press.

Garrett, Edward 1996. Wh-in-situ and the syntax of distributivity. In: Edward Garrett and Felicia Lee (eds.), *Syntax at Sunset*, pp. 129–145. UCLA Working Papers in Syntax and Semantics 1. Los Angeles, CA: UCLA, Department of Linguistics.

Gawron, Mark and Stanley Peters 1990. *Anaphora and Quantification in Situation Semantics*. Stanford: CSLI Publications.

Gentzen, Gerhard 1935/1969. Untersuchungen über das logische Schliessen. *Mathematische Zeitschrift* 39: 176–210, 305–431. English translation in M. E. Szabo (ed.), *The Collected Papers of Gerhard Gentzen*, pp. 68–131. North-Holland.

Geurts, Bart 2000. Indefinites and choice functions. *Linguistic Inquiry* 31/4: 731–738.

Geurts, Bart 2006. Take *five*: the meaning and use of a number word. In: Svetlana Vogeleer and Liliane Tasmowski (eds.), *Non-Definiteness and Plurality*, pp. 311–329. Amsterdam: John Benjamins.

Geurts, Bart and Frans van der Slik 2005. Monotonicity and processing load. *Journal of Semantics* 22/1: 97–117.

Geurts, Bart and Rick Nouwen 2007. *At least* et al.: the semantics of scalar modifiers. *Language* 83/3: 533–559.

Giannakidou, Anastasia 1998. *Polarity Sensitivity as (Non)Veridical Dependency*. Amsterdam: John Benjamins.

Giannakidou, Anastasia 2000. Negative ... concord? *Natural Language and Linguistic Theory* 18: 457–523.

Giannakidou, Anastasia 2004. Domain restriction and the arguments of quantificational determiners. In: *Proceedings of Semantics and Linguistic Theory XIV*, pp. 110–128. Ithaca: Cornell.

Gil, David 1982. Quantifier scope, linguistic variation, and natural language semantics. *Linguistics and Philosophy* 5/4: 421–472.

Gil, David 1990. Markers of distributivity in Japanese and Korean. In: Hajime Hoji (ed.), *Japanese/Korean Linguistics*, pp. 385–393. Stanford: CSLI Publications.

Gil, David 1995. Universal quantifiers and distributivity. In Bach et al. (1995), pp. 321–363.

Gil, David 2008. Conjunctions and universal quantifiers. In: Martin Haspelmath, Matthew S. Dryer, David Gil, and Bernard Comrie (eds.), *The World Atlas of Language Structures Online*, Chapter 56. Munich: Max Planck Digital Library. http://wals.info/feature/description/56.

Glanzberg, Michael 2006. Quantifiers. In: Ernest Lepore and Barry Smith (eds.), *The Oxford Handbook of Philosophy of Language*, pp. 794–821. Oxford: Oxford University Press.

Glanzberg, Michael 2008. Quantification and contributing objects to thoughts. *Philosophical Perspectives* 22/1: 207–231.

Grice, H. P. 1975. Logic and conversation. In: Peter Cole and Jerry L. Morgan (eds.), *Syntax and Semantics: Speech Acts*, Vol. 3, pp. 41–58. New York: Academic Press.

Groenendijk, Jeroen and Martin Stokhof 1984. *The Semantics of Questions and the Pragmatics of Answers*. PhD dissertation, University of Amsterdam.

Groenendijk, Jeroen and Martin Stokhof 1990. Dynamic Predicate Logic. *Linguistics and Philosophy* 14: 39–100.

Groenendijk, Jeroen and Martin Stokhof 1991. Dynamic Montague Grammar. In: László Kálmán and László Pólos (eds.), *Papers from the Second Symposium on Logic and Language*, pp. 3–48. Budapest: Akadémiai.

Grosu, Alex and Julia Horvath 2006. Reply to Bhatt and Pancheva's "Late Merger of Degree Clauses": the irrelevance of (non)conservativity. *Linguistic Inquiry* 37: 457–483.

Gutiérrez-Rexach, Javier 1997. Questions and generalized quantifiers. In: Szabolcsi (1997b), pp. 409–453.

Gutiérrez-Rexach, Javier 2001. The semantics of Spanish plural existential determiners and the dynamics of judgment types. *Probus* 13: 113–154.

Hackl, Martin 2000. *Comparative Quantifiers*. PhD dissertation. MIT, Cambridge, MA.

Hackl, Martin 2002. Comparative quantifiers and plural predication. In: Karine Megerdoomian and Leora Anne Bar-el (eds.), *Proceedings of WCCFL 20*, pp. 234–247. Cascadilla Press.

Hackl, Martin 2009. On the grammar and processing of proportional quantifiers. *Most* versus *more than half*. *Natural Language Semantics* 17/1: 63–98.

Halle, Morris and Alec Marantz 1994. Some key features of Distributed Morphology. In: *MIT Working Papers in Linguistics* 21: 275–288.

Hallman, Peter 2000. *The Structure of Predicates: Interactions of Derivation, Case and Quantification*. PhD dissertation, UCLA.

Hamblin, Charles 1973. Questions in Montague English. *Foundations of Language* 10: 41–53.

Harley, Heidi and Rolf Noyer 2003. Distributed Morphology. In: Lisa Cheng and Rint Sybesma (eds.), *The Second State-of-the-Article Book*, pp. 463–497. Berlin: Mouton de Gruyter.

Haspelmath, Martin 1995. Diachronic sources of 'all' and 'every'. In: Bach et al. (1995), pp. 363–382.

Haspelmath, Martin 1997. *Indefinite Pronouns*. Oxford: Clarendon Press.

Heim, Irene 1982. *The Semantics of Definite and Indefinite Noun Phrases in English*. PhD dissertation, UMass, Amherst.

Heim, Irene 1985. Notes on comparatives and related matters. Ms., University of Texas, Austin.

Heim, Irene 1990. E-Type pronouns and donkey anaphora. *Linguistics and Philosophy* 13: 137–177.

Heim, Irene 1992. Presupposition projection and the semantics of attitude reports. *Journal of Semantics* 9: 183–221.

Heim, Irene 2001. Degree operators and scope. In: C. Féry and W. Sternefeld (eds.), *Audiatur Vox Sapientiae: A Festschrift for Arnim von Stechow*, pp. 214–240. Studia Grammatica 52. Akademie Verlag.

Heim, Irene 2004. Notes on superlatives. Ms., MIT. SemanticsArchive.net

Heim, Irene 2006a. Remarks on comparative clauses as generalized quantifiers. Ms., MIT. SemanticsArchive.net

Heim, Irene 2006b. Little. In: *Proceedings of Semantics and Linguistic Theory XVI*. Ithaca: Cornell. SemanticsArchive.net

Heim, Irene and Angelika Kratzer 1998. *Semantics in Generative Grammar*. Oxford: Blackwell.

Hendriks, Herman 1993. *Studied Flexibility: Categories and Types in Syntax and Semantics*. PhD dissertation, University of Amsterdam.

Henkin, Leon A. 1963. A theory of propositional types. *Fundamenta Mathematica* 52: 323–344.

Herburger, Elena 2000. *What Counts: Focus and Quantification*. Cambridge, MA: The MIT Press.

von Heusinger, Klaus 1992. *Epsilon-Ausdrücke alse Semanteme für definite und indefinite Nominalphrasen und anaphorishe Pronomen*. PhD dissertation, Universität Konstanz.

von Heusinger, Klaus 2001. The reference of indefinites. In: Klaus von Heusinger and Urs Egli (eds.), *Reference and Anaphoric Relations*, pp. 247–267. Dordrecht: Kluwer.

von Heusinger, Klaus 2004. Choice functions and the anaphoric semantics of definite NPs. *Research on Language and Computation* 2: 309–329.

von Heusinger, Klaus 2008. Verbal semantics and the diachronic development of differential object marking in Spanish. *Probus* 20: 1–33.

von Heusinger, Klaus and Edgar Onea 2008. Triggering and blocking effects in the diachronic development of DOM in Romanian. *Probus* 20: 71–116.

von Heusinger, Klaus and Udo Klein 2008. Two indefinite articles in Uzbek. In: Reiko Vermeulen and Ryoskuke Shibagaki (eds.), *MIT Working Papers in Linguistics. Proceedings of the 5th Workshop on Formal Altaic Linguistics (WAFL 5)*. Cambridge, MA: MIT.

Heycock, Caroline 1995. Asymmetries in reconstruction. *Linguistic Inquiry* 26: 547–570.

Higginbotham, James 1991. *Either/or*. In: Tim Sherer (ed.), *Proceedings of NELS* 21, pp. 143–157. Amherst: GLSA.

Higginbotham, James 1993/2004. Interrogatives. In: Ken Hale and S. J. Keyser (eds.), *The View from Building 20: Essays in Linguistics in Honor of Sylvain Bromberger*. Reprinted in: Steven Davis and Brendan S. Gillon (eds.), *Semantics: A Reader*. 687–710. Oxford-New York: Oxford University Press.

Higginbotham, James and Robert May 1981. Questions, quantifiers and crossing. *The Linguistic Review* 1/1: 41–80.

Hintikka, Jaakko 1962. *Knowledge and Belief: An Introduction to the Two Notions*. Cornell University Press, Ithaca, NY.

Hintikka, Jaakko 1974. Quantifiers vs. quantification theory. *Linguistic Inquiry* 5: 153–177.

Hintikka, Jaakko 1997. No scope for scope? *Linguistics and Philosophy* 20: 515–544.

Hintikka, Jaakko and Gabriel Sandu 1997. Game-theoretical semantics. In: J. van Benthem and A. ter Meulen (eds.), *Handbook of Logic and Language*, pp. 361–410. Cambridge, MA: The MIT Press.

Hoji, Hajime 1985. *Logical Form Constraints and Configurational Structures in Japanese*. PhD dissertation. Seattle: University of Washington.

Honcoop, Martin 1998. *Dynamic Excursions on Weak Islands*. PhD dissertation, Leiden University.

Horn, Laurence R. 2004. Implicature. In: Laurence R. Horn and Gergory Ward (eds.), *The Handbook of Pragmatics*, pp. 3–28. Oxford: Blackwell.

Hornstein, Norbert 1995. *The Grammar of Logical Form from GB to Minimalism*. Oxford: Blackwell.

Horvath, Julia 2006. Separating "focus movement" from focus. In: S. Karimi et al. (eds.), *Clever and Right: A Festschrift for Joe Emonds*. Berlin: Mouton de Gruyter.

Huang, Shi-Zhe 1996. *Quantification and Predication in Mandarin Chinese: A Case Study of dou*. PhD dissertation, University of Pennsylvania.

Hunyadi, László 1989. On the procedural nature of quantification in Hungarian. Ms., LSA Linguistic Institute, Tucson, AZ.

Hunyadi, László 1999. The outlines of a metrical syntax of Hungarian. *Acta Linguistica Hungarica* 46: 69–94.

Iatridou, Sabine 1994. On the contribution of conditional *then*. *Natural Language Semantics* 2: 171–199.

Ionin, Tanya 2006. *This* is definitely specific: specificity and definiteness in article systems. *Natural Language Semantics* 14/2: 175–234.

Ionin, Tanya and Ora Matushansky 2006. The composition of complex cardinals. *Journal of Semantics* 23/4: 325–360.

Ioup, Georgette 1978. Some universals for quantifier scope. In: John P. Kimball (ed.), *Syntax and Semantics* 4, pp. 37–58. New York: Academic Press.

Jackson, Scott 2006. Prosody and logical scope in English. *19th Annual CUNY Conference in Sentence Processing*, New York, NY, March 24, 2006.

Jacobson, Pauline 1994. Binding connectivity in copular sentences. In: *Proceedings of Semantics and Linguistic Theory IV*, pp. 161–179. Ithaca: Cornell.

Jacobson, Pauline 1999. Towards a variable-free semantics. *Linguistics and Philosophy* 22: 117–184.

Jacobson, Pauline 2002. The (dis)organization of grammar. *Linguistics and Philosophy* 25: 601–626.

Jäger, Gerhard 2005. *Anaphora and Type-Logical Grammar*. Dordrecht: Springer.

Jayaseelan, K. A. 2001. Questions and question-word incorporating quantifiers in Malayalam. *Syntax* 4: 63–83.

Jayaseelan, K. A. 2005. Comparative morphology of quantifiers. Paper based on talk at *Strategies of Quantification*, July 15–17, 2004, University of York. CIEFL, Hyderabad.

Jayez, Jacques and Lucia M. Tovena 2006. Epistemic determiners. *Journal of Semantics* 23/3: 217–251.

Johnson, Kyle 2007. Determiners and movement. Ms., UMass, Amherst.

Johnson, Kyle and Satoshi Tomioka 1997. Lowering and mid-size clauses. In: Graham Katz, Shin-Sook Kim, and Winhart Haike (eds.), *Proceedings of the Tübingen Workshop on Reconstruction*, pp. 185–206. Tübingen, Germany.

Johnson-Laird, Philip N. 1983. *Mental Models: Towards a Cognitive Science of Language, Inference, and Consciousness*. Cambridge, MA: Harvard UP.

Johnson-Laird, Philip N. and Ruth Byrne 1991. *Deduction*. Hillsdale, NJ: Erlbaum.

Junker, Marie-Odile 1995. *Syntax et sémantique des quantifieurs flottants tous et chacun: distributivité en sémantique conceptuelle*. Genève: Librarie Droz.

Kadmon, Nirit 1993. *On Unique and Non-unique Reference and Asymmetric Quantification*. Garland. New York.

Kadmon, Nirit 2001. *Formal Pragmatics*. Oxford: Blackwell.

Kallulli, Dalina and Antonia Rothmayr 2008. The syntax and semantics of indefinite determiner doubling in varieties of German. *Journal of Comparative Germanic Linguistics* 11: 95–136.

Kamp, Hans 1981/2002. A theory of truth and semantic representation. In: Paul Portner and Barbara H. Partee (eds.), *Formal Semantics: The Essential Readings*. Oxford: Blackwell, pp. 189–223, 2002.

Kamp, Hans and Uwe Reyle 1993. *From Discourse to Logic*. Dordrecht: Kluwer.

Karttunen, Lauri 1977. The syntax and semantics of questions. *Linguistics and Philosophy* 1: 1–44.

Karttunen, Lauri and Stanley Peters 1979. Conventional implicature. In: C.-K. Oh and D. A. Dinneen (eds.), *Syntax and Semantics, Presupposition*, Vol. 11, pp. 1–56. New York, NY: Academic Press.

Kang, Beom-Mo 2002. Categories and meanings of Korean floating quantifiers – with some reference to Japanese. *Journal of East Asian Linguistics* 11: 375–398.

Kayne, Richard S. 1989. Facets of Romance past participle agreement. In: P. Benincà (ed.), *Dialect Variation on the Theory of Grammar*, pp. 85–104. Dordrecht: Foris.

Kayne, Richard S. 1994. *The Antisymmetry of Syntax*. Cambridge, MA: The MIT Press.

Kayne, Richard 1998. Overt vs. covert movement. *Syntax* 1: 128–191.

Kayne, Richard S. 2000. Past participle agreement in French and Italian. In: *Parameters and Universals*, pp. 10–25. Oxford and New York: Oxford University Press.

Kayne, Richard S. 2005a. *Movement and Silence*. Oxford: Oxford University Press.

Kayne, Richard S. 2005b. On some prepositions that look DP-internal. In: Kayne (2005a), pp. 136–176.

Kayne, Richard S. 2005c. A note on the syntax of quantity in English. In: Kayne (2005a), pp. 176–215.

Kayne, Richard S. 2007. *Several, few* and *many*. *Lingua* 117: 832–858.

Keenan, Edward L. 1987. A semantic definition of "indefinite NP". In: Eric Reuland and Alice ter Meulen (eds.), *The Representation of (In)definiteness*, pp. 286–317. Cambridge, MA: The MIT Press.

Keenan, Edward L. 1992. Beyond the Frege boundary. *Linguistics and Philosophy* 15/2: 199–221.

Keenan, Edward L. 1996. The semantics of determiners. In: S. Lappin (ed.), *Handbook of Contemporary Semantic Theory*, pp. 41–63. Oxford: Blackwell.

Keenan, Edward L. 2000. Quantification in English is inherently sortal. *History and Philosophy of Logic* 20: 251–265.

Keenan, Edward L. 2001. Logical objects. In: A. Anderson and M. Zeleny (eds.), *Logic, Meaning and Computation*, pp. 149–180. Dordrecht: Kluwer.

Keenan, Edward L. 2003. The definiteness effect: semantics or pragmatics? *Natural Language Semantics* 11: 187–216.

Keenan, Edward L. 2008. Quantification in Malagasy. In: Matthewson (2008), pp. 319–353.

Keenan, Edward L. (ed.) in progress. *Cross-linguistic Quantifiers Book*.

Keenan, Edward L. and Leonard M. Faltz 1985. *Boolean Semantics for Natural Language*. Dordrecht: Reidel.

Keenan, Edward L. and Jonathan Stavi 1986. A semantic characterization of natural language determiners. *Linguistics and Philosophy* 9: 253–326.

Keenan, Edward L. and Dag Westerståhl 1997. Generalized quantifiers in linguistics and logic. In: J. van Benthem and A. ter Meulen (eds.), *Handbook of Logic and Language*, pp. 837–893. Elsevier: Amsterdam.

Kennedy, Christopher 1997. Antecedent-contained deletion and the syntax of quantification. *Linguistic Inquiry* 28/4: 662–688.

Kennedy, Christopher 1999. *Projecting the Adjective*. PhD dissertation, UC Santa Cruz.

Keshet, Ezra 2008. *Good Intensions: Paving Two Roads to a Theory of the De Re / De Dicto Distinction*. PhD dissertation, MIT.

Khalaily, Shamir 1995. QR and the minimalist theory of syntax: the case of universally and negative quantified expressions in Palestinian Arabic. Ms., University of Leiden.

Kinyalolo, Kasangati 1990. *Syntactic Dependencies and the Spec-Head Agreement Hypothesis in KiLega*. PhD dissertation, UCLA.

Kiss, Katalin É. 1981. Structural relations in Hungarian, a "free" word order language. *Linguistic Inquiry* 12: 185–213.

Kiss, Katalin É. 1991. Logical structure in linguistic structure. In: James T. Huang and Robert May (eds.), *Logical Structure and Linguistic Structure*, pp. 387–426. Dordrecht: Kluwer.

Kiss, Katalin É. 1994. Sentence structure and word order. In: Ferenc Kiefer and Katalin É. Kiss (eds.), *The Syntactic Structure of Hungarian. Syntax and Semantics*, Vol. 27, pp. 1–90. San Diego: Academic Press.

Kiss, Katalin É. 2002. *The Syntax of Hungarian*. Cambridge: Cambridge University Press.

Kiss, Katalin É. 2008. Free word order, (non)configurationality, and phases. *Linguistic Inquiry* 2008, 39/3: 441–475.

Kiss, Katalin É. 2009. Scalar adverbs in and out of focus. In: Katalin É. Kiss (ed.), *Adverbs and Adverbial Adjuncts at the Interfaces*. Berlin: Mouton de Gruyter.

Klima, Edward 1964. Negation in English. In: Jerry Fodor and Jerrold Katz (ed.), *The Structure of Language: Readings in the Philosophy of Language*, pp. 246–323. New York: Prentice Hall.

Kobuchi-Philip, Mana 2003. *Distributivity and the Japanese Floating Numeral Quantifier.* PhD dissertation, CUNY Graduate Center.

Koller, Alexander and Joachim Niehren 1999. Scope underspecification and processing. *ESSLLI Reader.* http://ps.unisb.de/Papers/abstracts/./ESSLLI:99.ps

Koopman, Hilda 2001. Inside the noun in Maasai. Paper presented at the *Workshop on Head Movement*, October 2001, UCLA.

Koopman, Hilda 2005. On the parallelism between DPs and clauses: evidence from Kisongo Maasai. In: Andrew Carnie, Sheila Ann Dooley, Heidi Harley, and Shiela Ann Dooley-Collberg (eds.), *Verb First*, pp. 281–303. Amsterdam: John Benjamins.

Koopman, Hilda and Dominique Sportiche 2008. The *que/qui* alternation: new analytical directions. http://ling.auf.net/lingBuzz/000638

Koopman, Hilda, Dominique Sportiche, and Edward Stabler (to appear). *An Introduction to Syntactic Analysis and Theory.* Oxford: Blackwell.

Kornfilt, Jaklin and Klaus von Heusinger 2008. Specificity and partitivity in some Altaic languages. In: R. Vermeulen(ed.), *MIT Working Papers in Linguistics. Proceedings of the 5th Workshop on Formal Altaic Linguistics (WAFL 5).* Cambridge, MA: MIT.

Koster-Moeller, Jorie, Jason Varvoutis, and Martin Hackl 2008. Verification procedures for modified numeral quantifiers. In: Natasha Abner and Jason Bishop (eds.), *Proceedings of WCCFL 27.* Somerville, MA: Cascadilla Press.

Kratzer, Angelika 1989. An investigation of the lumps of thought. *Linguistics and Philosophy* 12: 607–653.

Kratzer, Angelika 1991a. Conditionals. In: Arnim v. Stechow and Dieter Wunderlich (eds.), *Handbuch Semantik/Handbook Semantics*, pp. 651–656. Berlin and New York: de Gruyter.

Kratzer, Angelika 1991b. Modality. In: Arnim v. Stechow and Dieter Wunderlich (eds.), *Handbuch Semantik/Handbook Semantics*, pp. 639–650. Berlin and New York: de Gruyter.

Kratzer, Angelika 1996. Severing the external argument from its verb. In: Johan Rooryck and Laura Zaring (eds.), *Phrase Structure and the Lexicon*, pp. 109–137. Dordrecht: Kluwer.

Kratzer, Angelika 1998. Scope or pseudo-scope? Are there wide scope indefinites? In: S. Rothstein (ed.), *Events and Grammar*, pp. 163–196. Dordrecht: Kluwer.

Kratzer, Angelika 2002. Facts: Particulars or information units. *Linguistics and Philosophy* 25: 655–670.

Kratzer, Angelika 2003. A note on choice functions in context. SemanticsArchive.net

Kratzer, Angelika 2004. Covert quantifier domain restrictions. Talk at the *Milan Meeting*, Palazzo Feltrinelli, Gargnano.

Kratzer, Angelika 2005. Indefinites and the operators they depend on: from Japanese to Salish. In: G. N. Carlson and F.J. Pelletier (eds.), *Reference* and *Quantification: The Partee Effect*, pp. 113–142. Stanford: CSLI Publications.

Kratzer, Angelika and Junko Shimoyama 2002. Indeterminate pronouns: the view from Japanese. In: Yukio Otsu (ed.), *The Proceedings of Third Tokyo Conference in Psycholinguistics.* Tokyo: Hituzi Syobo.

Krifka, Manfred 1989. Nominal reference, temporal constitution and quantification in event semantics. In: R. Bartsch, J. van Benthem, and P. von Emde Boas (eds.), *Semantics and Contextual Expression*, pp. 75–115. Dordrecht: Foris Publication.

Krifka, Manfred 1990. Four thousand ships passed through the lock: object-induced measure functions on events. *Linguistics and Philosophy* 13: 487–520.

Krifka, Manfred 1998. Scope inversion under the rise fall contour in German. *Linguistic Inquiry* 29: 75–112

Krifka, Manfred 1999. At least some determiners aren't determiners. In: Ken Turner (ed.), *The Semantics/Pragmatics Interface From Different Points of View, Volume 1 of Current Research in the Semantics/Pragmatics Interface*, pp. 257–291. Elsevier Science B.V.

Krifka, Manfred 2001. Quantifying into question acts. *Natural Language Semantics* 9: 1–40.

Krifka, Manfred 2006. Association with focus phrases. In: Valéria Molnár and Susanna Winkler (eds.), *The Architecture of Focus*, pp. 105–136. Berlin: Mouton de Gruyter.

Kruijff, Geert-Jan and Richard Oehrle (eds.) 2003. *Resource-sensitivity, Binding and Anaphora.* Dordrecht: Kluwer.

Kuroda, Yuki 1982. Indexed predicate calculus. *Journal of Semantics* 1: 43–59.

Kurzman, H.S. and M.C. MacDonald 1993. Resolution of quantifier scope ambiguities. *Cognition* 48/3: 243–279.

Kusumoto, Kiyomi 2005. On the quantification over times in natural language. *Natural Language Semantics* 13/4: 317–357.

Ladusaw, William 1980. *Polarity Sensitivity and Inherent Scope Relations.* New York: Garland.

Ladusaw, William 1992. Expressing negation. In: *Proceedings of Semantics and Linguistic Theory II*, pp. 236–259. Columbus, OH: OSU.

Ladusaw, William 1994. Thetic and categorical, stage and individual, weak and strong. *Proceedings of Semantics and Linguistic Theory IV*, pp. 200–229. Ithaca: Cornell.

Lahiri, Utpal 2000. Quantificational variability in embedded interrogatives. *Linguistics and Philosophy* 23: 325–389.

Lahiri, Utpal 2002. On the proper treatment of "expletive wh" in Hindi. *Lingua* 112: 501–540.

Landman, Fred 1991. *Structures for Semantics.* Dordrecht: Kluwer.

Landman, Fred 2000. *Events and Plurality: The Jerusalem Lectures.* Dordrecht: Kluwer.

Landman, Fred 2004. *Indefinites and the Type of Sets.* Oxford: Blackwell.

Lappin, Shalom and Tanya Reinhart 1988. Presuppositional effects of strong determiners: a processing account. *Linguistics* 26: 1021–1037.

Larson, Richard 1990. Double objects revisited: reply to Jackendoff. *Linguistic Inquiry* 21: 589–632.

Lasersohn, Peter 1995. *Plurality, Conjunction, and Events*. Dordrecht: Kluwer.

Lasersohn, Peter 1998. Generalized distributivity operators. *Linguistics and Philosophy* 21: 83–93.

Lasnik, Howard 1999. Chains of arguments. In: Samuel Epstein and Norbert Hornstein (eds.), pp. 189–217. *Working Minimalism*. Cambridge, MA: The MIT Press.

Lassiter, Daniel 2009. The algebraic structure of amounts: evidence from comparatives. To appear in T. Icard and R. Muskens (eds.), *Interfaces: Explorations in Logic, Language, and Computation*. Dordrecht: Springer.

Lechner, Winfried 2007. Interpretive effects of head movement. http://ling.auf.net/lingBuzz/000178

Lee, Felicia 2008. On the absence of quantificational determiners in San Lucas Quaviní Zapotec. In: Matthewson (2008), pp. 353–383.

Leu, Thomas 2008. *The Internal Syntax of Determiners*. PhD dissertation, New York University. In identical form in: *Groninger Arbeiten zur Germanistischen Linguistik* Vol. 47. http://gagl.eldoc.ub.rug.nl/

Leu, Thomas 2009. The internal syntax of *jeder* 'every'. To appear in *Linguistic Variation Yearbook*.

Lewis, David 1970. General semantics. *Synthèse* 22: 18–67.

Lewis, David 1975. Adverbs of quantification. In: Edward L. Keenan (ed.), *Formal Semantics of Natural Language*, pp. 3–15. Cambridge: Cambridge University Press.

Li, Y.-H. Audrey 1999. Plurality in a classifier language. *Journal of East Asian Linguistics* 8: 75–99.

Lin, Jo-wang 1998. Distributivity in Chinese and its Implications. *Natural Language Semantics* 6: 201–243.

Lin, Tzong-Hong 1998. On *ge* and other related problems. In Liejiong Xu (ed.), *The Referential Properties of Chinese Noun Phrases*, pp. 209–253. Paris: Ecoles des Hautes Estudes en Sciences Sociales.

Lindström, P. 1966. First-order predicate logic with generalized quantifiers. *Theoria* 32: 186–195.

Lindström, P. 1969. On extensions of elementary logic. *Theoria* 35: 1–11.

Link, Godehard 1983. The logical analysis of plural and mass terms: a lattice-theoretical approach. In: R. Bäuerle, C. Schwarze, and A. von Stechow (eds.), *Meaning, Use and Interpretation of Language*, pp. 302–323. Berlin: Walter de Gruyter.

Link, Godehard 1987. Generalized quantifiers and plurals. In: P. Gärdenfors (ed.), *Generalized Quantifiers: Linguistic and Logical Approaches*, pp. 203–235. Dordrecht: Reidel.

Liu, Feng-hsi 1997. *Specificity and Scope*. Amsterdam: John Benjamins.

Livitz, Inna 2009. *Both* – distributive and collective. Ms., New York University.

Löbner, Sebastian 1998. Polarity in natural language: predication, quantification, and negation in particular and characterizing sentences. *Linguistics and Philosophy* 23: 213–308.

Ludlow, Peter and Stephen Neale 1991. Indefinite descriptions: in defense of Russell. *Linguistics and Philosophy* 14: 171–202.

Marantz, Alec 1982. Re reduplication. *Linguistic Inquiry* 13: 435–482.

Martí, Luisa 2008. The semantics of plural indefinite noun phrases in Spanish and Portuguese. *Natural Language Semantics* 16/1: 1–37.

Mascarenhas, Salvador 2009. Referential indefinites and choice functions revisited. Ms., New York University.

Matthewson, Lisa 1999. On the interpretation of wide scope indefinites. *Natural Language Semantics* 7: 79–134.

Matthewson, Lisa 2001. Quantification and the nature of cross-linguistic variation. *Natural Language Semantics* 9: 145–189.

Matthewson, Lisa (ed.) 2008. *Quantification: A Cross-linguistic Perspective.* North-Holland Linguistic Series: Linguistic Variations, Volume 46. Bingley: Emerald Books Publishing.

May, Robert 1977. *The Grammar of Quantification.* PhD dissertation, MIT.

May, Robert 1985. *Logical Form: Its Structure and Derivation.* Cambridge, MA: The MIT Press.

May, Robert 1989. Interpreting Logical Form. *Linguistics and Philosophy* 12: 387–435.

McConnell-Ginet, Sally 2005. A few thoughts on Angelika Kratzer's "Covert quantifier restrictions in natural languages". *Content and Context Workshop,* LSA Linguistic Institute, MIT/Harvard. SemanticsArchive.net

McKay, Thomas 2006. *Plural Predication.* Oxford: Oxford University Press.

Milner, Judith and Jean-Claude Milner 1972. La morphologie du groupe nominal en allemand. *Documentation et recherche en linguistique allemande contemporaine, Vincennes. (DRLAV)* 2. Univ. de Paris VIII.

Milsark, Gary 1977. Toward an explanation of certain peculiarities of the existential construction in English. *Linguistic Analysis* 3: 1–29.

Miyamoto, Yoichi 2006. On locative empty pronouns and anti-quantifier *zutsu* in Japanese. In: Emily Elfner and Martin Walkow (eds.), *Proceedings of NELS 37.* Amherst: GLSA.

Moltmann, Friederike 1995. Exception sentences and polyadic quantification. *Linguistics and Philosophy* 18: 223–280.

Moltmann, Friederike 1997. Intensional verbs and quantifiers. *Natural Language Semantics* 5: 1–52.

Moltmann, Friederike 2007. Intensional verbs and their intentional objects. *Natural Language Semantics* 16: 239–270.

Moltmann, Friederike and Anna Szabolcsi 1994. Scope interactions with pair-list quantifiers. In: Mercé González (ed.), *Proceedings of NELS 24,* pp. 381–395. Amerst: GLSA.

Montague, Richard 1974a. The proper treatment of quantification in ordinary English. In: R. Thomason (ed.), *Formal Philosophy: Selected Papers of Richard Montague,* pp. 247–271. New Haven and London: Yale University Press.

Montague, Richard 1974b. Universal grammar. In: R. Thomason (ed.), *Formal Philosophy: Selected Papers of Richard Montague,* pp. 222–246. New Haven and London: Yale University Press.

Moortgat, Michael 1996. Generalized quantifiers and discontinuous type constructors. In: Harry Bunt and Arthur van Horck (eds.), *Discontinuous Constituency*, pp. 181–207. Berlin: Mouton de Gruyter.

Mostowski, Andrzej 1957. On the generalization of quantifiers. *Fundamenta Mathematicae* 44: 12–36.

Nakanishi, Kimiko 2007. Measurement in the nominal and verbal domains. *Linguistics and Philosophy* 30: 235–276.

Neale, Stephen 1990a. Descriptive pronouns and donkey anaphora. *Journal of Philosophy* 87: 113–150.

Neale, Stephen 1990b. *Descriptions*. Cambridge, MA: The MIT Press.

Neale, Stephen 2000. On being explicit: comments on Stanley and Szabó, and on Bach. *Mind and Language* 15: 284–94.

Nilsen, Øystein 2003. *Eliminating Positions: Syntax and Semantics of Sentence Modification*. PhD dissertation, Utrecht University.

Nishigauchi, Taisuke 1990. *Quantification in the Theory of Grammar*. Dordrecht: Kluwer.

Obenauer, Hans-Georg 1992. L'interpretation des structures WH et l'accord du participe passé. In: Hans George Obenauer and Anne Zribi-Hertz (eds.), *Structure de la phrase et théorie du liage*, pp. 9–11. Paris: Presses Universitaires de France.

Oh, Sei-Rang 2001. Distributivity in an event semantics. In: *Proceedings of Semantics and Linguistic Theory XI*, pp. 326–346. Ithaca: Cornell.

Pafel, Jürgen 2006. *Quantifier Scope in German*. Amsterdam, Philadelphia: John Benjamins.

Papafragou, Anna and Jeff Musolino 2003. Scalar implicatures: experiments at the semantics-pragmatics interface. *Cognition* 86: 253–282.

Partee, Barbara 1986. Noun phrase interpretation and type-shifting principles. In: Jeroen Groenendijk, Dick de Jong, and Martin Stokhof (eds.), *Studies in Discourse Representation Theory and the Theory of Generalized Quantifiers*, pp. 115–143. Dordrecht: Foris.

Partee, Barbara 1991. Topic, focus, and quantification. In: S. Moore and A. Z. Wyner (eds.), *Proceedings of Semantics and Lingustic Theory I*, pp. 159–188. Ithaca: Cornell.

Partee, Barbara 1995. Quantificational structures and compositionality. In: Bach et al. (1995), pp. 541–601.

Partee, Barbara 2004. Weak NP's in *have*–sentences. In: *Compositionality in Formal Semantics*, pp. 282–291. Oxford: Blackwell.

Paul, Ileana 2005. *Or*, *wh*- and *not*: free choice and polarity in Malagasy. In: Jeffrey Heinz and Dimitrios Ntelitheos (eds.), *UCLA Working Papers in Linguistics* 12: 359–367.

Penka, Doris and Hedde Zeijlstra 2005. Negative indefinites in Dutch and German. http://ling.auf.net/lingBuzz/000192

Percus, Orin 2000. Constraints on some other variables in syntax. *Natural Language Semantics* 8: 173–229.

Pereltsvaig, Asya 2008a. Russian *nibud*-series as markers of co-variation. In: Natasha Abner and Jason Bishop (eds.), *Proceedings of WCCFL* 27, pp. 370–378. Somerville, MA: Cascadilla Press.

Pereltsvaig, Asya 2008b. Variations in distributivity. Paper presented at the *Workshop on nominal and verbal plurality*, Paris, CNRS, November 7–8, 2008.

Perlmutter, David. 1970. The two verbs *begin*. In: Roderick Jacobs and Peter Rosenbaum (eds.), *Readings in English Transformational Grammar*, pp. 107–119. Waltham, MA: Blaisdell.

Pesetsky, David 1982. *Paths and Categories*. PhD dissertation. MIT.

Peters, Stanley and Dag Westerståhl 2006. *Quantifiers in Language and Logic*. Oxford: Oxford University Press.

Pietroski, Paul 2005. *Events and Semantic Architecture*. Oxford: Oxford University Press.

Plotkin, Gordon 1975. Call-by-name, call-by-value and the λ-calculus. *Theoretical Computer Science* 1: 125–159.

Postal, Paul M. 1974. *On Raising*. Cambridge, MA: The MIT Press.

Pratt, Jan and Nissim Francez 2001. Temporal generalized quantifiers. *Linguistics and Philosophy* 24: 187–222.

Pylkkänen, Liina 2008. Mismatching meanings in brain and behavior. *Language and Linguistics Compass* 2/4: 712–738.

Pylkkänen, Liina and Brian McElree 2006. The syntax-semantics interface: online composition of sentence meaning. In: M. Traxler and M.A. Gernsbacher (eds.), *Handbook of Psycholinguistics*, 2nd edition, pp. 537–577. New York: Elsevier.

Quine, Willard Van Orman 1948. On what there is. *The Review of Metaphysics* 2: 21–28. Reprinted in: *From a Logical Point of View*. New York: Harper and Row, 1953.

Quine, Willard Van Orman 1960. Variables explained away. *Proceedings of the American Philosophical Society* 104: 343–347.

Ramchand, Gillian 1997. Questions, polarity and alternative semantics. In: Kiyomi Kusumoto (ed.), *Proceedings of NELS* 27, pp. 383–396. Amherst, MA: GLSA. Longer version at http://ling.auf.net/lingBuzz/000183.

Ramchand, Gillian 2007. Events in syntax: modification and predication. *Language and Linguistics Compass* 1/5: 476–497.

Rapoport, Vlad 2000. Structure and interpretation of Russian quantifier phrases. Ms., New York University.

Recanati, Francois 2002. Unarticulated constituents. *Linguistics and Philosophy* 25: 299–345.

Reinhart, Tanya 1979. Syntactic domains for semantic rules. In: Franz Günthner and J. S. Schmidt (eds.), *Formal Semantics and Pragmatics for Natural Languages*, pp. 107–130. Dordrecht: Reidel.

Reinhart, Tanya 1983. *Anaphora and Semantic Interpretation*. London: Croom Helm.

Reinhart, Tanya 1997. Quantifier scope: how labor is divided between QR and choice functions. *Linguistics and Philosophy* 20: 335–397.

Reinhart, Tanya 1998. Wh-in-situ in the framework of the Minimalist Program. *Natural Language Semantics* 6: 29–56.

Reinhart, Tanya 2006. *Interface Strategies*. Cambridge, MA: The MIT Press.

Rescher, Nicholas 1962. Plurality-quantification. *Journal of Symbolic Logic* 27: 373–374.

Richards, Norvin 2008. Can A-scrambling reorder arguments? http://ling.auf.net/lingBuzz/000613

Rips, Lance 1994. *The Psychology of Proof*. Cambridge, MA: The MIT Press.

Ritter, Elizabeth 1991. Two functional categories in noun phrases: evidence from Modern Hebrew. In: Susan Rothstein (ed.), *Syntax and Semantics 26*, pp. 37–62. San Diego: Academic Press.

Ritter, Elisabeth 1995. On the syntactic category of pronouns and agreement. *Natural Language and Linguistic Theory* 13/3: 405–443.

Rizzi, Luigi 1997. The fine structure of the left periphery. In: Liliane Haegeman (ed.), *Elements of Grammar: Handbook of Generative Syntax*, pp. 281–337. Dordrecht: Kluwer.

Rizzi, Luigi. 2001. Reconstruction, weak island sensitivity, and agreement. In: Carlo Cecchetto, Gennaro Chierchia, and Maria Teresa Guasti (eds.), *Semantic Interfaces: Reference, Anaphora and Aspect*, pp. 145–176. Stanford: CSLI Publications.

Roberts, Craige 1990. *Modal Subordination, Anaphora, and Distributivity*. New York and London: Garland Publishing, Inc.

Roberts, Craige 1995. Domain restriction in dynamic semantics. In: Bach et al. (1995), pp. 661–700.

Romero, Maribel 1998. *Focus and Reconstruction Effects in Wh-phrases*. PhD dissertation, UMass, Amherst.

Rooth, Mats 1992. A theory of focus interpretation. *Natural Language Semantics* 1: 75–116.

Rullmann, Hotze 1995. *Maximality in the Semantics of Wh-constructions*. PhD dissertation, UMass, Amherst.

Ruys, Eddy 1992. *The Scope of Indefinites*. PhD dissertation. OTS, University of Utrecht.

Ruys, Eddy and Yoad Winter 2008. Quantifier scope in formal linguistics. To appear in: Dov Gabbay (ed.), *Handbook of Philosophical Logic*, 2nd edition.

Safir, Kenneth and Timothy Stowell 1988. Binominal *each*. In: James Blevins and Juli Carter (eds.), *Proceedings of NELS* 18, Vol. II, pp. 426–450. Amherst, MA: GLSA.

Sanford, Anthony J. and Patrick Stuart 2002. Depth of processing in language comprehension: not noticing the evidence. *Trends in Cognitive Science* 6/9: 382–386.

Sauerland, Uli 2004. Scalar implicatures in complex sentences. *Linguistics and Philosophy* 27/3: 367–391.

Sauerland, Uli, Jan Andersen, and Kazuko Yatsushiro 2005. The plural involves comparison. In: S. Kesper and M. Reis (eds.), *Linguistic Evidence*. Berlin: Mouton de Gruyter.

Scha, Remko 1981/2003. Distributive, collective and cumulative quantification. In: J.A.G. Groenendijk, T.M.V. Janssen, and M.B.J. Stokhof (eds.), *Formal Methods in the Study of Language*, Part 2. Amsterdam: Mathematisch Centrum, 1981, pp. 483–512. Reprinted in: Javier Gutiérrez-Rexach (ed.),

Semantics: Critical Concepts in Linguistics, Vol. III: *Noun Phrase Classes*, Chapter 40. Routledge, 2003.

Schein, Barry 1993. *Plurals and Events*. Cambridge, MA: The MIT Press.

Schein, Barry 2009. *Conjunction Reduction Redux*. Ms., University of Southern California.

Schlenker, Philippe 1999. *Propositional Attitudes and Indexicality (A Cross-Categorial Approach)*. Ph dissertation, MIT.

Schlenker, Philippe 2004. Sequence phenomena and double access readings generalized. In: Lecarme and Guéron (eds.), *The Syntax of Time*, pp. 555–597. Cambridge, MA: The MIT Press.

Schlenker, Philippe 2006a. Scopal independence: a note on branching and wide scope readings of indefinites and disjunctions. *Journal of Semantics* 23: 281–314.

Schlenker, Philippe 2006b. Ontological symmetry in language: a brief manifesto. *Mind and Language* 21/4: 504–539.

Schwarz, Bernhard 2004. Indefinites in verb phrase ellipsis. *Linguistic Inquiry* 35: 344–353.

Schwarzschild, Roger 1996. *Pluralities*. Dordrecht: Kluwer.

Schwarzschild, Roger 2002. Singleton indefinites. *Journal of Semantics* 19: 289–314.

Schwarzschild, Roger and Karina Wilkinson 2002. Quantifiers in comparatives: a semantics of degree based on intervals. *Natural Language Semantics* 10: 1–41.

Sharvit, Yael 2002. Embedded quantifiers in *which-* and *whether*-questions. In: *Proceedings from Semantics and Linguistic Theory XVII*, pp. 266–285. Ithaca: Cornell.

Sharvit, Yael and Penka Stateva. 2002. Superlative expressions, context, and focus. *Linguistics and Philosophy* 25:453–505.

Sher, Gila 1990. Ways of branching quantifiers. *Linguistics and Philosophy* 14: 393–422.

Shimoyama, Junko 2001. *Wh-constructions in Japanese*. PhD dissertation, UMass, Amherst.

Shimoyama, Junko 2007. Indeterminate noun phrase quantification in Japanese. *Natural Language Semantics* 14/2: 139–173.

Shlonsky, Ur 1991. Quantifiers as functional heads: a study of quantifier float in Hebrew. *Lingua* 84: 159–180.

Shu, Chih-hsiang 2009. Sentential adverbs as focusing adverbs. Presented at the *7th GLOW in Asia*. Ms., University of Stony Brook.

Spector, Benjamin 2003. Plural indefinite DPs as plural-polarity items. In: Josep Quer, Jan Schroten, Mauro Scorretti, Petra Sleeman, and Els Verheugd (eds.), *Romance Languages and Linguistic Theory 2001: Selected Papers from 'Going Romance'*, pp. 295–313. Amsterdam: John Benjamins.

Spector, Benjamins 2007. Aspects of the pragmatics of plural morphology: on higher-order implicatures. In: Uli Sauerland and Penka Stateva (eds.), *Presupposition and Implicature in Compositional Semantics*, pp. 243–281. Palgrave-Macmillan.

Spector, Benjamin 2008. Interpreting numerals: 'Pragmatics' and grammar. Slides for talk at IJN, November 28, 2008, Paris.

Sportiche, Dominique 1988. A theory of floating quantifiers and its corollaries for constituent structure. *Linguistic Inquiry* 19: 425–449.

Sportiche, Dominique 2005. Division of labor between Merge and Move: strict locality of selection and apparent reconstruction paradoxes. In: *Proceedings of the Workshop Divisions of Linguistic Labor. The La Bretesche Workshop.* http://ling.auf.net/lingBuzz/000163

Sportiche, Dominique 2006. Reconstruction, binding, and scope. In: Martin Everaert and Henk van Riemsdijk (eds.), *The Blackwell Companion to Syntax*, pp. 35–94. Oxford: Blackwell.

Stabler, Edward 1997. Computing quantifier scope. In: Szabolcsi (1997b), pp. 155–183.

Stanley, Jason 2000. Context and Logical Form. *Linguistics and Philosophy* 23/4: 391–434.

Stanley, Jason 2002a. Making it articulated. *Mind and Language* 12: 149–168.

Stanley, Jason 2002b. Nominal restriction. In: Gerhard Peters and Georg Preyer (eds.), *Logical Form and Language*, pp. 365–390. Oxford: Oxford University Press.

Stanley, Jason and Zoltán Gendler Szabó 2000. On quantifier domain restriction. *Mind and Language* 15: 219–261.

von Stechow, Arnim 1984. Comparing semantic theories of comparison. *Journal of Semantics* 3: 1–77.

von Stechow, Arnim 2003. Feature deletion under semantic binding: tense, person, and mood under verbal quantifiers. Ms., Tübingen.

von Stechow, Arnim 2004. Binding by verbs: tense, person, and mood under attitudes. In: Horst Lohnstein and Susanne Trissler (eds.), *The Syntax and Semantics of the Left Periphery*. Berlin: de Gruyter.

Steedman, Mark 2000. *The Syntactic Process*. Cambridge, MA: The MIT Press.

Steedman, Mark 2009. *The Grammar of Scope*. Submitted book ms.

Sternefeld, Wolfgang 1993. Plurality, reciprocity, and scope. SfS-Report 13–93, Universität Tübingen, Tübingen.

Sternefeld, Wolfgang 2001. Semantic vs. syntactic reconstruction. In: H. Kamp, A. Rossdeutscher, and C. Rohrer (eds.), *Linguistic Form and its Computation*, pp. 145–182. Stanford: CSLI Publications.

Strawson, Paul F. 1952. *Introduction to Logical Theory*. London: Methuen.

Surányi, Balázs 2003a. Differential quantifier scope: Q-Raising versus Q-feature checking. In: Olivier Bonami and Patricia Cabredo Hofherr (eds.), *Empirical Issues in Syntax and Semantics 5. Proceedings of CSSP 2003*, pp. 215–240. www.cssp.cnrs.fr/eiss5/index_en.html

Surányi, Balázs 2003b. Quantifier interaction and differential scope-taking. *Studies in Modern Grammar* 34: 31–70.

Surányi, Balázs 2004. The left periphery and Cyclic Spellout: the case of Hungarian. In: David Adger, Cecile de Cat, and George Tsoulas (eds.), *Peripheries and Their Effects*, pp. 49–73. Dordrecht: Kluwer.

Sutton, Melody 1993. *Binominal "each"*. Master's Thesis, UCLA.

Szabó, Zoltán Gendler 2008. Bare quantifiers. Paper at the *Philosophy and Linguistics Workshop*, May 2008, Rutgers University.

Szabó, Zoltán Gendler 2009. Specific, yet opaque. In: Maria Aloni et al. (eds.), *Pre-proceedings of the Seventeenth Amsterdam Colloquium*, pp. 22–32. ILLC, University of Amsterdam.

Szabolcsi, Anna 1981. Compositionality in focus. *Folia Linguistica Societatis Europaeae* 15: 141–161.

Szabolcsi, Anna 1982. Model theoretic semantics of performatives. In: Ferenc Kiefer (ed.), *Hungarian General Linguistics*, pp. 515–536. Amsterdam: John Benjamins.

Szabolcsi, Anna 1986. Comparative superlatives. In: Naoki Fukui, Tova Rapoport, and Elisabeth Sagey (eds.), *Papers in Theoretical Linguistics. MIT WPL 8*, pp. 245–266. Cambridge, MA: MIT.

Szabolcsi, Anna 1992. Combinatory grammar and projection from the lexicon. In: Ivan A. Sag and Anna Szabolcsi (eds.), *Lexical Matters*, pp. 241–269. Stanford: CSLI Publications.

Szabolcsi, Anna 1994. The noun phrase. In Ferenc Kiefer and Katalin É. Kiss (eds.), *The Syntactic Structure of Hungarian. Syntax and Semantics*, Vol. 27, pp. 179–275. New York: Academic Press.

Szabolcsi, Anna 1995. On modes of operation. In: Paul Dekker and Martin Stokhof (eds.), *Proceedings of the Tenth Amsterdam Colloquium*, pp. 651–669. Amsterdam: ILLC/Department of Philosophy.

Szabolcsi, Anna 1997a. Strategies for scope taking. In: Szabolcsi (1997b), pp. 109–154.

Szabolcsi, Anna (ed.) 1997b. *Ways of Scope Taking*. Dordrecht: Kluwer.

Szabolcsi, Anna 1997c. Quantifiers in pair-list readings. In: Szabolcsi (1997b), pp. 311–342.

Szabolcsi, Anna 1997d. Background notions in lattice theory and generalized quantifiers. In: Szabolcsi (1997b), pp. 1–29.

Szabolcsi, Anna 2000. The syntax of scope. In: Mark Baltin and Chris Collins (eds.), *Handbook of Contemporary Syntactic Theory*, pp. 607–634. Oxford: Blackwell.

Szabolcsi, Anna 2003. Binding on the fly: cross–sentential anaphora in variable-free semantics. In: Geert-Jan Kruijff and Richard Oehrle (eds.), *Resource-sensitivity, Binding, and Anaphora*, pp. 215–231. Dordrecht: Kluwer.

Szabolcsi, Anna 2006. Strong vs. weak islands. In: Martin Everaert and Henk van Riemsdijk (eds.), *The Blackwell Companion to Syntax*, Vol. 4, pp. 479–532. Oxford: Blackwell.

Szabolcsi, Anna 2008. Scope and binding. To appear in Claudia Maienborn, Klaus von Heusinger, and Paul Portner (eds.), *Semantics: An International Handbook of Natural Language Meaning*. Berlin: Mouton de Gruyter.

Szabolcsi, Anna 2009. Overt nominative subjects in infinitival complements cross-linguistically: data, diagnostics, and preliminary analyses. In: Patricia Irwin and Violeta Vázquez Rojas (eds.), *NYU Working Papers in Linguistics, Vol. 2. Papers in Syntax, Spring 2009*. www.nyu.edu/gsas/dept/lingu/nyuwpl/

Szabolcsi, Anna and Frans Zwarts 1993/1997. Weak islands and an algebraic semantics for scope taking. *Natural Language Semantics* 1: 235–285. Reprinted in Szabolcsi (1997b), pp. 217–263.

Szabolcsi, Anna and Bill Haddican 2004. Conjunction meets negation: a study in cross-linguistic variation. *Journal of Semantics* 21/3: 219–249.

Takahashi, Shoichi 2006. More than two quantifiers. *Natural Language Semantics* 17: 57–101.

Thijsse, Elias 1985. Counting quantifiers. In: Johan van Benthem and Alice ter Meulen (eds.), *Generalized Quantifiers in Natural Language*, pp. 127–147. Dordrecht: Foris.

van Benthem, Johan 1986. *Essays in Logical Semantics*. Dordrecht: Reidel.

van der Does, Jaap 1992. *Applied Quantifier Logics*. PhD dissertation, University of Amsterdam.

van Geenhoven, Veerle 1998. *Semantic Incorporation and Indefinite Descriptions*. Stanford: CSLI Publications.

Vázquez Rojas, Violeta 2009. *Puros*. Ms., New York University.

Verkuyl, Henk 1981. Numerals and quantifiers in X-bar syntax and their semantic interpretation. In: Jeroen Groenendijk, Theo Janssen, and Martin Stokhof (eds.), *Formal Methods in the Study of Language*, pp. 567–600. Mathematical Centre Tracts 136. University of Amsterdam.

Villalta, Elisabeth 2003. The role of context in the resolution of quantifier scope ambiguities. *Journal of Semantics* 20: 115–162.

Villalta, Elisabeth 2008. Mood and gradability: an investigation of the subjunctive mood in Spanish. *Linguistics and Philosophy* 31: 467–522.

Wedgwood, Daniel 2005. *Shifting the Focus: From Static Structures to the Dynamics of Interpretation*. Amsterdam: Elsevier.

Westerståhl, Dag 1985. Determiners and context sets. In: J. van Benthem and A. ter Meulen (eds.), *Generalized Quantifiers in Natural Language*. Dordrecht: Foris.

Westerståhl, Dag 1987. Branching generalized quantifiers and natural language. In: P. Gärdenfors (ed.), *Generalized Quantifiers*, pp. 45–73. Dordrecht: Reidel.

Westerståhl, Dag 1989. Quantifiers in formal and natural languages. In: D. Gabbay and F. Guenthner (eds.), *Handbook of Philosophical Logic*, Vol. IV, pp. 1–131. Dordrecht: Kluwer.

Wiggins, David 1980. "Most" and "all": some comments on a familiar programme. In: Mark Platts (ed.), *Reference, Truth and Reality: Essays in the Philosophy of Language*, pp. 318–346. London: Routledge.

Williams, Edwin 1986. The reassignment of the functions of LF. *Linguistic Inquiry* 17: 265–299.

Williams, Edwin 1988. Is LF distinct from S-structure? A reply to May. *Linguistic Inquiry* 19: 135–147.

Williams, Edwin 2003. *Representation Theory*. Cambridge, MA: The MIT Press.

Wiltshire, Caroline and Alec Marantz 2000. Reduplication. In: *Morphology: An International Handbook of Inflection and Word Formation*, Vol. 1, pp. 557–568. Berlin: de Gruyter.

Winter, Yoad 1997. Choice functions and the scopal semantics of indefinites. *Linguistics and Philosophy* 20: 399–467.

Winter, Yoad 2000. DP structure and flexible semantics. In: M. Hirotani, A. Coetzee, N. Hall, and J. Kim (eds.), *Proceedings of NELS* 30. Amherst, MA: GLSA.

Winter, Yoad 2001. *Flexibility Principles in Boolean Semantics*. Cambridge, MA: The MIT Press.

Winter, Yoad 2004. Functional quantification. *Research on Language and Computation* 2: 331–363.

Wurmbrand, Susi 2008. Word order and scope in German. Ms., University of Connecticut.

Yanovich, Igor 2005. Choice-functional series of indefinites and Hamblin semantics. In: *Proceedings of Semantics and Linguistic Theory XV*, pp. 309–326. Ithaca: Cornell.

Yanovich, Igor 2008. Ordinary property and identifying property *wh*-words: two *kakoj*-s in Russian. In: Franc Marušič and Rok Žaucer (eds.), *Proceedings of Formal Descriptions of Slavic Languages 6.5*, pp. 309–324. Frankfurt-am-Main: Peter Lang.

Yanovich, Igor 2009. Certain presuppositions and intermediate readings, and vice versa. To appear in: *Proceedings of Berlin workshop on Funny Indefinites*.

Yatsushiro, Kazuko 2002. The distribution of *mo* and *ka* and its implications. In: M. Cuervo, D. Harbour, K. Hiraiwa, and S. Ishihara (eds.), *Proceedings of FAJL 3. MIT Working Papers in Linguistics 41*, pp. 181–198. Cambridge, MA: MIT.

Zamparelli, Roberto 2000. *Layers in the Determiner Phrase*. New York: Garland.

Zamparelli, Roberto 2008. On singular existential quantifiers in Italian. In: Ileana Comorowski and Klaus von Heusinger (eds.), *Existence: Semantics and Syntax*, pp. 293–328. Dordrecht: Springer.

Zerbian, Sabine and Manfred Krifka 2008. Quantification across Bantu languages. In: Matthewson (2008), pp. 383–415.

Zimmermann, Malte 2002a. A compositional analysis of anti-quantifiers as quantifiers. In: *Proceedings of Semantics and Linguistic Theory XII*, pp. 322–338. Ithaca: Cornell.

Zimmermann, Malte 2002b. *Boys Buying Two Sausages Each: On the Syntax and Semantics of Distance-distributivity*. PhD dissertation, University of Amsterdam.

Zimmermann, Malte 2007. Overt existential closure in Bura (Central Chadic). In: *Proceedings of Semantics and Linguistic Theory XVII*, pp. 333-350. Ithaca: Cornell.

Zimmermann, Malte 2008. Quantification in Hausa. In: Matthewson (2008), pp. 415–477.

Zimmermann, Malte 2009. Variation in the expression of universal quantification and free choice: the case of Hausa *koo-wh* expressions. In: Jeroen van Craenenbroeck (ed.), *Linguistic Variation Yearbook 2008*, pp. 179–232. Amsterdam: John Benjamins.

Zimmermann, Thomas Ede 1993a. Scopeless quantifiers and operators. *Journal of Philosophical Logic* 22: 545–561.

Zimmermann, Thomas Ede 1993b. On the proper treatment of opacity in certain verbs. *Natural Language Semantics* 1: 149–179.

Zucchi, Alessandro 1995. The ingredients of definiteness and the definiteness effect. *Natural Language Semantics* 3: 33–78.

Zwarts, Frans 1983. Determiners: a relational perspective. In: Alice G. B. ter Meulen (ed.), *Studies in Model-theoretic Semantics*, pp. 37–63. Dordrecht: Foris.

Zweig, Eytan 2005a. Nouns and adjectives in numeral NPs. In: Leah Bateman and Cherlon Ussery (eds.), *Proceedings of NELS* 35, pp. 663–679. Amherst, MA: GLSA.

Zweig, Eytan 2005b. The implications of dependent plurals. In: Christopher Davis, Amy Rose Deal, and Youri Zabbal (eds.), *Proceedings of NELS* 36, pp. 735–750. Amherst, MA: GLSA.

Zweig, Eytan 2008. *Dependent Plurals and Plural Meaning*. PhD dissertation, New York University.

Zweig, Eytan 2009. Number-neutral bare plurals and the multiplicity implicature. *Linguistics and Philosophy* 32: 353–407.

Index

Language index